D1743331

NATIONAL INSTITUTE FOR SOCIAL WORK TRAINING SERIES

No. 3

SOCIAL POLICY AND ADMINISTRATION

Publications by the
National Institute for Social Work Training
Mary Ward House, London, W.C.1,
England.

NO. 1 SOCIAL WORK AND SOCIAL CHANGE
by Eileen Younghusband

NO. 2 INTRODUCTION TO A SOCIAL WORKER
produced by the National Institute
for Social Work Training

NO. 3 SOCIAL POLICY AND ADMINISTRATION
by D. V. Donnison, Valerie Chapman and others

NO. 4 SOCIAL WORK WITH FAMILIES
edited by Eileen Younghusband

NO. 5 PROFESSIONAL EDUCATION FOR SOCIAL WORK
IN BRITAIN
by Marjorie J. Smith

NO. 6 NEW DEVELOPMENTS IN CASEWORK
compiled by Eileen Younghusband

NO. 7 THE FIELD TRAINING OF SOCIAL WORKERS
by S. Clement Brown and E. K. Gloyne

NO. 8 DECISION IN CHILD CARE
by R. A. Parker

NO. 9 ADOPTION POLICY AND PRACTICE
by Iris Goodacre

NO. 10 SUPERVISION IN SOCIAL WORK
by Dorothy E. Pettes

NO. 11 CARING FOR PEOPLE
Report of a Committee of Enquiry into the
Staffing of Residential Homes set up by
The National Council of Social Service

NO. 12 SOCIAL WORK AND SOCIAL VALUES
Compiled by Eileen Younghusband

NO. 13 MOTHER AND BABY HOMES
by Jill Nicholson

SOCIAL POLICY AND ADMINISTRATION

STUDIES IN THE DEVELOPMENT OF SOCIAL SERVICES
AT THE LOCAL LEVEL

BY

D. V. DONNISON AND VALERIE CHAPMAN

MICHAEL MEACHER, ANGELA SEARS
AND KENNETH URWIN

London

GEORGE ALLEN & UNWIN LTD

RUSKIN HOUSE   MUSEUM STREET

FIRST PUBLISHED IN 1965
SECOND IMPRESSION 1967
THIRD IMPRESSION 1970

PRINTED IN GREAT BRITAIN
in 11 on 12 point Fournier type
BY C. TINLING AND CO. LTD
LONDON AND PRESCOT

FOREWORD

Many people have contributed to this book. The research on which
it is based began for the purpose of teaching future social workers
taking the course in Applied Social Studies at the London School of
Economics and Political Science. Thanks to a grant from the school's
research funds, Mrs Valerie Chapman was able to spend two years
exploring the literature and making five of the case studies presented
here. These were used for several years by students, at the school and
elsewhere, whose comments helped to improve the presentation and
discussion of the cases. At a later stage two more case studies were
made by Michael Meacher, Miss Angela Sears and Councillor Kenneth
Urwin, who were then graduate students at the school. The book was
completed during a period of leave from the school which I spent at
the National Institute for Social Work Training. I owe a great deal to
Robin Huws Jones, the Institute's Principal, and his colleagues.
Besides providing secretarial services and shelter from visitors and
the telephone, they joined in regular and critical discussions of my
drafts, inviting three others who also made exceedingly valuable
contributions to these meetings—Miss Geraldine Aves, CBE, recently
Chief Welfare Officer at the Ministry of Health, Dr Roy Parker of the
London School of Economics, and Derek Newman, Principal of the
Glacier Institute of Management. Meanwhile the whole project depended from start to finish on the directors and staff of local units of
the social services who permitted us to study their work and record
their endeavours to develop these services. They gave a great deal of
their time and experience to the making of these studies and to the
correction and improvement of successive drafts. Their generosity
must not be allowed to implicate them in any errors that remain, all of
which are the authors' responsibility.

D.V.D.

CONTENTS

PART I

CHAPTER 1

THE PURPOSE AND PLAN OF THIS BOOK

THIS book is written for specialists with the hope that it may also interest a wider audience. Students intending to work in the social services are the special group we have in mind. For them there is now a growing literature on the social services, their structure, powers and policies, and the needs these services are designed to meet; but little has been written about the practice of social administration itself. In the social services, as elsewhere, administrators are usually expected to pick up whatever skills they require from experience gained on the job. Indeed, many would assert that the art of administration can *only* be learnt in this way—and the books and teaching methods so far available justify no confident rejection of that view. Yet the continuing lack of any specific preparation for administrative work in the social services contrasts oddly with the proliferation of professional training for other branches of these services; untrained teachers and social workers find it increasingly difficult to get jobs, and no one wants an untrained medical officer, health visitor, surveyor or treasurer. But many of these people devote a great deal of their time to the general management and development of their services—tasks for which their professional training provides scant preparation. In a recent study of seven children's departments it was found that professional staff spent only half their time on work directly concerned with individual children, and only 2 per cent of their time in conversation with children.[1] While the professional training of child care officers includes considerable study of the history and structure of the social services, it is mainly

[1] Tom Burns and Susan Sinclair, *The Child Care Service at Work*. Edinburgh, Scottish Education Department, 1963.

designed to deepen their understanding of human behaviour and to equip them to offer competent, sensitive help to the people whom they serve. It does little to equip them in any systematic fashion for administration and policy-making. This is not the fault of those who teach the skills of social casework and other professions. If administrators had been as successful as the social workers, teachers, doctors and nurses have been in analysing and recording what they do and devising methods for teaching others how to do it, then professional and administrative staff could both be offered a more comprehensive and appropriate training.

The conventions of professional training in many fields still owe a great deal to traditions established in the last century when the skills and the technical equipment required for professional work were rudimentary, and the work itself was often done single-handed or by small groups of partners and their apprentices. What the doctor, the teacher or the architect could offer was in those days contained largely within their own heads and applied through a technique of personal relationships, with the aid of equipment that could be carried in a small bag. For members of such professions the capacity to handle face-to-face contacts with their clients still remains vital but few of them could get far today on this basis alone, for their professional skills are now increasingly employed and applied by complex organizations providing a wide variety of specialist services that depend on massive technical and administrative resources and the close co-ordination of teams of workers in a network of different organizations. A man may be a surgeon by virtue of his training, but he cannot practice his profession effectively without the aid of pathologists, anaesthetists, administrators, nurses and technicians of many kinds, or without operating theatres, laboratories, x-ray equipment and all the other resources of a modern hospital. A man may be a scholar by virtue of his training, but he cannot be a university teacher without libraries, lecture halls, computers, and all the administrative, technical and financial resources required for the selection and maintenance of students, the conduct of examinations, and the organization and publication of research. The newer professions are even more deeply enmeshed in the administrative framework of the organizations that employ them. Social workers, whatever their training, cannot actually practise as probation officers, child care officers, almoners and so on, without an increasingly elaborate supporting organization of courts, clinics, foster homes, cash allowances and other resources. Their ability to draw on these resources effectively, to bring organizations other than their own to the aid of their clients, and to modify and develop the services within which they operate is no longer a peripheral concern but a central feature of their professional equipment. In this and other professions the conventions of training have yet to be properly adapted to these changes.

But we cannot teach anything about administration until we have studied it more thoroughly, and we cannot do that effectively until we have determined the purposes and developed the methods of research in this field. This book explores the administration of the social services in order to clarify what a student of the subject should be studying and what kind of conclusions might emerge from his work. It is no more than a reconnaissance. The next step must be to make more systematic and extensive analyses of social administration which can provide a sound basis for teaching.

Those working in the social services or preparing to do so are by no means the only people now grappling with these questions. In recent years social scientists of all kinds have been led by the logic of their studies to examine human organizations more closely. Political scientists concerned with power, economists concerned with the distribution of scarce resources, sociologists concerned with the structure and development of society, and psychologists concerned with human motivation and behaviour must all at some point examine the organizations through which power is exercised, the organizations in which decisions about the allocation of resources are made and implemented, the organizations that go far to determine the structure of our society and the perceptions and aspirations of its members. Thus administration is not a self-contained specialism; it is the meeting point and common concern of all these disciplines. Indeed it is the concern of all who live in an industrial, urban country. For if 'administration' is the management of human organizations, then all of us—as employees and customers, patients and pupils, voters and taxpayers—are familiar with many aspects of it; and in a country which devotes about a sixth of its gross national product to social services, 'social' administration constitutes a major part of this familiar process.

The work of administrators in the social services may not differ fundamentally from that of administrators and managers in many other fields. Nevertheless the organizations discussed in this book are part of a large array of welfare services which has developed in particular ways to meet particular needs over a long period of time, and research on these services and their problems also has distinctive characteristics and a considerable history—starting more than a century ago in royal commissions, public health departments, local statistical societies and other bodies, to which universities have added their contribution since they took up the subject before the First World War.

Thus the organizations to be examined and the questions to be asked about them cannot be understood without some knowledge of the pedigree of both. This book therefore begins with a brief historical essay on the development of 'social administration', dealing with both meanings of that term: the work of those who administer the social services, and the academic study of these services and the problems they deal with. This should enable us to pose more clearly the questions we propose to examine, and to distinguish our own approach to the study of administration from that of others working in this field. Chapter 3 explains this approach and some of the methods and concepts that may help in the analysis of administration. The second and longest part of this book presents a number of administrative case studies dealing with local units of social services provided by central and local government and by voluntary bodies. It begins with an account of the methods used in selecting and compiling these studies, and each study concludes with a brief discussion of ideas that may be derived from it. The cases have been arranged in a sequence that has some cumulative effect, so that ideas derived from earlier studies can be applied to later ones. Our discussion of each may be read as a running commentary on the results of our research—a commentary which leads to the more comprehensive analysis that appears in the third part of the book. Although the studies presented here are not sufficiently numerous or representative to justify any firm conclusions, we have endeavoured to draw our findings together and construct on this basis some hypotheses about the development of social administration and the parts played in that development by people at different levels and in different branches of the social services—hypotheses that have a sufficiently general application to be interesting, while being sufficiently precise to be tested in further research. The implications of our findings for other social scientists concerned with the behaviour and evolution of organizations are also discussed in this final chapter. Two appendices follow: the first presents an introduction to the literature on administration, and the second offers some suggestions that may help those who wish to use our case studies in training courses of various kinds. The book ends with an index presented in three parts dealing, respectively, with administrative concepts and processes, with organizations and services, and with the names of people.

CHAPTER 2

THE DEVELOPMENT OF SOCIAL ADMINISTRATION[1]

THE problems people discern in the social services, and hence the questions they pose for researchers and policy makers in this field, are derived from their assumptions about the character and function of the services themselves. They may assume that 'The essential marks of a social service are: (a) that it is rendered by, or on behalf of, the community *to an individual* or at most *to a family*, and appropriated to his or its exclusive use; and (b) that it contains an element of redistribution, i.e. that the majority of the individuals or families who avail themselves of it are receiving more than they give.' If so, it is natural for them to continue: 'The question therefore which poses itself is not, "Should a means test be applied to a social service?" but "Why should any social service be provided *without* test of need?".'[2] If, in more uplifting fashion, they feel that: 'the generally accepted hallmark of social service is that of direct concern with the personal well-being of the individual' and its 'basis . . . is . . . to be found in the obligation a person feels to help another in distress' it is natural that they should ask whether the 'multiplication of statutory social services' has produce a 'decline in initiative and repudiation of personal and family responsibility'.[3] Few authors express their views about the functions of the social services so clearly as those we have quoted, but similar views are frequently implied.

With variations of detail and emphasis, it is widely assumed that the social services—'the moving frontier of social conscience'—were first established by religious and charitable pioneers and later consolidated by the state, under pressure from the Labour movement, to provide benefits for the relatively poor at the expense of the

[1] Much of this chapter appeared in *The Development of Social Administration. An Inaugural Lecture*, D. V. Donnison. London School of Economics and Political Science, 1962.

[2] Iain McLeod and Enoch Powell, *The Social Services. Needs and Means.* Conservative Political Centre, 2nd Ed. 1954, pp. 5 and 9.

[3] Penelope Hall, *The Social Services of Modern England.* Routledge and Kegan Paul, 1959, pp. 3-4 and 7.

relatively rich—benefits which enable the poor to have some of the
things that the rich can furnish for themselves unaided.

Within these assumptions there is still plenty of room for disagreement. At one extreme are those who regard the social services
as a charitable burden borne on the back of the 'productive' institutions of the economy. To them these services are a 'residual' function
of government, a temporary expedient to be dispensed with as soon
as growing wealth and enlightenment enable the poor to meet their
own needs through the 'normal' mechanisms of the market. At the
other extreme are those who regard these services as a necessary,
permanent and growing feature of a 'progressive' economy, producing not only a gradual socialization of the national income but
also an increasingly just, classless and efficient society in which the
major decisions will be based on rational and humane criteria. But,
whether they look upon them as a dangerous intrusion upon normality or as a good deed in a naughty world, advocates at both
extremes tend to regard the social services as distinctive institutions
operating according to economic, political and moral 'rules' which
differ from those that apply elsewhere. These assumptions encourage
the belief that the problems of social administration are equally
distinctive, that the analysis of these problems constitutes a distinctive academic discipline, and that distinctive 'principles of social
policy' can be devised for their solution. Before accepting or rejecting
these views it would be wise to examine the history of the social
services. It may provide a more realistic understanding of their
character and functions and thus clarify the character and functions
of research upon them.

One strand in the story of the social services is the continuing
endeavour to provide the environment required for industrial progress. The industrial revolution imposed a clear-cut distinction
between those who were in work and those who were not—between
the self-supporting and the dependent. It called for a mobile, disciplined and increasingly educated labour force. As a labour market
developed, from which the young and the old were gradually
excluded, and as rising living standards extended the expectation of
life and hence the number of elderly dependants, so the poverty
cycle afflicting children, their parents and the aged was greatly
intensified. Industrialization brought the ruin of obsolete industries
and the threat of recurring unemployment in every industry; it also
created the big city, with its new problems of public health and
public order. 'The age of great cities,' said Walter Bagehot, 'requires

strong government.'[1] But neither working men nor their employers could wait on government. In the friendly societies working men endeavoured to organize their own labour exchange, medical service, sick pay, unemployment benefits and funeral grants. Employers, too, attempted to create the conditions for profitable industrial progress when the opportunity arose. In the nineteenth century new towns, created by the railways and other industries, showed the kind of environment industry required, with police forces, medical services, savings banks, schools, pension schemes and housing—all provided or supported by the companies that established them. Though scarcely typical of the 'bleak age', these communities were no Utopian experiment, but a hard-headed business investment. When at last the state assumed responsibility for elementary education, the Grand Junction Railway Company increased its contributions to the denominational schools of Crewe for reasons that were frankly explained by its chairman: 'What is done at Crewe . . . in subscribing to schools, is only done after most careful consideration as to whether it is cheaper for the shareholders to pay a subscription or to pay the rate necessary to support a school board, the only consideration moving the directors being the economy which can be effected to the shareholders.'[2]

This strand in the development of social administration is still to be seen today as continuing industrial progress throws up new needs and intensifies old ones. In Britain company chairmen may bewail the crippling weight of taxation and the debilitating effects of the state's welfare services in the opening paragraphs of their annual reports, but they go on to record the increasingly generous pension schemes and health services, the cheap canteens, the interest-free loans for house purchase and the other benefits they provide (at the consumer's expense) for their employees. Employers in other countries have gone even further in providing for the welfare of their workers. They point out that such benefits reduce absenteeism and labour turnover, help to recruit managerial staff and key workers, improve morale and promote efficiency. Meanwhile, private insurance to meet the costs of education and medical care is booming, and the state has been called in to alleviate the poverty cycle amongst the rich by redistributing their income over the life-span with the aid of tax allowances that grow more elaborate every year.

[1] Mrs Russell Barrington, *Life of Walter Bagehot*, 1914, pp. 393-5. Quoted by O. R. McGregor, 'Sociology and Welfare', *Sociological Review Monograph No. 4*, 1961.
[2] W. H. Chaloner, *The Social and Economic Development of Crewe, 1780-1923* Manchester University Press, 1950, p. 224.

Clearly there is no argument about the necessity—the growing necessity, amongst rich and poor alike—for collective action of many kinds to redistribute income over the life-span, to spread the risks and meet the needs that cannot be effectively met through personal expenditure from individual incomes. But who should distribute the benefits and levy the payments for them, and on what principles should they proceed? That is what we argue about.

The defence of the nation against economic and military rivals forms a second and closely related strand in the history of the social services. Sweat and courage were devalued by the industrialization of production and warfare. Ninety years ago it was clear that a nation must also be equipped with health and trained intelligence if it was to survive, militarily or economically. The Prussians, it was being said, had defeated the greatest military power in Europe because their soldiers could read and write and the French could not. To such requirements 'total war' added the elusive but vital concept of 'civilian morale' derived from a sense of common purpose and confidence in the justice of the nation's social and political system. The implications for social administration of these discoveries were spelled out in the social reforms that followed from every major war. And today the 'space race' and the growing pace of international economic competition seem likely to bring about a development of educational systems which has been called for on less compelling grounds for a generation or more.

The continually rising aspirations of ordinary people—aspirations often created by the social services themselves—form a third strand in the story. In Britain the first school attendance officers had a difficult task compelling hostile parents to send their children to school, with the uncertain backing of magistrates who might themselves be employing the children concerned. But in the first decade of this century this problem seems to have dwindled to a numerically trivial scale—intractable though it still remains.[1] That change probably came about because the first generation for whom a universal system of elementary schooling had been provided began at this time to send their own children to school. The numbers of people seeking help from the health services—particularly the mental health services—appear to be increasing in many countries, though there is no evidence of a comparable increase in the disorders to be treated. The provision of new and better services has raised the aspirations, or lowered the 'pain thresholds', of the afflicted. In a recent study

[1] Julia Dixon, *School Attendance Officers*. University of Manchester. MA thesis, 1956.

of homeless families in London, it was clear that there are still families in Britain's richest city who fall below subsistence level.[1] Sixty years ago there were thousands in this position: they clothed themselves in rags, starved themselves and their children and crowded into cellars and garrets. But today children are adequately fed and clothed, and neither parents nor their landlords are willing to tolerate housing conditions that used to be commonplace. Thus families become homeless, and the state must provide if they are not to disintegrate altogether—their offspring scattered amongst relatives and children's homes.

Meanwhile, for technological and other reasons, the prices of the services upon which these rising aspirations are focused—particularly the prices of education, medical care and housing—tend to rise more rapidly than other prices. Thus the development of social services does not hasten the day when people can provide for themselves through the 'normal' mechanisms of the market, but renders it less likely that this state of affairs will ever be attained.

Britain embarked on her industrial revolution early, towards the end of a century in which the powers of central government had been severely and deliberately limited, at a time when the sea and the Royal Navy relieved government of its most onerous responsibility—the maintenance of a standing army. With such a rudimentary government machine, collective action to soften the hardships of industrialism had often to be initiated by friendly societies, employers, and religious and charitable bodies, and for many years the state confined itself mainly to relieving the destitute. But in countries which have been industrialized more recently the state has frequently taken the lead in creating social services, partly owing to the example of neighbouring governments, but also because collective action for the advancement of social welfare was seen to be a means of promoting and sustaining industrial growth itself. Britain has also experienced this reversal of its own traditional pattern. In the boom years since the Second World War it has often been forgotten that the proposals for 'subsistence level' insurance benefits and variable contributions made in the Beveridge Report gained support partly because they provided a means of maintaining consumer demand through the post-war depressions then widely anticipated. Similar arguments are reappearing now that British governments are again concerned about economic growth and the maintenance of effective

[1] John Greve, *London's Homeless*. Occasional Papers on Social Administration, No. 10. Welwyn, Codicote Press, 1964.

demand. The steps recently taken to increase the output of housing followed a period of several years during which no attempt was made to plan or predict the total rate of building. But the first statement of these new aspirations came not from the Ministry of Housing and Local Government but from the NEDC.[1] If a rapid rate of economic growth is to be achieved, further developments in the social services may soon be required to ensure a market for the nation's increased output.

The creation of public services requires the recruitment and training of a growing number and variety of workers who in turn play a major part in extending and shaping the services themselves. The contribution of these groups—particularly those we call 'professions' —is a fifth strand in the story. Their history is a record of conflict— conflicts between the younger and older generations within the profession, conflicts with laymen and well established neighbouring professions, and sometimes a conflict between the sexes. All are to be seen in the letters of Florence Nightingale. 'The whole reform in nursing . . . has consisted in this,' she said to one of her protégees who had just been appointed a hospital matron: 'to take all power over the nursing out of the hands of the men, and put it into the hands of *one female trained* head and make her responsible for everything . . . Usually it is the medical staff who have injudiciously interfered . . . How much worse it is when it is the Chaplain . . . *There is no worse matron than a chaplain.*'[2] Sometimes the professionals do battle with the administrators—the staff who are responsible for the development of the organization itself rather than for the provision of services for its individual clients. Thus a medical commission, investigating London's poor law infirmaries in 1865, reported that 'with regard to the powers entrusted to the surgeon we are of opinion that great need for reform exists. At present, owing to his nominal inferiority of rank to the master [of the poor law institution], an official who is nevertheless (save in exceptional instances) socially below him, an antagonism is often set up, and in many cases leads to the most vexatious and mischievous interference of the master with the purely medical orders of the surgeon . . .'[3] A sphere of expertise—'purely medical'—is being carved out, and its practitioners

---

[1] National Economic Development Council, *Growth of the United Kingdom Economy, 1961–1966.* London, HMSO, 1963.

[2] Letter from Miss Nightingale, 1867. Quoted by Brian Abel-Smith, *A History of the Nursing Profession.* London, Heinemann, 1960, p. 25.

[3] *Report* of the Lancet Sanitary Commission *for Investigating the State of the Infirmaries of Workhouses, 1866,* pp. 31-2.

seek the status needed to secure their hold upon it. In their plan for the break-up of the poor law, the Webbs—those inveterate technocrats—proposed a wholesale eviction of laymen from positions of power in local administration, and their replacement by paid professional and administrative staff who would be co-ordinated and supervised in every county and county borough by a new official, the Registrar of Public Assistance. One of their opponents attacked the scheme, saying that Englishmen would become 'sheep shepherded by an enormous and apparently irresponsible bureaucracy . . . But stay—did I say irresponsible? To whom should an official be responsible but to an official? Behind the local superintendent there looms a greater figure—the unique glory of the Minority Report— that bureaucrat of bureaucrats, the Registrar—peripatetic, absolute and wielding, as the sword of his spirit, nothing less than a card index.'[1] The conflict between the minority and the majority in this commission—two groups who agreed on so many radical reforms that their disputes now seem tragically trivial—can only be understood if we bear in mind the division between those who put their faith in the paid professional and those who preferred the lay volunteer.

The commitment of these professional groups to the development of their work has repeatedly led them to demand more and better social services. They have been disturbed by the knowledge that children cannot be taught unless they are first fed, that patients cannot be cured unless they are decently housed, that young delinquents cannot be tamed if they have no legitimate playground— for their primary responsibilities are not to the taxpayers or the organization that employs them, but to their profession and the people whom they serve. The erosion of the poor law system in many countries, as more and more of its functions were taken over by new services, was partly due to the lack of any generally enforced system of training for poor law officials, and their failure to acquire the expansive outlook and influential status of a profession.

Each profession seeks to stress and develop those features of its work which are peculiar to itself, which distinguish it most effectively from other groups and protect it from what are seen as extraneous or 'unprofessional' commitments. Partly as a result of this tendency to specialization—sometimes fruitful, sometimes merely protective— each tends to promote the growth of satellite specialisms whose

[1] T. Hancock Nunn, *The Minority Report*, National Poor Law Reform Association (undated), p. 10.

practitioners later seek professional status on their own account. The cluster of medical occupations offers the most highly developed example of this, though the same process can be seen elsewhere. Doctors needed midwives and medical social workers to assist in their work. The qualified midwife would not do the domestic and childminding chores undertaken by her predecessor, the 'handy woman', and domestic help and child care services developed partly to take over these functions. Home help organizers now have their own association (and an international association) and are pressing for training and registration. Meanwhile medical social workers are seeking the appointment of specially trained assistants to relieve them of their clerical and routine welfare work.

The struggle for the resources needed to provide an effective service and the struggle for 'professional freedom' (freedom, largely, from lay interference) have frequently led the professions to call for bigger administrative units and increasing intervention on the part of central government—as witness, for example, the contribution of the medical profession to the development of the health services, and the parts played by many professional groups in the recent debates about the reform of London's government. Thus the growth of a new social service depends on the growth of new professions and new administrative organizations which then proceed to expand, subdivide and multiply. Thenceforth the service can only be modified with their consent. It may be easier (as the Curtis Committee concluded) to create a new service and a new profession than to make radical changes in the habits of existing organizations and professions.

While the form and function of public services are often shaped by the professions they employ, the form and function of the professions may in turn be shaped by the administrative structure within which they develop. The relationship between the two can often be seen most clearly when comparisons are made between similar professions in different countries. Thus in the United States the practice and outlook of social workers owes a great deal to the voluntary family casework agencies whose contribution to the development of this profession has been much greater than their size alone would suggest. These agencies have the right to select their own clients and restrict their caseloads, their material resources are limited but they have considerable freedom to determine their own functions, they have a relatively simple administrative structure and operate alongside a wide variety of other services largely created by local initiative and largely financed from local resources. Voluntary services of this kind exist in Britain, too, but here they operate on a smaller scale alongside a more extensive national system of statutory services in which most of the country's social workers are employed. Social work in this country has been regarded as one aspect of social administration; in America it has more often been regarded as an independent professional activity. This contrast helps to explain why social workers in Britain have long been more subdivided, and more concerned with the provision of practical help, the exercise of statutory powers and duties and the study of social administration, while their American colleagues have gone further in analysing and developing the skills of personal relationships and the practice of community organization. So brief and dogmatic a generalization cannot do justice to the complexity of this comparison, but it may serve to illustrate the link between the structure and the function of social service professions and the need to consider the influence of each upon the other.

We have argued that the social services are not an unproductive frill tacked on to the economy as a charitable afterthought, but an integral and (in some form or other) a necessary part of our economic and social system—a form of collective provision required to meet the needs of an expanding industrial society and to provide a market for its products. They are developed, differentiated, and developed again, in accordance with the changing aspirations of those who work in them and those whom they serve.

Since they are so deeply embedded in society, it follows that they cannot grow in a stable, liberal democracy without the consent of the major interests—political, industrial, religious or administrative —that hold power in such a society. This leads to a final strand in their history: the continuous endeavour to prevent or contain disruption of the social order. Some services—the penal system and much of the poor law, for example—were established wholly or partly as a means of social control, but similar motives appear in surprising places. 'An ill-educated and undisciplined population,' the House of Commons was once told by one of its members, '... is one that may be found most dangerous to the neighbourhood in which it dwells, and ... a band of efficient schoolmasters is kept up at much less expense than a body of police or soldiery.'[1] Octavia Hill opposed the building of houses in courts or culs-de-sac for 'the poorer class of London labourers' because '... it is much more difficult to keep order in them. Where I own them, I feel very much more

Quoted in *Education in Wales, 1847-1947*. HMSO, 1948, p. 5.

strongly the difficulty of keeping any public opinion or order in them, than the difficulty of getting air . . .'[1] But many social services have revolutionary potentialities. Thus the schools teach the illiterate to read, call for taxation on a new scale, and take over social functions hitherto performed by the family, the church and employers. Such services cannot develop until those with the power to prevent them are satisfied that they present no serious hazard to the existing social order. In this country the provision of elementary education was delayed for a generation as a result, and our secondary schools are only now beginning to free themselves from the assumption that there are three kinds of Englishman—officers, NCO's and other ranks, as it were—for whom different types of schooling must be provided. Until very recently the universities, too, still tailored their size and functions to the needs of the late nineteenth-century society in which their traditions took shape. Perhaps they bear in mind that classic statement of their duty to preserve the existing social order pronounced by one of Oxford's most distinguished sons. His ideal university would be a place in which 'people should be taught a wisdom, safe from the excesses and vagaries of individuals, embodied in institutions which have stood the trial and received the sanction of ages, and administered by men . . . supported by their consistency with their predecessors and with each other.'[2]

This brief sketch of the development of the social services does not completely discredit the popular assumptions about their origins and functions outlined at the start of this chapter. Many of these services were indeed designed to assist the poor at the expense of income and property taxes to which the rich made the heaviest contributions. Many of those who founded these services and many who now work in them have indeed been moved by the desire to help the distressed. It is clear, too, that churches, friendly societies and charitable bodies of various kinds have played a major part in creating and shaping our social services. So has the Labour movement. Such motives, however, and the history of voluntary bodies which afforded a means for their expression, cannot provide a convincing explanation for the development of collective provision for human needs—collective provision which appears in one form or another, even in countries which lack the political movements and charitable traditions which characterize our own. The history of

[1] *Royal Commission on the Housing of the Working Classes, 1884-5.* Minutes of evidence. C.4402, para. 8886.
[2] John Henry Cardinal Newman, *The Idea of a University.* London, Longmans Green 1893, p. xii.

voluntary action frequently explains the *forms* the social services take and the *order* in which they develop—the late start of our primary education, for instance, and the cumbersome pattern of flat-rate contributions and benefits that has restricted the scope of our social insurance system. But whatever the form and order adopted, the state has had to assume major responsibilities for the advancement of social welfare in every industrial country.

However, the social services, narrowly defined, form only a part of the collective provisions which have grown up in such countries to meet the needs that the open market cannot adequately cater for. The redistribution of incomes brought about by fiscal systems in which taxation is adjusted to promote the welfare of children, old people and other selected groups; the pensions, welfare services and other non-monetary benefits provided by employers; the 'semi-public' and 'non-profit-making' bodies (more common abroad than in this country) which operate under public supervision, with the aid of tax privileges, subsidies and government loans, to provide housing, medical care, pensions and other services—all these are parts of the same framework, although the use made of different institutions within this framework and the methods and policies each adopt vary from time to time and from country to country.[1]

Thus the student of social administration must examine the whole framework and cannot restrict his studies to those institutions which happen at a particular time and place to be classified as 'social services'. He will find that the questions posed by traditional definitions of this subject matter (Should social services be provided without test of need? Do they produce a decline in initiative and personal responsibility?) are not the most interesting problems on his agenda, important though they may be. We live in a period of rapid demographic, economic and social change: are these changes producing new human needs or sharpening old ones? How are such needs perceived and what priorities are they accorded by different classes of the population and by those in the administrative, professional and political organizations concerned with the development and implementation of social policies? What is being done—and what can be done—through collective action on the part of government, employers, consumers and voluntary organizations to meet these needs? When new forms of collective provision are established, what

[1] Richard M. Titmuss, in *The Social Division of Welfare* (Eleanor Rathbone Memorial Lecture, Liverpool University Press, 1956, reprinted in *Essays on 'The Welfare State'*, Allen and Unwin, 1958) made the first, and still the most comprehensive, analysis of this framework.

impact do they have on the nation's social structure and the distribution of income and power, and what new problems do they
produce? These are the fundamental questions that students of social
administration are concerned with. Political scientists, sociologists,
and historians—economic, social and demographic—are often best
equipped to answer such questions. Only when dealing with the
practice and potentialities of the social services and related institutions
can the student of social administration make any claim to special
expertise. Even here he needs the help of scholars from other disciplines, and his conclusions, as our final question shows, will have
implications for social scientists of every kind.

Thus social administration is not an academic discipline of the
traditional sort. The major social sciences each endeavour to accumu-
late a valid body of knowledge, to develop and refine consistent
theoretical systems, and to perfect appropriate methods of study.
But the distinctive feature of social administration is neither its body
of knowledge (for most of this could be incorporated in other disciplines), nor its theoretical structure (for it has very little), and it is
not concerned with methodology for its own sake. We are concerned
with an ill-defined but recognizable territory: the development of
collective action for the advancement of social welfare. Our job is
to identify and clarify problems within this territory, to throw light
upon them—drawing light from any discipline that appears to be
relevant—and to contribute when we can to the solution of these
problems. Thus the best developed and most fruitful branches of the
subject are often those in which other disciplines play the most
active part—criminology, for example, which rests mainly in the
capable hands of sociologists, lawyers and statisticians.

The study of social administration first entered the universities
as the major component in training courses for social workers. From
the first it was recognized that the subject could not be taught in a
merely descriptive or narrowly vocational fashion. '. . . since half the
thought and money spent on relieving existing evils would probably
have prevented many of them from coming into existence at all,
it is, on a long view, more important to lay bare causes than to plan
immediate remedies . . .' said R. H. Tawney, inaugurating what later
became the Social Administration Department of the London School
of Economics and Political Science.[1]

[1] R. H. Tawney, *Inaugural Lecture, Memoranda on Problems of Poverty, No. II*.
London, The Ratan Tata Foundation, The London School of Economics, 1913,
p. 10.

More recently the subject has been developed by a broader partnership of the social sciences—the particular disciplines involved depending largely on the interests of the scholars concerned, and the structure and past history of their universities. Social administration is now studied by a growing number of students who are not entering social work.[1] Teachers of the subject are occasionally, but increasingly, invited to contribute to the education of doctors, town planners, magistrates, architects, administrators and others. While the study of social administration will always play a major part in the education of social workers, its future development is likely to be of interest to people in many other fields. Armed with this understanding of our subject and its location on the academic map we can return to the research presented in this book.

It should now be clear that a social service is not a static institution applying well-tried methods to well-defined problems; likewise the framework of collective provision within which such services operate is not a completed or permanent edifice—as the phrase 'welfare state' too often suggests. The social services are a continually developing response to continually changing needs and problems. The same could be said of the motor industry, the construction industry or any other sector of the economy that is subject to changes in demand and technology. But in these fields the general aims of an enterprise can often be specified fairly clearly—to 'stay in business' for example, or to 'secure a larger share of the market'. And once the current means for achieving these ends have been decided, most of the people in the enterprise can devote themselves to attaining specified objectives as efficiently, quickly and profitably as possible. A professional engineer, it is true, is not merely a technologist—he is equipped to apply and develop a systematic intellectual discipline —but the specifications to which he works can be made reasonably precise. Nevil Shute illustrates the point in his account of the building of the airship R.100.

'... it was stipulated in contractual form that the airship must attain a speed of seventy miles an hour and that her tare weight should not exceed ninety cubic feet, giving her a disposable load of sixty-two tons; she was to do English trials according to a definite schedule, ending up with a forty-eight hour endurance flight. When these conditions had been complied with the contract would be

[1] See Barbara N. Rodgers, 'The Careers of Social Studies Students', *Occasional Papers on Social Administration* No. 11, Codicote Press, 1964

finished and the ship would be accepted, and our expenditure on her would be at an end.'[1]

The specifications in this case were clear; they constituted a task to be completed, and on completion it was possible to compare intention and outcome, costs and returns, and arrive at some measure of the success achieved. Similar specifications, measurements and comparisons could doubtless be applied more frequently in the social services. But the social administrator is often faced with a different kind of task. The specifications for a national health service or for some local branch of it—from the Act itself to a county council's decision to establish a new clinic to provide maternity and child welfare services—are of necessity vague, and subject to continual change. Many of the tasks to be performed have no completion date, and there is often no conclusive way of measuring how successfully they are being carried out. This lack of specifications and standards is partly due to remediable ignorance: those responsible for the social services could sometimes secure more precise and comprehensive information about the character, coverage and achievements of their work. But often the problem is of a more fundamental kind. All would agree that an aircraft should fly safely, economically and reliably. But what *is* 'health'? What *is* a 'good education'? Would an improved child care service take *more* children from their homes, or *fewer*? What *is* a 'fair rent'? Should a legal aid scheme help *more* people to pay for divorce proceedings? Such questions cannot be answered in a fashion that commands unquestioning assent. Thus specifications of the aims and functions of the social services can at best be temporary, and liable to revision whenever attitudes change or a new election is held. Even when general aims are agreed, the methods appropriate for attaining them are open to questions of more than a technical nature. At a case conference the Education Department's representative may urge that a child be removed from his home to ensure that he attends school, a child care officer may argue that the family should be kept together and moved to better housing, and the Housing Department may object that other families' needs must be met first. The aims of each service and their practical application cannot be determined or reconciled without a continual exercise of moral judgement. The development of these aims is thus one of the principal responsibilities of social administrators and their professional staff, and poses the central questions for research in this field. Those who run a social service can never justify their policies

[1] Nevil Shute, *Slide Rule—the Autobiography of an Engineer*. Heinemann, 1954, p. 134.

by arguing that they serve to keep an organization in being or to extend its share of a 'market'. The history of the social services shows how diverse are the motives from which such aims are derived. We have outlined half a dozen strands of thought that have played a part in the development of these services, but many others could have been added—and the more clearly each motive or 'guiding principle' is stated, the more certainly we shall find another that conflicts with it. Attempts to reconcile equality with equality of opportunity, social justice with liberty, freedom of choice with efficiency, or the interests of one class or age group with those of another lead generally to compromises that are liable to be upset before long. Thus there can be no generally and permanently valid 'principles of social policy' and no book of rules for the social administrator.

Yet even the search for fruitful and enduring compromises between diverse interests can be a sufficiently difficult and important task. And on occasion the social administrator may enable those concerned with his service to create something bigger and more enduring than a mere compromise between rival interests.

How can he prepare himself for such work? Ideally, he requires a general knowledge of the social sciences and the ability to apply these disciplines to problems arising in his field—an ability which studies of social administration are designed to foster. No one with a career to make has time to explore so vast a territory thoroughly; nevertheless the educated man of today can acquire some understanding of the outlook and methods of sociologists, psychologists and political economists—just as his predecessors acquired some understanding of classical literature, ancient history and the Bible—without gaining degrees in each of these subjects.

With this background of general knowledge it may then be worth his while to make some more detailed and systematic study of the processes of administration in the social services. Development and change—not stability and equilibrium—are the dominant features of the social services. The evolution of these services is not an impersonal or automatic response to the external pressures of supply and demand, neither is it simply dictated by legislation; it is largely brought about by the people who work in the services. How do these services develop? How do new services begin, how do changes come about in the scope and character of existing services, why do such changes take place, and what parts are played in this process by different people, different interests and groups? These are the principal questions that research should deal with. The answers to them will not teach anyone the techniques of good administration, but they may help him to understand the administrative process and to discern the salient features of its development more surely; they may enable him to grasp opportunities for change, to accept the limits that confine the scope for change, and to pose more clearly the questions he must answer for himself—the questions no book can answer for him. The resources and methods at his command he owes to his predecessors; the history of his organization and the history of the society within which it operates are his principal assets, and sometimes his principal obstacles. The future of his organization and of the community to which it contributes is for him and his colleagues to create with the help of their fellow citizens. The rest of this book is designed to throw some light on this task of linking the past to the future.

CHAPTER 3

THE ANALYSIS OF ADMINISTRATION

THE previous chapter dealt with the evolution of social policies on a long-term national scale, and explained the features of this process to be explored in the next chapters. There the same process is dealt with in microscopic fashion, through a description and discussion of relatively short-term developments in local units of the social services. But before embarking on these case studies our approach to the analysis of administration and some of the concepts we employ call for further clarification. They are derived from various sources which will be fully acknowledged in an appendix which surveys the literature in this field, but our debt to Herbert A. Simon and his collaborators will be obvious to those who are familiar with this literature.

The administrator's job is to get something done, and his agency or department will not interest us for its own sake but only as a means to that end. In common parlance his agency may be described as an 'organization', and studies of administration often take such units as their focal point. But administrative organization consists of a set of people collaborating and communicating with each other in a systematic and continuing fashion for the performance of a common task, and different tasks call different patterns of collaboration into being. Since one person may play a part in several tasks he may in this stricter sense be a member of several 'organizations', and these organizations are not necessarily coterminous with the unit in which he happens to be employed. 'Organization', in our sense, does not exist in its own right: it is simply a way of describing certain types of human collaboration, and the description required depends on the task to be performed. Neither the structure of organization nor the process of administration can be identified or explained until this task has been specified.

This is why increasing use has been made of case studies in recent literature on administration. They permit the student of administration to explore and analyse the performance of particular tasks without the restrictions imposed by inappropriate definitions of his subject matter. The drawback of many collections of case studies lies in their authors' reluctance to explain precisely what they are making case studies *of* and what lessons are to be derived from the exercise—but these are not inevitable features of the method.

Our own case studies deal with 'developments' or 'changes' in the work of local units of the social services. (The procedures for selecting these cases and the methods of research employed will be explained in the next chapter.) Thus the *tasks* that form the basis of the studies that follow consist of one or more developments in the work of an administrative agency. The administrative *process*, or history, traced in each study consists of the work done to accomplish these tasks. The *organization*, or structure, of administration consists of the more or less specialized roles played by those who accomplished the task, and the pattern of collaboration and communication linking these people together. These three concepts—task, process and organization—provide the means for an analysis of administration. The meaning of each depends on the others. Once a task has been specified it is possible to discover the processes that play a part in its accomplishment, and once the process has been traced it becomes possible to abstract the pattern of roles, rules and relationships which constitutes the administrative organization for this work.

But the meaning of such concepts is always uncertain. Like most of the vocabulary of administration, they can be interpreted in four different ways. (a) Many agencies have tasks, procedures and an organization which are written into their constitutions, operating manuals and organization charts. This is the 'official' or 'authorized' version. (b) When questioned, however, the people who work in such agencies often give their own interpretation of the system, explaining that the 'official' version has in practice been developed and modified through the interplay of practical necessity, historical accident, personal idiosyncrasy and other local circumstances. (c) But anyone who studies the agency may come to the conclusion that even this interpretation provides an inadequate account of the way in which it *really* works. His own conclusions about the organization will also be a subjective interpretation but they are designed to approximate as closely as possible to a third concept: 'administration as it really is'. (d) Meanwhile he and others may form opinions about the tasks, organization and procedures that the agency *ought* to adopt. This pattern, which is usually harder to specify or describe in detail, may be regarded as a direction of development that is being advocated for the future.

Thus, although the words employed may remain the same, administrative concepts may be endowed with different meanings by being discussed in any of these four 'tones of voice'. In some of the literature on this subject these usages have been termed 'manifest' (the officially approved version), 'assumed' (the interpretation offered by the individuals concerned), 'extant' (the reality), and 'requisite' (or recommended).[1]

It will be helpful to bear these distinctions in mind and to note that they may be related to each other in time, constituting an approximate but recurring progression in human experience and in the thinking derived from that experience. Administrators endeavour to formulate an explanation of their doings—the agency's 'assumed' organization. This is their attempt to identify and explain the continually developing reality—the 'extant' organization—and to provide an account of it that is comprehensible and reliable, yet not too far removed from the official, or 'manifest', organization they may be expected to uphold. At the same time they look ahead to devise plans for the future, advocating a 'requisite' organization. As they take shape, these plans for the future may eventually call for a codification and reformulation of the original aims and procedures, providing a new version of 'manifest' organization. The cycle may then be repeated. Whether or not this is the normal pattern of development, the illustration may serve to show that in a changing world administrators will inevitably give varying and approximate interpretations of their work and its organization. Divergences between official principles, practical interpretations, the reality itself and aspirations for the future need not be a sign of confusion or error. Provided they constitute a continuing and fruitful progression and are neither extreme nor contradictory, such divergences may be a means of adaptation and a sign of vigour.

We can now return to a more detailed analysis of the basic concepts to be employed in our analysis. The *tasks* to be examined in the studies that follow were thought to constitute important changes or developments in the work of the agencies concerned. Some of them amounted to changes in the service provided for the agency's clients, some were changes in the organization and procedures for the provision of these services, and most of them involved changes of both

---

[1] See Wilfred Brown, *Exploration in Management* (London, Heinemann, 1960), p. 289, whose definition of the fourth term mentioned differs slightly from our own.

types. Some of these changes were foreseen, planned and carried through as a specific and deliberate project—they were 'tasks' in the normal sense of that word. Other changes 'worked themselves out' gradually, and their meaning and importance were only appreciated after they had taken place—they could only be identified as 'tasks' with the aid of hindsight, after completion.

The *process* of administration consists of a sequence of events. But 'events' are not discrete or concrete objects waiting, like fossils, to be discovered by the explorer. They are incidents and aspects of human experience, selected, named and interpreted by men for their own purposes. (Thus people may agree that a particular committee met between the hours of two and four on a given day and that certain decisions were recorded in the minutes, but one person giving an account of that afternoon may say the committee decided that two departments should be combined, another may say that new budgeting procedures were adopted, and a third may say that the head of one department was prematurely pensioned off. All may be referring to the same occurrences. Have they described one event or three? Is one version correct and the others wrong? All three versions may be true, and all are interesting—if only for the light they throw on the selective perceptions and memories of the speakers.) The selection of the events to appear in an account of administrative processes should include any—and any versions of them—that help to explain the evolution and performance of the tasks being studied. The same criterion should be applied, so far as time and resources permit, when deciding how far back into the past the story should be traced.

The story assembled in this way may be regarded as a continuous series of 'decisions' or 'choices', and this can be a helpful concept, provided its artificial and abstract character is remembered: the people concerned may not in practice be aware of choosing or deciding. Each time a choice is made—and even the decision to do nothing is still a decision, provided action of some kind is possible —those who choose depend on their knowledge of the situation and hence on communication, past and present, with other people. That is to say the decision is partly an outcome of organization. Moreover each choice is both a decision to do something and a decision *not* to do other things. At the start of the story the participants can select from amongst all the choices practicable at that time. Each decision that is made thereafter reduces the number of alternatives still available, until the last act is reached which determines the final outcome of the story in question. At certain stages in this process decisions are taken which select one route and exclude many others potentially available up to that point. These major junctions in the map across which the administrator travels are the crucial stages in his progress; the assumptions he makes, the ends he pursues and the communications available to him at these points are the crucial elements in the story.

This account of administrative processes makes them appear deceptively systematic and continuous. In practice the performance of a particular task, or the carrying through of a particular development, seldom fills the working day of those responsible for it. It may consist of one item towards the end of a crowded committee agenda, a telephone call made the following month, a memorandum prepared over the weekend dealing mainly with other matters, then a hurried departmental meeting followed by a chance conversation between two people on their way to lunch. Such are the scattered incidents —if the researcher is fortunate enough to trace them—which should be threaded together to produce what the participants may later regard as an unrecognizably coherent story.

The administrative process consists of a series, or many related series, of actions taken by individuals and groups. These people collaborate with each other in a reasonably systematic and predictable manner, they treat each other in distinctive ways and play specialized parts in the administrative story: that is to say their behaviour is 'organized'. *Organization* is again an abstract concept; it consists of the specialized roles of each person concerned in the development to be studied, and the relationships between these roles. Like the tasks and processes of administration, it may be discussed in terms of its 'manifest', 'assumed', 'extant' or 'requisite' content. Like the processes, too, it is not something concrete that lies around waiting to be discovered: features of organization which are relevant for one task may be irrelevant for others, and people concerned with different tasks will often describe administrative organization in very different terms, even though all of them are employed in the same agency.

The descriptions of administrative organization given in the chapters that follow are compiled by listing the people involved in the development to be studied and describing the parts they play in it and their relationships to each other. Who should be regarded as being 'involved' is a matter of judgement: anyone whose behaviour appears to influence the outcome of the development should be included in the list—whether or not he holds any official position, belongs to any particular agency or is aware of the contribution he makes. Those on the list thus compiled will fall into distinguishable groups, some of which may constitute separate units or agencies. These units or working groups may form a single hierarchy responsible to one person or committee—consisting of head office, sub-departments and local field offices of one social service, for example. But often this will not be so: the administrative organization for the performance of one task may include independent units and structures responsible to no common authority. Moreover one person may play a part in several overlapping systems of organization; he might, for example, be a member of a public health department and of a co-ordinating committee (on which many departments are represented) and of the local branch of his professional association. The selection and definition of the agencies and groups to be included in any account of administrative organization must again be a matter of judgement: it is a good selection in so far as it is useful, and useful in so far as it explains the performance of the particular tasks studied. Thus neither the process nor the organization of administration can be understood in isolation from each other: they are two different ways of describing the same phenomena.

Administration may be regarded as a set of procedures for linking those who control the resources necessary for certain tasks (the members of a municipal council or the shareholders in a company, for example) with those who use the goods or services produced from these resources (pupils, patients, tenants, customers, etc.). The administrator has to maintain and develop collaboration between those who control or provide resources, those who perform the tasks that convert these resources into goods and services, and those who use the products or outcome of this work. If these three groups are not effectively and continuously linked, the work cannot be done and the agency responsible for doing it will eventually go out of business. A single-handed ice-cream vendor might be regarded as 'linking' his suppliers and customers, but it is only when the process grows sufficiently complex to require a variety of people performing specialized tasks and systematic procedures for the co-ordination of their work that 'administration' can be said to take place.

The co-ordinating relationships which create an 'organization' of the individuals participating in the task to be performed arise from the fact that these individuals have neither time, knowledge, power nor ability to decide all their actions independently. They cannot decide everything 'for themselves', but depend repeatedly on others for the information, guidance and instructions that enable them to do their work. The organization determines the timing, direction and content of the communications on which they depend and many of the assumptions and aims that guide them. Each time they rely on past or present communications with someone else when making a decision they confer 'power' of some kind on the person upon whom they rely. An analysis of the relationships which make up an administrative organization can therefore be made by distinguishing the different forms taken by this exercise of power or influence.

Within most organizations specific officers or groups (committees, boards, etc.) are required to make certain decisions. The appointment or dismissal of staff, the determination of salaries, the decision to pursue particular policies, to purchase or issue certain types of equipment—these are typical of the kinds of decision involved. The individuals or groups concerned may largely determine for themselves what should be done, or they may merely approve the recommendations put to them by others in the organization. But a decision cannot strictly be said to have been taken until the designated person or group has approved it. This type of power may be called 'formal authority'.

Formal authority is an important but strictly limited type of power. It may too easily be confused with the general influence exercised by senior staff over more junior members of their service or agency, and borderline cases arise in which the two cannot be clearly distinguished. (It may be difficult to tell whether the junior does as his boss tells him because the boss has formal authority to determine what should be done, because he likes, respects or fears the boss, because he has a habit of doing what he is told or because both share the same concern for the service in which they work and normally agree on the action required.) The general influence exercised by senior staff may more usefully be regarded as the exercise of one form of 'prestige'. Prestige, which takes many other forms, may be attached to certain posts or groups within the organization, or to certain skills; it may be a peculiarly personal matter, derived from the character and past history of the person concerned; it may be exercised on senior members of the organization by their juniors, or in the reverse direction.

Prestige is often attached to 'advisers'—indeed without the support of some measure of prestige and mutual confidence the adviser is likely to find his recommendations disregarded. Nevertheless 'advice' is worth distinguishing from other forms of influence. The adviser has a particular sphere of competence about which he is supposed to be in some measure expert, and he often has specific terms of reference which define the questions on which his advice is sought. But he does not hold formal authority in the sphere upon which he advises. He recommends but does not decide. Advisers may hold full-time posts within the agency concerned. If brought in from outside they are sometimes called 'consultants', but this word has too many meanings to have much general value. (Compare, for example, the role of a 'management consultant' brought in to advise a firm on a particular administrative problem, and that of a 'consultant surgeon' directly responsible for a department within a hospital). In practice the power of the adviser may depend more upon his prestige than his knowledge. It may also be difficult to distinguish from formal authority; those with formal authority may not be compelled to accept the advice they are given, but in practice the only alternative open to them may be to find another adviser who is likely to recommend a similar course of action. Thus accountants, legal and medical advisers and other experts effectively determine many of the decisions taken by those holding formal authority to make these decisions.

The adviser may give some, but rarely all, of the information on which his advice is based. It is his responsibility to decide how much to tell those whom he advises. This aspect of his role constitutes another form of power that appears in many relationships which are not of an advisory character—the power of 'filtering' communications. Communication systems are devised for the transmission of selected and summarized information. That is to say, the withholding or suppression of information is one of their principal functions. The 'filterer's' job is to communicate selected data to selected people at appropriate times. Since communication proceeds 'upwards', 'sideways', and 'downwards' within an administrative hierarchy, filtering also operates in all these directions, and the longer the lines of communication are, the greater tends to be the power and the heavier the responsibilities of those who act as filters. Their influence also depends heavily on their reputation or prestige: the higher it stands, the more willingly people accept the selection of information they transmit.

Thus far we have distinguished types of power largely by distinguishing types of communication. All assume a willingness to communicate on the part of those involved. But their participation in the process only continues on certain conditions, and there is always the possibility that people may withhold the labour or resources they command, or respond so rarely and perversely to the communications they receive that they become absentees in effect if not in fact. There may never be a resignation or a strike, the organization's suppliers may continue to provide what is wanted, and its customers may accept what it produces; but the possibility that such people may refuse to participate can nevertheless compel it to do, or refrain from doing, certain things, even if the use of this ultimate weapon is never explicitly threatened.

Thus the emphasis given to communication in this analysis should not suggest that 'administrative man' is a kind of machine whose responses can be determined by the character and timing of the stimuli to which he is subjected. People bring with them their own ambitions, assumptions and attitudes which dispose them to act in certain ways, and the history and structure of the organizations in which they work will modify these dispositions, whether by accident or by design. They have to take so many decisions that the administrative process would break down altogether if they were not capable of handling most of them without stopping to communicate with others. Therefore the development of appropriate attitudes and habits of thought, derived from technical knowledge and frames of reference which enable people to perceive a situation and react to it in an appropriate fashion, are central parts of the administrator's work. The training and organization which constitute a 'profession' provide one method of standardizing and controlling the performance of staff and their participation in the administrative process. A profession operates within a particular field as an 'institutional conscience', sanctioning behaviour which would otherwise depend only on the conscience of the individual and the outlook of the groups in which he happened to work. But professions are themselves a form of organization, established to achieve particular aims that may sometimes conflict with those of other professions and of the organizations in which their members serve. They may be a source of conflict as well as a means to unity.

We have attempted to introduce and illustrate some of the concepts and methods that throw light on the practice of administration. Anyone studying administration would do well to start by asking: 'the administration of *what*?' He is dealing with a purposive activity; the organization and processes relevant to his studies are not 'given', but depend on the tasks he is examining. Once the task or development to be studied has been selected he can explore its history and the human relationships which constitute the organization through which that history is enacted. Their exploration is rendered possible by the conditions that bring the organization into being—by people's inability to decide everything for themselves, 'from nothing' as it were. Since they are not omniscient they need information, guidance, instructions and a code of behaviour to enable them to make choices and decisions, and these influences, the traditions and institutions from which they are derived and the means of communicating them, are accessible to the research worker. Thus the series of decisions and choices which constitute the administrative process can be pieced together—with hard work, good fortune and the help of administrators themselves. Some phases of the process, and the communications and influences brought to bear at these points, will in retrospect appear crucial and call for specially detailed study.

We should endeavour to clear our minds of conventional assumptions about the manner in which organizations are supposed to work, and search out the influences actually operating as best we can. In doing so, we may find that formal authority is more limited in scope and more rarely used in practice than we had supposed, that the aims and functions of organizations are ill-defined and subject to dispute and change, that advisers and filterers of communication are more powerful than might at first appear, that personal prestige and influence sometimes operate in surprising directions, and that the networks of communication and power are complicated, continually shifting and often fail to conform to any uniform or unitary hierarchical pattern. We may find, too, that an account of the official or formal structure and procedures of an organization tells little about the work it actually does and less about the scope for changes in that work. The outlook of those who play a part in the story—arising from their own past history and that of the agency in which they work—goes far to determine their response to the communications they receive and their capacity to sieze opportunities for innovation.

In common parlance the word 'administration' often refers to a special form of work which may be contrasted with other kinds of work—with 'policy-making' or 'professional work' for example. Though this usage may be convenient for distinguishing different aspects of the administrative process, and the capacities required at different points in an administrative hierarchy, it too often restricts and confuses the questions the serious student of the subject should be asking. 'Administration', for him, should include *all* the activities and influences that determine the character and outcome of the tasks he is studying. He is interested in *all* who participate in these processes and contribute to their outcome—whether or not they happen to be called 'administrators', and whether or not they are employed by the agency whose work he is studying. (A voluntary social work agency included in the studies that follow had an area office which occupied a corner of a municipal building, and it was found that the porters at the main entrance played a large part in directing those who called at this building to various offices within it. Thus the people who sought this agency's help were partly selected by these men. Since the porters helped to determine the character of the agency's work they participated in its administration.) The activities of 'policy-makers' and 'professional staff' are just as much a part of the administrative process as those of the staff who are called 'administrators'. The activities of receptionists, clerical workers, staff in neighbouring administrative units and the clients of the service are likewise a part of this process, and the student of administration should be alert to all of them.

PART II

CHAPTER 4

THE CASE STUDIES

THE approach to the study of social administration explained in the preceding chapters dictates the character of the case studies presented in the second part of this book. Our social services are not a self-contained, static or completed edifice. They are part of a more general and continually evolving collective response to the changing needs of an industrial society. Their objectives, derived from diverse pressures and motives, are continually developing and continually disputed. Their organization has no validity in its own right; it can only be evaluated in the light of the tasks it has to perform. Thus neither the ends nor the means of social administration can be taken as 'given'; they must be considered, and questioned, together. Moreover these ends and means are not determined, once and for all, by Parliament: they are repeatedly reshaped and re-interpreted by people at all levels in the social services and by the changing needs and expectations of their clients.

The central purpose of our studies is therefore to throw light on the evolution of the aims and methods of the social services, and the contribution made to that evolution by different groups and individuals. They deal with change, and the manner in which it comes about. No attempt is made to pass judgement on the social services; although the reader may form his own judgements from time to time, our purpose has been to explain, not to evaluate, the development of social policies. These studies are a small part of the broader academic enterprise of exploring the ways in which societies evolve. They call for the aid of other disciplines that deal with human behaviour and social structure, and their debt to these disciplines will be repaid in so far as they succeed in elucidating the particular aspects of social change to which they are directed. In the concluding chapter we comment briefly on the implications our work may have for other social sciences.

The administrative units which formed the starting point for our studies were local offices of social services provided by central and local government and by voluntary organizations—the kind of unit that will employ those for whom this book is primarily designed. All but one of these units operated in the London area. We approached the officials responsible for them and asked: 'What are the most important developments or changes which have taken place in your department (or local office) in the last few years?' In some cases we were assured that no 'developments' or 'changes' had occurred for many years. If this view was maintained in subsequent discussion we proceeded no further—even though we were sometimes aware that changes of some importance had taken place. In other cases, one or more 'developments' were mentioned, and we then selected whatever seemed most important (and accessible to research) in consultation with the head of the local unit concerned. Clearly these developments cannot be regarded as a random sample of the administrative process, or of the work of London's social services. They may have been chosen because they were expected to interest a University Department of Social Administration, or because they were easily identified and analysed, or because they were unlikely to discredit the service being studied. Nevertheless they were chosen, not by outsiders who might have misapprehensions about the most important features of the work to be studied, but by those directly responsible for the administrative units concerned. The outcome may prove less dramatic than a series of studies chosen because they were 'interesting' or likely to provide 'good teaching material', but it may afford a more realistic and representative picture of important local developments in social administration—developments more important than the reorganization of record-keeping procedures or a typing pool, but more local than a change in central government policy or the nationwide implementation of new legislation. Having selected our material in this fashion, we felt bound to include all the studies we could publish, even though some of them contribute relatively little to the general themes pursued in the third part of this book. To exclude those which do not support our conclusions would clearly destroy whatever merits our selection procedure may have.

Our methods of research were simple though laborious; we read all the relevant documents we could find and interviewed those who had been most closely concerned with the events to be traced. Some of the developments chosen were still in progress, but most of them had been completed months earlier. Human forgetfulness or reticence and the failure to make or preserve records inevitably prevented us from securing the complete story in some cases. Publication had then to be approved by senior officials, and at times it seemed that our studies were either dull, because we had not discovered the full story, or unpublishable—because we had. But with the passage of time we have arrived at versions of the studies which include all we were able to discover that appeared to us to be of real importance. The only study omitted deals—ironically enough—with a University: in this case the authorities concerned gave permission for publication but after long and painful deliberation we decided that publication at this stage could not be reconciled with other obligations of its author.

These studies have been written without theoretical presuppositions or technical terminology. While there is nothing more revealing than a valid theory, few things can be so stultifying and misleading as an inappropriate one. Since it was the lack of enlightening and tested theories of administration which prompted this research in the first place, it seemed best to present our studies in a descriptive fashion, without attempting to illustrate or prove any general conclusions, so that the reader could be enabled, as far as possible, to draw his own conclusions and reject ours. Each study is followed by a brief discussion of the light it throws on the evolution of social policies —a marginal commentary that is drawn together and reappraised in the third part of the book. The differing interests of our readers will prompt them to look for different things in these studies, and some may be bewildered by the aspects of them which we have chosen to explore in our discussions. The purpose of these discussions may become clearer if our concluding chapter and the two appendices that follow it are read before the case studies.

We owe a great debt to all those who helped us compile and revise these studies. Any errors and distortions still to be found in them are the authors' responsibility. The officials who helped in this research knew it was unlikely to be of any immediate practical value to them and might even prove harmful—if only in the demands it made on the time of busy people. We hope their patience and generosity may encourage others to assist in future work of this kind. Meanwhile, it must constantly be borne in mind that the studies do *not* provide a complete or typical picture of the organizations and services concerned, nor were they intended to do so; they deal only with particular developments within them and particular phases of their history. Many of these services have changed considerably since the periods covered by our research, and no attempt has been made to bring the studies up to date. Their purpose is *not* to provide an account of current social policies, but an analysis of the manner in which such policies are formulated, implemented and modified at the local level.

Finally we must draw attention to an omission so obvious that it may too easily be overlooked. Our resources only permitted us to read records and interview many of the staff who participated in the developments examined. We did not seek the other side of the story —the views of clients and consumers. The contribution they made to the development of these services is glimpsed from time to time, but to explore it systematically would have required extensive interviews with clients and potential clients. This we hope to do in the future. Meanwhile it must be remembered that this book presents an analysis of social administration which is derived from one side of the counter only.

CHAPTER 5

———

SLUM CLEARANCE BEGINS AGAIN
IN BETHNAL GREEN

The first study in this series provides a useful introduction to the framework of local government which forms the setting for several subsequent studies. A change in the resources available for a service brought about a redirection of policy, the character of which was dictated by the aims of the elected Council. The administrative processes involved took place in various departments of the local authority, and at other levels of government too. Co-ordination of the whole development depended heavily on one official. The change in policy was perceived in different ways by those concerned.

THIS study, carried out in 1958, began in the Housing Manager's Department of the Metropolitan Borough of Bethnal Green. The Housing Manager had no hesitation in naming the most important recent development in the work of her department: it was the return to slum clearance or—as she first described it—the change from rehousing people selected from the Borough's waiting lists to rehousing people whose houses were to be demolished. This development was traced through the records of the Borough—those in particular of the Housing Committee and its Housing Management Sub-Committee —and in discussions with the Chairman of the Housing Committee, the Housing Manager and her staff, the Deputy Town Clerk, the Medical Officer of Health and his staff of Public Health Inspectors.

Our report begins with a brief outline of housing policy in England between 1945 and 1958, followed by an account of the bodies responsible for implementing various aspects of this policy in the Borough. The changeover to slum clearance is then described.

But first a warning should be given. 'Slum clearance', the Chairman of the Housing Committee reminded us, is a technical term, referring to the demolition of houses unfit for human habitation: it implies no evaluation of the people who live in this property. These people have lived longer in Bethnal Green than anyone else and are the

Borough's most respected citizens; if there *were* any 'slum people' in Bethnal Green, he remarked, they would be found elsewhere in the Borough.

Housing Policy since the War

For about eight years after the war, housing *policy* presented few problems; the problems were mainly of *method*—how to build houses as fast as possible in all parts of the country with the resources available, and how to restrict the programme to a level these resources would permit.[1] The Housing (Temporary Provisions) Act of 1944 extended to 'general needs housing' the subsidies provided for slum clearance under the Housing (Financial Provisions) Act of 1938. The Ministries of Works and Health were empowered by further legislation to construct, distribute and erect prefabricated houses that were to go on sites provided by the local authorities. In 1946 the Housing (Financial and Miscellaneous Provisions) Act established the basis for new and more generous subsidies which were continued, with minor modifications in 1949 and further increased in 1952, until the Housing Subsidies Act of 1956 drastically reduced 'general needs' subsidies (as a first step to abolishing them altogether) and concentrated Exchequer contributions for new building on slum clearance projects, on 'overspill' housing built in new and expanded towns and in other places outside the authority for which the houses were provided, and to a lesser extent on housing for old people. Until 1954, housing policy for most authorities was, in principle at least, a fairly straightforward matter: Mr Tomlinson, introducing the first post-war housing Bill, said housing 'should be tackled as one would tackle a military operation'. Mr Bevan, introducing the 1949 Housing Bill, had no doubts about the aims of this operation: 'We shall, of course, go on providing additional houses until we have reached the position of providing a separate home for every family in the country . . .' The local authorities were the chosen instruments for this operation —their programmes could be planned and controlled, and they could allocate the new houses to those most in need of them. When private building began again, the local authorities were told (by Labour and Conservative Governments alike) that new houses built for private owners 'must go and be seen to go to persons in need of homes'.[2] Provisions were made in the 1949 Housing Act for the encourage-

[1] D. V. Donnison, *Housing Policy Since the War*. Occasional Papers on Social Administration, No. 1. Welwyn, Codicote Press, 1959.
[2] Ministry of Health Circular, 108/48 of June 25, 1948. Similar instructions were given in the Ministry of Housing and Local Government's Circular 73/51 of November 27, 1951.

ment of repairs and improvements to existing houses (through loans, grants and technical advice). This policy was developed further in the 1954 Housing Repairs and Rents Act and in a number of subsequent Circulars and policy statements, but it had achieved little by 1958. During the period covered by this study, proposals for slum clearance thus constituted the only seriously considered alternative to the over-riding policy of increasing the country's stock of homes. These proposals were first taken up with conviction in a Circular issued in March 1954, which withdrew earlier instructions to hold up clearance projects and asked local authorities to 'take up again, as a matter of urgency, the campaign of slum clearance which the war interrupted.'[1] The Housing Repairs and Rents Act of that year required all authorities to submit slum clearance proposals to the Ministry of Housing and Local Government, and there followed a period of discussion and planning brought to a head two years later —amidst bitter political controversy—by the Housing Subsidies Act which compelled many authorities to switch their efforts from 'waiting list' rehousing to slum clearance rehousing.

Under slum clearance procedures local authorities may deal with individual buildings by serving demolition orders. Larger areas containing a sufficient proportion of unfit houses can be declared to be 'clearance areas' with the approval of the Minister. The authority may then compel the owners of property in the area to demolish it and later make compulsory purchase of the land if they fail to redevelop it; or it may (and normally does) acquire the land by agreement or compulsion and itself demolish and rebuild. Alternatively, large groups of buildings in urban areas may be declared to be 'redevelopment areas', provided they contain at least fifty 'working class' houses of which at least one-third are unfit for habitation or congested or overcrowded; or the declaration may be based on grounds of overall planning needs, regardless of the character of the property involved. The procedure for redevelopment is the same as that for slum clearance.[2] Objections may be made to compulsory purchase or clearance orders and these are considered at public local enquiries conducted by a representative of the Minister.

In this study an attempt will be made to show how one Metropolitan Borough came to make the change from building for 'general needs' to slum clearance and rebuilding. It is not suggested that

[1] Ministry of Housing and Local Government Circular 30/54 of March 2, 1954.
[2] The Town and Country Planning Act of 1947, and Part III of the consolidating Housing Act of 1957 contain the relevant powers for redevelopment and clearance.

developments in this Borough were typical of those taking place on a national scale. This development was not chosen as an example of housing policy, but as an illustration of administrative processes. Since the time of this study there have been further developments in national housing policies and a radical reform of London's local government, but they need not be recorded here.

Housing Administration in Bethnal Green

Bethnal Green covers a compact 760 acres between Shoreditch, Stepney, Hackney and Poplar in the east end of London. Its population in 1955 was 54,000—just half what it was in 1931. Ninety-three per cent of those in work were in skilled (55%), partly skilled (13%) or unskilled (25%) manual jobs.[1] Rows of two-storey terrace houses are crowded amongst small factories and workshops, a few squares and parks, new council flats, Victorian tenement houses, and the main railway lines running eastwards and northwards from Liverpool Street Station. In Bethnal Green a penny rate raised less revenue than in any other London Borough. Many of the Borough's houses were condemned as long ago as 1920 when its first thorough survey of housing conditions was made.

Unlike some of the other public services considered in this series of studies, the provision of housing is not the responsibility of a single authority or department but of several. The smaller Metropolitan Boroughs presented an extreme example of this system.

In 1958 the London County Council and the Metropolitan Boroughs had joint housing powers. Major questions of planning, the allocation of responsibility for redevelopment areas, major building projects, and building that took place outside the County Council's boundaries were among the more important issues to be decided by the County Council, working to a considerable extent through the District Offices of its Housing Management Department. The Eastern District Office covered the Boroughs of Stepney, Poplar, Hackney, Bethnal Green, and parts of Shoreditch, Finsbury and Woolwich. Bethnal Green's surveys and the five-yearly development plans called for by the Town and Country Planning Act of 1947 were discussed with the London County Council, and areas for clearance and redevelopment were divided between the two authorities—the County generally taking the largest. The Borough was not compelled to secure the County's approval for its housing programme, but in practice the two collaborated closely, partly owing to the fact that the Borough had to

[1] Census 1951.

rely on the County Council for help in rehousing any families that could not be accommodated in Bethnal Green. Unlike other housing authorities, the Metropolitan Boroughs were not permitted to build outside their own boundaries. A Borough as densely populated as Bethnal Green could seldom find homes for all those whose houses were to be demolished in clearance schemes, but the County Council normally provided for half the resulting 'overspill'. Owing to its small population, limited resources and serious housing problems, Bethnal Green had always relied on close collaboration with the London County Council for help in its housing programmes. Boroughs with less daunting problems to face, larger resources and a different political complexion, tended to collaborate less happily with the County.[1]

The Ministry of Housing and Local Government and its predecessors, the Ministry of Local Government and Planning and the Ministry of Health, used to exercise detailed control over the numbers, types and location of houses to be built, the volume of building licences to be issued, the purposes for which they were to be used, and so on. But building licences, 'zonal conferences' of local housing authorities, housing allocations and restrictions on the use of materials had come to an end before the period with which this study is mainly concerned. At that time the size of the housing programme was mainly limited by the rising cost of building, the high level of interest rates and the restriction of subsidies. The Ministry still supervised building standards, approved all plans for demolition, clearance and redevelopment, and sanctioned loans raised by the local authorities.

The Borough's Housing Committee, through its Housing Manager and assistants, was responsible to the Council for preparing a building programme, selecting the tenants to go into Council flats, and arranging transfers and exchanges between tenants in Council and private property. The Borough had no architect of its own, and its buildings were designed by four private firms of architects who worked closely with the Borough's officers, attending Housing Committee meetings when necessary and conducting negotiations on the Borough's behalf with contractors, the County Council and the Ministry. For the actual construction of houses and flats the Borough normally employed private contracting firms, but some of its new building and much of its maintenance work was carried out by its

---

[1] Evidence submitted to the Royal Commission on Local Government in Greater London by the Boroughs of Hampstead, St. Marylebone and Bethnal Green illustrates this contrast.

Surveyor's Department. The Borough Treasurer was responsible for raising loans—at one time from the Public Works Loan Board but in 1958 from the open market—in order to finance building schemes. He was also responsible for collecting rents on Council property and for advising the Committee when they fixed these rents. The Medical Officer of Health was responsible for the selection and 'representation' of unfit buildings and areas. This work was largely handled by the Public Health Inspectors in his Department; they attempted to make regular surveys and inspections, but this was difficult owing to the acute shortage of these officers, only two of whom were available for housing work. Decisions about the 'fitness' of housing had to be made in consultation with the County Council but in practice the Medical Officers of the two authorities applied rather different standards. The County's criteria had to be applied throughout its territory, but a Borough which had made good progress with its clearance programme could afford to apply more rigorous standards.

It should now be clear that the provision and management of housing do not constitute a separate, self-contained 'service', directed by one official and his committee; they are the responsibility of half a dozen independent bodies, including private architects and various Departments of the London County Council, working under the general supervision of the Ministry. In this Borough the co-ordination of the activities of these different bodies was largely due to the Clerk's Department and in particular to the Deputy Town Clerk.[1] A few examples may illustrate how the system worked.

Slum clearance projects begin with the selection of sites suitable for clearance. Every five years a 'preliminary survey' was made of the whole Borough and a general plan of action discussed and agreed with the County Council. Detailed surveys were then made by the Public Health Inspectors who brought bad spots to the attention of the Medical Officer of Health. He might also receive information from other sources, official and unofficial. The position was discussed with the Deputy Town Clerk, and the Medical Officer himself made a survey of the areas selected. He would then prepare an 'official representation' of certain areas which was submitted to the Public Health and Housing Committees and then to the Council. The Medical Officer might be asked to make changes in the general programme derived from the preliminary survey, and he was usually

---

[1] All reports made to the Council on housing questions appeared over the name of the Town Clerk, but in practice the Deputy Town Clerk assumed responsibility for preparing these reports.

prepared to accept some modifications of the original scheme, perhaps altering the priorities for demolition or increasing the size of the whole clearance programme. Since this Council was entirely dominated by one Party, the effective debate on such questions occurred in Committees and in Labour Party Group meetings where the representatives of different wards might call for prompter action in their own areas. Clearance plans for individual areas were communicated to the London County Council and then went to the Minister for approval, with a census of the population involved and an undertaking to rehouse the people within a specified period. The Borough had at the same time to publish its plan for the area to be cleared and within six months serve clearance or compulsory purchase orders on the owners of the property concerned. The latter might make objections to the Minister who notified the Borough (which then made a further survey of the area) and conducted a public local enquiry. At this enquiry it was the Town Clerk's responsibility to present the Borough's case; his Deputy generally handled this, though counsel might act for the Borough in some cases. The Borough Surveyor and the Medical Officer of Health were the main expert witnesses called on the Borough's behalf. The order would then be confirmed, amended or rejected. The administrative procedures required before demolition could begin normally took more than a year to complete.

Decisions about the type of housing to be built on the site were made by the Council, on the recommendation of the Housing Committee where the matter was discussed with the Deputy Town Clerk, the Housing Manager and the architects. Usually there was considerable discussion of these problems before they reached the Committee —the architects perhaps favouring larger flats which are more economical to build, and the Housing Manager hoping for an increase in the scarce supply of small dwellings. The Housing Committee was unlikely to be faced with a difficult decision unless its officers and the architects had been unable to reach agreement. The sizes and types of dwellings built were related as nearly as possible to the character of the households to be catered for, but since plans for flats might have to be drawn up four or five years before the tenants moved in this was an extremely difficult task. It is not surprising that in the days of the waiting list an applicant's chance of being rehoused depended to a considerable extent upon the size of house he needed. The selection of tenants was made by the Housing Manager from a waiting list compiled according to the 'points' system devised by the

Committee (up till 1955), or (later) from the property due to be demolished. In 1953 there were about 2,800 households on the Borough's waiting list. Since then the numbers are likely to have become increasingly misleading because many who knew of the slum clearance policy and the abandonment of the waiting lists would not have bothered to get their names on the lists. Tenants were not necessarily transferred direct from condemned to new property; much of the Housing Manager's time was spent in arranging exchanges —sometimes three- or four-cornered exchanges—which made for greater flexibility in rehousing policy than might at first appear possible. It frequently happened that people whose homes were to be demolished ('decanted' tenants, in official language) preferred to move to repaired property or to pre-war flats rather than to more expensive new buildings which might be in a less favoured part of the Borough, or might call for an embarrassing jump in living costs. Exchanges were sometimes arranged with the London County Council, or with other Boroughs within or beyond the London area. These arrangements were designed to meet individual needs, and did not necessarily involve new property. Where they did, the principle was observed that in each set of transfers one new dwelling must be provided for someone whenever a household was moved from condemned property. Rents were fixed at levels comparable with those currently charged for London County Council property, though neither authority kept in step with subsequent changes made by the other.

Slum Clearance Begins Again

By the end of 1953 repairs to war damaged houses capable of further use had been completed (though general deterioration could not be so easily set right) and 643 new houses had been built by the Borough. Few Boroughs had suffered so much destruction—altogether 3,120 homes had been destroyed and practically every house had suffered in some way—and for some time there was no shortage of sites. Those rehoused were selected from several waiting lists (drawn up for households of different sizes) ranked according to points systems which changed from time to time but in general gave priority to those overcrowded or with no home of their own, those with children, those who had been waiting longest, and those suffering from illnesses likely to be exacerbated by their housing conditions.

In 1951 Bethnal Green, like other Metropolitan Boroughs, embarked on a five-year housing plan, worked out in consultation with the London County Council. The Borough's officers were already aware that the policy of building new houses and flats as quickly as possible could not go on much longer, for there would soon be no more sites left to build on. They demolished 236 unfit houses during this period, but clearance would soon be needed on a larger scale. Rehousing from the waiting lists must therefore be brought to a halt while there were still sufficient unallocated houses in the course of construction to take the growing numbers of people whose homes were to be demolished.

The second five-year plan came up for discussion in April 1954, just after the appearance of the Ministry's Circular urging authorities to resume slum clearance. The Deputy Town Clerk, Medical Officer of Health and Housing Manager discussed the situation and there followed a joint meeting of the Housing and Health Committees at which plans for slum clearance were considered. The Deputy Town Clerk presented a report on the situation, pointing out that '. . . the housing programme of the Council was, in effect, only the consequent redevelopment upon this slum clearance programme . . .' The Council was eager to set about clearing the slums, particularly in view of the failure of the London County Council to fulfil its own (considerably larger) plans for clearance in this area. The Borough's officers persuaded the Council to reduce its first ambitious estimates since the resources available for this work were unlikely to be sufficient, and somewhat reluctantly agreement was reached on a more modest demolition programme during the second five-year programme. The Medical Officer of Health and the Deputy Town Clerk were responsible for working out these figures. Between 1956 and 1960, 510 unfit houses were demolished in Bethnal Green by the County and 550 by the Borough. Large numbers of 'grey' houses (not technically unfit) were pulled down in the same clearance areas.

In October 1955 the Deputy Town Clerk presented a report to the Joint Public Health and Housing Committee outlining the five-year plan finally agreed with the London County Council and submitted to the Minister. In it '. . . members' attention is specifically drawn to the following assumptions upon which the programme has been devised: (1) That no dwellings becoming available during the next five years will be allocated to the housing waiting list unless such persons on the waiting list, by coincidence, happen to be in clearance areas . . .' Since this decision was the inevitable concomitant of the clearance programme which all were determined to start on, it was accepted without much comment and discussion was confined to the timing and details of the programme. No new flats were completed between June 1955 and April 1957, a long gap that seems to have been due mainly to the ambitious nature of the project completed in 1957, which included a number of high flats requiring extensive piling. The meeting in October 1955 thus constituted a watershed between the old policy and the new. The last block of flats completed in 1955 was let to people moved from a clearance site, and after that only one new letting and two 'relets' were offered to families on account of their position on the waiting list. Two of these families were flagrantly overcrowded and the third moved from a house which could then be used for rehousing a large family whose home was due to be demolished.

Each year thereafter, the Deputy Town Clerk presented a report on the housing programme to the newly appointed Housing Committee. Each year his report repeated the assumptions on which the policy was based. But while no serious objection has ever been offered to what constitutes, in effect, a closing of the waiting lists, no public announcement of the decision to abandon the lists was ever made.[1] Indeed, strictly speaking, no such decision was ever taken—it was merely the outcome of the decision to switch resources to slum clearance which was forced on an authority that had no more vacant building sites and was not permitted to build outside its own boundaries. After the Housing Subsidies Act of 1956 many other authorities were encouraged or compelled by the central government to adopt similar policies and the abandonment of the waiting list was then more explicitly recognized by the Bethnal Green Council.

The outcome of this change in policy appears in the distribution of new housing and of vacancies in existing housing. Between 1953 and 1958 the Borough had an average of 135 new lettings and 75 vacancies in older housing to dispose of each year. During the first three of these years, 24 per cent of all lettings were allocated to the waiting lists, and 43 per cent went to tenants 'decanted' from slum property or to others exchanging flats in a manner designed to meet the needs of decanted tenants. During the next three years decanted tenants and exchanges organized on their behalf accounted for 75 per cent of all lettings, and only two lettings went to the waiting lists— though many of those who were rehoused on account of slum clearance were also on the waiting lists. The remaining lettings during this period

---

[1] This may be contrasted with the policy of the London County Council and other authorities which have publicly announced their decisions to curtail or abandon the rehousing of those on waiting lists.

were exchanges and transfers unrelated to slum clearance, and a small number provided for caretakers, for people moved out of requisitioned property, and for special cases of various kinds. The shift from waiting list to slum clearance rehousing took place in the new lettings about a year earlier than in the re-letting of older property, but the change was effectively complete in both types of letting by 1956, and began several years before that.

The Housing Manager described this development as a change in the selection of tenants involving the virtual elimination of the waiting lists as an instrument of selection. The Deputy Town Clerk described the development in rather different terms. The growing shortage of building sites and the fact that the Borough was restricted to building within its own boundaries compelled the Council to choose between abandoning its housing programme or embarking on slum clearance. The Council's determination to press on with building left the choice in no doubt. This implied an end to rehousing from the waiting lists, but no formal decision was taken, or required, on that question. The smooth progress of this change in policy was largely due to the Deputy Town Clerk's work as co-ordinator of the various departments and authorities who were required to play a part in it. The central government's policy took a similar turn at about the same time, but Bethnal Green's change in policy was dictated by other necessities and was not greatly affected by developments in Whitehall.

DISCUSSION

The change in policy traced in this brief study may not appear momentous. Yet it deprived many families whose cramped housing conditions placed them near the top of the waiting lists of the opportunity of securing a new flat, transferring these opportunities to people living in condemned housing. The County Council's waiting lists remained open and continued for a time to provide an avenue of escape from bad housing conditions. But as other Boroughs were compelled to make the same choice that had faced Bethnal Green, and as the County's own slum clearance programme got under way, that avenue dwindled to a narrow path through which few could be admitted. This change in policy, coupled with the effects of the 1957 Rent Act, the disposal of requisitioned property (virtually completed in 1960) and the continued growth of employment in the London region, rendered it increasingly difficult to provide adequate housing in central London for families previously catered for through the waiting lists. It was no accident that the rising numbers of homeless families seeking the County Council's help and the growth of illegal and undesirable practices in London's rented housing market attracted increasing public attention from 1960 onwards. But although the development we have traced was part of a longer and more drastic trend affecting the whole of London, it presented no serious problems in Bethnal Green at the time. Once the blitzed building sites were exhausted, the legal powers of the housing authority (restricted to building within its boundaries), the densely populated area it was responsible for, and the determination of the Council to press on with the rebuilding of the Borough permitted only one course of action. The change in policy was provoked by a change in the resources (of land) available to the service, and its outcome was dictated by the structure and powers of the administrative system and the general objectives of all concerned. The Borough's housing powers might conceivably have been changed —by conferring on Bethnal Green the powers available to the near-by County Borough of West Ham, for instance—but since this would have called for a radical change in the principles of London's local government at a time when the central government was intent on persuading local authorities throughout the country to adopt the changes in policy already taking shape in this Borough, it was not surprising that no attempt was made to do this.

No more need be said here about this change in policy, but several features of the administrative organization bringing it about should be noted. This case vividly illustrates a point made in our preliminary discussion of administrative concepts—the fact that administrative 'organization' does not exist in its own right, but is simply a useful way of summarizing the relationships between people performing a specific task. Most of the actors in this story—the Chairmen of Housing and Health Committees, the Deputy Town Clerk, the Medical Officer of Health, the Borough Treasurer, and so on—were responsible for many other things besides the particular development studied here. The relationships between them—the patterns of communication, authority and influence that constitute the 'organizations' in which they played a part—could not be traced or described without specifying the work or task to which the organization is relevant. Even the most carefully drawn 'organization chart' can only be valid for specified tasks. Other work—the administration of the food and drug Acts, or the calculation of next year's rates, for example—would call a different pattern of organization into being, even if the same people appeared in it.

It is clear, too, that the development described could only have been brought about through the collaboration of many different administrative units. Different departments of the Borough, the County Council and the Ministry each played a part in the story, while the implementation of this change in housing policy called for an even wider collaboration, including firms of private architects, contractors, property owners, and the institutions of the money market. Bethnal Green had an exceptionally decentralized pattern of housing administration, arising from its past history and the relatively modest size of its housing programme. But even in authorities which have brought rent collection and much of the design, building and repair of housing within one department, there remain many aspects of this development which would have to be handled by separate administrative units, owing to the technical skills needed (in the field of local government finance, for example), the requirements of the law (only the Medical Officer can classify housing as 'unfit', for example), or the division of powers between separate levels of government (responsibility for town planning rests with the County Council, for example). Such a development cannot, therefore, be carried through within the framework of a single administrative hierarchy in which each person has only one superior and all are ultimately responsible to one person or group; it can only be carried through by a constellation of individuals working in parallel or completely independent administrative units, and subject to no single system of authority, sanctions or loyalties. Some authors have regarded such patterns of administration as abnormal or undesirable. Our own studies were not designed to evaluate administrative structures and do not provide the systematic assessments of administrative performance that such an evaluation demands. But it is clear that many important developments in policy *are* carried through in this way, and under a system of independent local government they must be. Only those concerned with organization for its own sake would make a general condemnation of such a system.

Since many of the people concerned in this story worked in independent units and were subject to no common authority, it follows that 'formal authority' played a fairly small part in bringing the development about. Other forms of administrative relationship had to be employed. The task of maintaining these relationships and bringing them into play in the proper time and sequence fell largely on the Deputy Town Clerk. Although exercising scant formal authority, he had great influence owing to his technical and diplomatic abilities, his seniority, and his general responsibilities for co-ordinating housing policy and preparing the necessary correspondence and memoranda. The initiation of discussions, the arrangement of informal meetings, the preparation of reports and draft decisions conferred on him the roles of adviser, influential colleague and 'filterer' of communications—used to crucial effect, for example, in securing (and repeating annually) the Housing Committee's formal decision to press on with slum clearance, and hence to abandon the waiting lists as a means for the selection of tenants. The experience of comparable housing authorities suggests that this field of social administration, calling for the collaboration and co-ordination of so many different units and levels of government, generally depends heavily on influential and far-sighted 'middlemen' of this kind. Where they are found is often a matter of chance: in other boroughs it may be the Surveyor, the Housing Manager, or even a member of the Council who do most of this work.

The role of the Council and its Committees is difficult to trace. Over the period in question the Labour Party held all the seats on the Council and was thus able to confine discussion of contentious issues to closed meetings of the Party Group, consisting of Council members and local representatives of the Labour movement. Thus there was no public recognition of the fact that the waiting lists were effectively closed. The battle between different wards for priority in the slum clearance programme and the resulting pressures occasionally exerted on the Medical Officer of Health were one outcome of the Group's discussions. The Council also compelled their officers to revise and increase the provisional clearance programme prepared for the years 1956-60, though they did not secure as large a programme as they had first hoped for. A considerable amount of the Housing Committee's time was devoted to consideration of individual problems of housing management and the Chairman of the Committee —always an influential figure in the Council—took a close interest in the Department's work. (One of the Chairmen during the period covered by this study was a bus conductor on a route passing close to the Town Hall, which enabled him to make frequent and unexpected calls on the Housing Manager.) But the influence of an elected Council and its Committees cannot be determined solely from its recorded decisions. It is clear that the officers of this Borough were never in doubt about the general determination of their Council to press on with rebuilding as fast as the available resources would permit. The Council is also responsible for the Borough's public relations—communicating official views and intentions to the electorate, the County Council and other bodies, as well as communicating the electorate's views to their officials. This work may be inadequately performed (other Councils have played a much more active part in explaining their abandonment of waiting lists, for example) but it can never be entirely forgotten—as can be seen from the remarks of the Housing Committee chairman quoted at the beginning of this report. Meanwhile the very existence of a Council and its Committees, and the regular monthly meetings they hold, provide a means for establishing and registering policy decisions, and for reconciling and codifying the views of the chief officers who must prepare the evidence and recommend the decisions to be considered by elected members.

CHAPTER 6

THE NATIONAL ASSISTANCE BOARD
TAKES ON NEW DUTIES

The next study deals with an entirely different situation. A national organization, with local offices operating throughout the country under close central control, was called upon to assess the incomes of people seeking a service provided by another agency. On the local level at which this study was conducted the task to be performed was clearly specified, presenting problems of a purely 'technical' nature. But the subdivision of responsibilities for different aspects of the service posed a number of problems; and the rules drawn up for the assessment of incomes may have restricted the scope of the service in ways not originally intended.

UNLIKE the others dealt with in this series, the National Assistance Board's services are provided by the central government and subject to uniform, centrally determined policies applied in a similar fashion throughout the country. In order to meet local needs some flexibility is permitted in the interpretation of the Board's rules, but major innovations in policy do not originate at the local levels where this study was made. In 1959, after discussing various proposals for research with the NAB's East Ham Area Officer, the Regional Controller and a member of the Headquarters staff, it was decided that the organization and reorganization of 'assessments' for Legal Aid in the East Ham Area Office constituted the most suitable recent 'development' for our purposes. The authors interviewed officials concerned with the Legal Aid Scheme at these three levels of the hierarchy, and read various documents on this subject prepared by the Board and others.

The National Assistance Board

The NAB was set up in 1948 to carry out provisions of the National Assistance Act of that year which deal mainly with financial assistance for those lacking adequate means to support themselves. The Board itself consists of six members appointed by the Crown. Like its predecessors, the Assistance Board and the Unemployment Assistance

Board, it is supposed to be independent of direct Parliamentary control in carrying out its work. But its spokesman in Parliament is the Minister of Pensions and National Insurance and its status and powers do not in practice differ appreciably from those of other central government departments. Day to day administration is carried out through a network of Area offices, numbering 427 in 1959, to which were attached 83 Local Advisory Committees whose members are selected for their local knowledge and status. Area Offices are grouped into Regions, nine of which covered England and Wales.

The Part Played by the NAB in the Legal Aid Scheme in 1959

Two years after it was set up the NAB took on additional duties under the Legal Aid and Advice Act of 1949. This Act empowered the government to assist people involved in litigation not covered by existing free legal aid schemes,[1] and the sections dealing with actions originating in the Supreme Court came into effect in October 1950. Since the scheme was intended only for those with 'small or moderate means', there were two aspects to its administration: legal and financial. Other services, such as the child care and home help schemes dealt with in this series of studies, also call for payments that are determined by means tests. But in those the provision of the service and the administration of means tests are carried out by the same organization: in this case, however, the two tasks were sharply distinguished and given to different organizations. The administration of the scheme's legal provisions rests in the hands of the Law Society, and is carried out through the Society's Area and Local Offices, subject to the requirements of the Act and the Legal Aid (General) Regulations. The financial sections of the Act, however, require the assessment of applicants' resources and their liability for contributions, and this function was allotted to the Board. The procedure is complicated; its general outline, including specific financial limits, is laid down in the Act itself and amplified by the Legal Aid (Assessment of Resources) Regulations. These Regulations are issued by the Lord Chancellor, with the Treasury's approval. The Board has no statutory part to play in drawing up or revising Legal Aid Regulations, although it does prepare the rules for its own services—the Regulations for Assistance issued by the Minister under the 1948 Act.

All applications for legal aid were made in the first instance to the Area or Local committees of the Law Society by whom they were sent

---

[1] Under the Criminal Appeal Act 1907. S.10, Poor Prisoners Defence Act 1930 S.1 & 2, or Summary Jurisdiction (Appeals) Act, 1933, S.2.

to the appropriate NAB office if the applicant appeared to have a prima facie case. The Law Society's Areas generally corresponded to the Regions of the NAB, which was administratively convenient, but in 1948 there were less than half as many Local committees as NAB Area Offices. It was realized that administration would be simplified were each local Law Society committee to refer to one NAB office only, and for this reason it was hoped either to concentrate legal aid work in one Area office in each committee's district, or to arrange for one office to provide for liaison with the committee. More important, however, was the Board's recognition that the new functions would require special knowledge and skills among the officers concerned and that the volume of legal aid work would not be great enough to occupy a full-time officer in each Area office. From the beginning, therefore, it was envisaged that in appropriate districts assessments for legal aid might be concentrated in a few specialized offices.

The procedure for assessment can now be described in greater detail. If the legal merits of the case appeared to be adequate, the part of the application referring to financial circumstances was sent from the local branch of the Law Society to the appropriate NAB office. All assessments (although, as will be shown, not all interviewing) had to be done by the office 'designated' for this work in the district where the applicant lived.

Interviews normally took place in the office but might be carried out at home if applicants were ill or disabled. In exceptional cases travelling expenses could be paid for applicants who lived a considerable distance from the office. At the interview the person applying for legal aid had to declare and prove all sources of income and capital, and all liabilities. Except in matrimonial disputes, this information was given for both the husband and wife. From this information the 'disposable income' was calculated—that is, the income likely to be received during the twelve months following the application, from which were deducted allowances made on account of major expenses necessary for the support of dependents, for rent, and so on. Capital assets had also to be taken into account, and after deductions for dependent relatives and other responsibilities a calculation was made of 'disposable capital'. In 1959, anyone with a disposable annual income of less than £156 and anyone receiving National Assistance was entitled to free legal aid. A disposable annual income of more than £420 or (with a few exceptions) a disposable capital of more than £500 disqualified the applicant from receiving any legal aid. With a disposable income between £156 and £420 and a disposable capital under £500 he was liable to make a maximum contribution of one half of the amount by which the disposable income exceeded £156, plus the amount by which the disposable capital exceeded £75.[1] The more generous provisions subsequently made in the Act of 1960 are shown in a footnote on page 67.

A 'determination' giving three figures (the disposable income, the disposable capital and the maximum contribution) together with other information relevant to the collection of contributions, was sent to the branch of the Law Society referring the case, which decided on the precise amount of the contribution and the way in which it was to be paid. Unless the applicant's circumstances changed sufficiently to warrant a re-assessment, that was the end of the NAB's part in the procedure. The Law Society had no power to amend or overrule the NAB's assessment, although it had some discretion in allowing assistance to people with disposable incomes below £420 who had been refused help because they had more than the maximum amount of capital.

The method of computation, the maximum allowances permitted for major items such as dependants and rent, and the amounts of supplementary income from pensions and insurance benefits which might be disregarded were laid down in the Act and in the Lord Chancellor's Regulations—unchanged between 1950 and the date of this study. Little discretion was allowed to the Area's officers, and particularly close control was exercised in the early years of the scheme.

Assessments were verified by the designated Area Officer before being returned to the Law Society, and some queries could be dealt with at that point. More serious problems, and cases falling into categories reserved for Headquarters' decision were passed on, in the first instance to the Regional office. Originally such referrals were fairly heavy and in the office of the London (Outer) Region, which included East Ham, the Legal Aid staff consisted of at least two full-time executive officers. The Region's discretion was also fairly limited. About 10 per cent of the cases referred to it were decided there and returned to the Area, sometimes after informal consultation with Headquarters. Collaboration between Regional and Headquarters staff was comparatively easy since both occupied the same building. The few fraudulent applications were returned to the Law Society for action. The remaining cases bearing the Region's preliminary opinion were sent to the Legal Aid Section at Headquarters. This consisted of

---

[1] For example, if the disposable income was £356, and the disposable capital £100, the maximum contribution would have been £125—that is, £100 from income and £25 from capital.

an Assistant Secretary, a Principal, a Higher Executive Officer, Executive Officer and Clerical Officer. At first the section received problem cases at the rate of approximately sixty each week. By 1958, with better training, growing expertise and greater discretion allowed to officers in the Areas, the number had been halved.

Most of these referred applications fell into two groups: first, those in which there might be a case for allowances more generous than those permitted under local discretion (for example, where there were large payments to be made to separated dependants, or heavy and necessary hire purchase commitments); and second, those in which complications arose from comparatively unusual factors (involving income tax, trust monies, or the resources of a step-father in a case involving a wife with a child from a previous marriage, for example). Difficulty commonly arose where the applicant's income was drawn from his own business—a man may run a Jaguar yet have a declared personal income of only £10 per week. These cases went to specialists in the Finance Division. Where legal problems arose, the Headquarters staff consulted the Board's Solicitor or the Law Society. Once a decision had been taken, cases were returned to the Area via the Regional Office. A straightforward assessment was dealt with by the Area within a fortnight (although much depended upon the co-operation of the applicant). Difficult assessments might take as much as three months.

The Development of Assessment Work in East Ham

The East Ham Area office was originally given responsibility for carrying out assessments for nine Areas in the metropolitan fringe of Essex, and for this purpose an Executive and a Clerical Officer were added to its staff of twenty executive and clerical officers. Along with their colleagues in other parts of the country, the special officers were given short training courses organized by Headquarters to equip them for their new duties. After the first rush of applications, reaching a total of 1,549 in 1951, the numbers of cases dealt with by these two officers fell steadily to an annual rate of 850-900 between 1955 and 1957. Most of the Area offices designated for this work elsewhere in the country had far fewer cases: in a sample fortnight in 1954 half of them received fewer than five applications. At that time the Board's Organization and Methods Division found the standards of assessment in the quieter Areas were disturbingly uneven and urged that the number of designated offices be reduced by about a half in order to achieve greater specialization and uniformity in this work. This step was delayed because the Government was considering extending the Legal Aid scheme to suits originating in County Courts, and the Board and the Law Society could not predict how caseloads would be affected. The extension came into effect on January 1, 1956, and applications rose by only 6 per cent in the following year—in East Ham by even less.

Regional Controllers were then encouraged to bring about a further concentration of assessment work in Area offices close to the Law Society's offices. Meanwhile the picture was complicated by the Government's drive to reduce the number of Regional offices in all government departments. Two of the NAB's Regional offices in south-eastern England were abolished, and in 1958 the East Ham Legal Aid section was given responsibility for assessments in nine more Areas. The applications dealt with doubled in that year and an extra Clerical Officer was appointed to help with the work. This growth in the territory to be covered hastened another development that had already gone a considerable way: the collection of the information required for assessment was separated from the assessment itself, and the special officers had to rely increasingly on their colleagues in other Areas to secure this information, bringing them together from time to time to explain what was required. Shortly after this study was concluded a further step was taken in this direction by transferring assessments for Essex to the South Kensington Area office and leaving East Ham to collect and pass on information about applications in the surrounding Areas. Legislation was introduced later to raise the income and capital limits governing the assessment procedure so that Legal Aid could be provided on a more generous basis, but that most important development, which brought an appreciable increase in the scope of the scheme and the number of cases dealt with, falls outside our study.[1]

Conclusion

This study traces the manner in which new duties were assumed by a service responsible for a much larger volume of different work. At the beginning the assessment procedure was unfamiliar and complicated. The volume of work to be done was unpredictable. The applications to be dealt with constituted a tiny and widely scattered fraction of the Board's total caseload. In 1954, besides the two assess-

---

[1] The Legal Aid Act of 1960 increased the disposable income limit of £420 to £700 and reduced the contributions from income to one third of the excess over £250 and from capital to the amount by which disposable capital exceeds £125. The revised Legal Aid (Assessment of Resources) Regulations also provided for a more generous definition of capital resources.

ment officers in East Ham, there were only twenty-seven others in the whole of England and Wales employed full-time on this work; the rest of it had to be done by a much larger number of officers, equivalent to seventy-one full-timers, most of whom spent only an hour or two a week on these assessments. It was therefore extremely difficult to maintain the standards of precision, promptness and uniformity required.

The Board adopted three approaches to the solution of these problems. (a) Short initiation and refresher courses were arranged for the staff doing the work. (b) The work itself was increasingly divided into two parts: the collection of the information required from applicants, and the calculation of the figures that formed the basis for assessing applicants' contributions. (c) The work of assessment was gradually concentrated in a reduced number of designated Area offices, to achieve greater skill among the officers thus enabled to specialise on it, and closer collaboration with local offices of the Law Society.

The Headquarters staff were responsible for these developments, and they were convinced that they improved the standards of work: certainly the proportion of unresolved cases that had to be sent to the Region and on to Headquarters for final decisions fell off considerably, and with growing experience staff in the Area offices designated for assessment work could be given greater discretion. But the maintenance of uniform and efficient standards of work among the interviewing officers who collected information from applicants remained a continuing problem that could never be finally resolved.

The principal objectives and methods of the assessment procedure could be clearly defined and were not changed during the period studied. Having no responsibility for the broader social and professional aims of the Legal Aid scheme, NAB staff could devote their energies to perfecting the procedure. In the Region studied the officials carrying out the work remained in the same posts for considerable periods of time, and such specialist training as they had was planned and provided by the NAB, not by independent professional institutions. Thus the development called for an intelligent organization and deployment of resources for the attainment of defined and agreed ends. Though technically complex, it was logically simple— and more completely a matter of administrative 'technique' than any of the others studied in this series.

But it should not be forgotten that the logical simplicity of these problems arose from the distinctive structure of the Legal Aid scheme.

The scheme itself and the service it was designed to provide, were administered by the Law Society and its members. It was they who actually decided whether Legal Aid should be granted. The Board only provided the information required by the Society for determining the contributions to be made by applicants whose cases were regarded by solicitors as meriting legal representation. Yet the NAB's task, though merely 'technical' in appearance, went far to shape the character of the whole scheme; for the assessments effectively determined who was entitled to Aid. But these assessments were performed according to prescribed rules, drafted by the Lord Chancellor's Department and the Treasury, which could not be altered without fresh legislation. The Law Society's first Report on the operation of the scheme pointed out that the contributions demanded of assisted persons were too high. A scheme originally designed for people of 'small or moderate means' was in danger of being restricted to the very poor. But these contributions remained unaltered through a decade of inflation that continually eroded the scope of the scheme. It was our impression that the Board's officers were well aware of this problem, and often did their utmost to exercise discretion in favour of applicants.

But the division of responsibilities for the operation of the Legal Aid scheme between the Law Society, the Lord Chancellor, and the NAB might have been designed to obscure these problems by ensuring that each of these authorities would concentrate its attention upon its own contribution to the scheme and none would be in a position to assess the service as a whole. The NAB's administration of assessments was simplified—and possibly rendered more 'efficient' in a technical sense—by the exclusion of these broader questions of policy from its sphere of responsibility. But some may conclude that the applicants and potential applicants paid a considerable price for this achievement.

The Legal Aid service itself lay outside the scope of our study, but those responsible for it were keenly aware of the restrictions imposed on it by the means test regulations. Rarely can an official advisory committee have made its views so monotonously clear:
'We have said in previous Reports that the rate of contribution in some cases imposes too great a hardship on assisted persons. The cost of living is still rising and, though in some cases wages and salaries have risen proportionately or more, there are many prospective litigants whose incomes are fixed and to them the rate of contribution is an increasing burden as the cost of living rises.' (*Fifth Report of the Law Society on the Operation and Finance of Part I of the Legal Aid and Advice Act, 1949, and the Comments and Recommendations made by*

the Advisory Committee. London, HMSO 1956. *Comments,* para. 19.)

'Nothing has occurred to alter the view expressed in our last four Reports that the rate of contribution does impose too great a hardship on some categories of assisted persons.' 'The basic figures in the Act and the Assessment of Resources Regulations have not been amended to take account of the changed economic circumstances. [Yet] Since the Regulations were made, the subsistence levels or "scale rates" contained in the National Assistance (Determination of Need) Regulations have been increased on four occasions.' (Ditto, 1957; paras. 11 and 12.)

'We cannot but take the view that after the thirteen years of rising prices, the scheme no longer adequately covers the section of the community, regarded in terms of income groups, which the Rushcliffe Committee intended' [in its Report of 1945.[1]]. (Ditto, 1958; para. 13.)

'The value of the £420 disposable income limit compared with 1949 money values is therefore only about £280. To bring it back to its real value in 1949 would require raising it to about £650, £50 more than we recommended in our last Report . . .' (Ditto, 1959; para. 5.)

But some relaxation was permitted at last, and the Advisory Committee was able to report in 1961:

'During the year, by the Legal Aid (Assessment of Resources) Amendment Regulations, 1959[2], your Lordship amended the . . . Regulations so as to make more favourable to applicants the rules for computing the allowances which are taken into account in determining their incomes and eligibility for legal aid. Largely as a result of those measures, there was, during the year under review, a considerable increase in the volume of legal aid work . . .' (Ditto, 1961; para. 2.)

DISCUSSION

The developments outlined in this case have more general implications that should be noted. The Legal Aid scheme is the only major independent service for which the NAB has been called on to carry out the investigation of means and the determination of contributions. But from its own resources the Board can also refund payments for National Health Service prescriptions, some have argued that it should carry

---

[1] *Report of the Committee on Legal Aid and Legal Advice in England and Wales.* Cmd. 6641; para. 147.
[2] S.I. 1959/1350.

out means tests to determine the rents paid by Council tenants, and those wishing to impose or increase payments for medical care and education sometimes have similar procedures in mind. This analysis of Legal Aid assessments may indicate some of the problems such procedures would pose. Our discussion of the case, however, is not designed to pursue its long-term social and political implications, but to throw light on the administrative processes involved.

The structure of the NAB differs from that of the other agencies dealt with in this series of studies. Its services are provided by Area offices within each of which individual officers and specialist sections are subject to the authority of one Area Officer; Areas are grouped under Regional offices, within each of which there are specialist sections responsible to a Regional Controller, and they in turn are subject to Headquarters and the Board itself. Throughout the country there is a clear 'line of command' from the officers interviewing applicants, through Area Officers and Regional Controllers, to Headquarters. Auxiliary and specialist services are required at these three levels, but although those providing them communicate with similar specialists at other levels of the hierarchy, they are directly responsible to the 'line' officer in charge of their unit and official communications pass through him. The complexity and variety of Legal Aid cases compelled some modification of this system (in that the Area office at East Ham, designated for assessment work, relied on officers in the surrounding Areas to gather much of the information it required), but difficult cases were passed for decision to the Region and on to Headquarters through the Area Officer and Regional Controller, and returned by the same route. Specialist staff at each level were given considerable, and increasing, discretion to make their own decisions on these cases but this discretion was interpreted in the light of the NAB's general policies, on the understanding that cases in which these policies afforded insufficient guidance would be passed to the 'line' officers who could forward them when necessary to more senior levels of the hierarchy.

In some of the earlier literature on administration this type of structure, typical of military organization, was regarded as a normal pattern and one to be widely advocated.[1] It clearly has many advantages. Necessary specialist services can be incorporated at appropriate points in the system and effectively co-ordinated without infringing the principle that everyone should be responsible to one, known

[1] Eg. L. Urwick, 'Organization as a Technical Problem', *Papers on the Science of Administration:* L. Gulick and L. Urwick, Eds. New York, Institute of Public Administration, 1937.

superior. A variety of knowledge and skills can be brought to bear on particular problems while ensuring that the duty of making decisions in each unit rests with one person who is responsible for the attainment of the more general objectives to which each specialist makes his contribution. The service to be provided can be deployed over a wide area, and staff who are transferred to different parts of the country and to different levels of the hierarchy can quickly get their bearings within units whose structure is already familiar to them. Without infringing the authority of 'line' officers, senior specialists can maintain effective contact with similar specialists in subordinate units, thus keeping abreast of developments in the field, ensuring adequate standards of performance, and watching over the careers of junior staff.

The NAB has certain characteristics which render it peculiarly well suited for such a system. It must provide prompt and effective help to meet needs that can potentially be a matter of life and death to the people concerned, and its work is subject to close and critical public scrutiny. The same could be said of hospitals and other services, but the NAB's call primarily for humanity, devotion to duty and a good working knowledge of rules and procedures—not for advanced technical skills derived from a high degree of training. More specialized skills, such as those provided by the Board's legal and financial officers, for example, can be treated as auxiliary or advisory services supporting the provision of assistance that is the Board's main task. The Assistance Regulations and the practical principles accumulated for their interpretation are the main criteria for the guidance of individual officers. These officers do not have the discretionary powers, the protection from public criticism or the opportunities for alternative employment that expert status and membership of a profession confer. Their education and experience is often fairly limited and the turnover of staff is considerable: those seeking promotion are often compelled to move to other departments of government. One of the Board's senior officers reports that there has been 'an exceptionally heavy and sustained turnover of staff'. '. . . one Area office in two years had 39 departures and 41 arrivals: the complement of the office is 40. At a smaller office, with a complement of 25, there were 23 departures and 25 arrivals. These are offices in Central London, and they are not untypical.'[1] It is essential that the services these officers provide should be immediately available in all parts of the country, and subdivision of the work to be done must therefore be based mainly on geographical

[1] K. R. Stowe, 'Staff Training in the National Assistance Board: Problems and Policies'. *Public Administration*, Vol. 39, Winter 1961, p. 331.

considerations, rather than on distinctions in expertise, techniques, the types of client to be served or other factors. At the same time close control, prompt communication and uniform practice must be ensured throughout this network of local offices. If the system appears to restrict discretion and the exercise of judgement, it should be remembered that discretion can be employed 'against' a client as well as 'for' him—particularly in cases involving litigation (in which divorce proceedings are the most common type of action). None of the other services considered in this book have this combination of administrative requirements or the structure that arises from them.

The provision of legal advice and the decision to embark on litigation in cases where the client's costs are partly or wholly met from public funds (while his opponent is likely to be meeting his own expenses) clearly pose technical, professional and ethical problems of the highest order. Only trained lawyers could provide such a service. Had they been recruited on a full-time salaried basis for this purpose, like the professional staff of other social services, eligibility and payment for the service could more easily have been determined by the organization responsible for providing it. But although some of them draw a large part of their income from this service, the lawyers remained in independent professional practice. Thus it was that another organization, equipped with the necessary expertise, was called upon to carry out the assessment of applicants' incomes.

This subdivision of responsibilities for the scheme, dictated by the legislation establishing it, focused the attention of the NAB's staff on the perfection of assessment procedures, and the need to ensure prompt and uniform decisions gradually brought about a centralization of the work in offices remote from the applicant himself. Meanwhile the lawyers devoted themselves to the professional services they were to provide. The manner in which responsibilities for the scheme were distributed among different authorities appears to have prevented effective reappraisal of the total scheme and probably restricted the operation of Legal Aid in ways that Parliament had not originally foreseen or intended. As in other cases considered here, the administrative structure established for a service played a large part in determining the work, the outlook and the general frames of reference of those engaged in providing it—and hence the contribution they were enabled to make to its development.

CHAPTER 7

THE FIRST TEN YEARS OF
A HOME HELP SERVICE

This study traces the development of a new social service. The service began to take effective shape when full-time organizers were appointed to run it. They were given considerable freedom to work out their aims and methods. The outcome, a decade later, appears to have been dictated largely by the demands made on the service by its clients and by 'neighbouring' organizations which needed its help in their own work.

WHEN the possibility of making a study in one of the nine geographical Divisions of the London County Council's Public Health Department was first discussed with the County Medical Officer of Health and senior members of his staff, half a dozen topics were suggested for research. After further discussion with the Divisional Medical Officer and members of his staff, it was decided that the evolution of the Home Help service provided the most suitable development to study in his area—Division 5 of the County Health Department. The research was carried out in 1959, and was based on interviews with the Medical Officer of Health and administrative officers at County Hall, the Divisional Medical Officer and his senior colleagues, the three Home Help Organizers in the Division and the President of the Institute of Home Help Organizers, and also on a number of departmental reports and memoranda, and on reports and circulars issued by the Ministry of Health.

Home Help Services before 1948

The Home Help service became nation-wide after 1948, but its origins lie sixty years further back. These origins are probably to be found in the growth of a specialized body of qualified midwives and the displacement of the old fashioned 'handy-woman' who not only delivered the baby but also cared for the home and family during the mother's confinement. This was work that a trained midwife would not do, and the gap had to be filled by someone—usually by the mother's relatives.[1] In London at the turn of the century a voluntary society concerned with infant welfare started to provide household helps to look after families during the mother's confinement. Results were good enough for the Local Government Board, predecessor of the Ministry of Health, to take up the idea in November 1914 when a circular was issued on the welfare of expectant and nursing mothers in wartime, recommending local authorities to consider among other things the possibility of employing and training 'household or, as they are sometimes termed, sick-room helps'. Four years later the Maternity and Child Welfare Act of 1918 gave general powers to local authorities to arrange for the care of expectant mothers and young children. It was followed by a circular explaining that one of the services which could be given under the Act, with the aid of a 50 per cent subsidy from the exchequer, was the provision of suitable women to take over a mother's ordinary domestic duties during the puerperium. Voluntary associations might be used as agents for this purpose.

During the next year eight local authorities and thirteen voluntary societies started such schemes, but recruitment was difficult and by 1924 only forty-two local authorities were providing this service, on a widely varying scale and with varying types of staff. At no time did the service absorb more than £7,000 per annum, or 0·5 per cent of the total subsidy for maternity and child welfare services. The Ministry realized that success depended upon constant supervision, and that local authorities could not afford to allot administrative staff solely to this work. The service dwindled to very small proportions: even after the renewal of powers under the Public Health Acts of 1936 only seven authorities in England and Wales had schemes, dealing in 1937 with a mere 262 cases.

The second world war placed a great strain on services for civilians and a Ministry of Health circular of November 1942 urged local authorities to maintain and improve home help schemes as a vital part of their maternity and child welfare services. Since recruitment was then more difficult than ever, the Ministry of Labour and National Service gave such work equal priority with hospital domestic duties. War-time conditions intensified the difficulties of all kinds of sick and disabled people, including the aged whose problems attracted the keenest attention. In 1944, Defence Regulation 68E gave Welfare Authorities the power to provide 'domestic helps' for non-maternity

---

[1] See *Report of the Working Party on Social Workers in the Local Authority Health & Welfare Services*. HMSO 1959, p. 57.

cases. A subsequent circular[1] explained the Ministry's intentions more fully. The service was intended for the kind of case where a wife was ill or had to leave her home to visit a husband in hospital, for cases in which illness struck several members of a family simultaneously (at this time the Ministry feared outbreaks of epidemic illness), and for the elderly infirm. Like the home help service it would be subsidized, could be operated through voluntary agencies, and the Ministry of Labour and National Service would assist with recruitment. Again the Ministry realized the need for special administrative staff, but did nothing to encourage such appointments. The service was regarded as experimental and thought to be unnecessary in rural areas.

The response was patchy and generally inadequate. A Ministry survey made in 1946 found that in the whole of England and Wales only two authorities—one metropolitan borough and one provincial city using the wvs—were operating fully successful schemes, and that their success largely depended on the existence of a full-time organizer. Recruitment still presented problems, but it was hoped that the establishment of the National Institute of Houseworkers would help to solve them by raising the status and quality of domestic work.

In November of the same year the National Health Service Act reached the statute book. Under Part III (Local Authority Services), Section 29 gave local health authorities power to supply domestic help to households where someone was ill, lying-in, expecting a baby, mentally deficient or aged, or where there were children under school leaving age. These powers replaced those granted under the 1936 Acts and Defence Regulation 68E, and amalgamated the home help and domestic help services. A Ministry circular (118/47) pointed out that although these powers were permissive the absence of such a service would greatly reduce the effect of other local authority services that were compulsory. In the event, all local health authorities provided the service. Like its predecessors, the service is grant-aided, but those able to pay for it may be called upon to do so. The circular stressed the need for full-time organizers.

The Structure of the Service in 1959

The National Health Service Act of 1946 came into operation on July 5, 1948. It transferred to the London County Council some of the health services which had previously been administered by the Metropolitan Borough Councils, the City of Westminster and the City of London Corporation. The services transferred included those for

[1] 179/44, dated 14 December, 1944.

maternity and child welfare, the prevention of tuberculosis, after-care for the tuberculous, chiropody and a restricted form of domestic home help, but some Boroughs did not operate all these services. Henceforth the day to day supervision of these services was carried out in nine newly created Health Divisions (co-terminous with similar Divisions for Education and, later, for Children's Services). Each Division covered the areas of a number of Metropolitan Boroughs. Health Division 5, in which the developments to be described took place, covered the City of London and the Metropolitan Boroughs of Bethnal Green, Poplar and Stepney.

The Public Health Department was directed from County Hall by the Medical Officer of Health, who was also the Principal School Medical Officer. He had a staff of medical, nursing, technical and administrative officers in County Hall and the Divisions. Matters of policy were dealt with by the Health Committee (subject to the approval of the Council) and the Committee's decisions transmitted to Divisional Health Committees. Each Divisional Health Committee consisted of about eighteen members; three or four (including the Chairman) were members of the Health Committee, ten (one of whom was the Vice-Chairman) were nominated by Metropolitan Borough Councils in its area, and the rest were nominees of the Local Medical Committee, Dental Committee, Pharmaceutical Committee, District Nursing Associations and the Royal College of Nursing. The Divisional Committee was responsible to the Health Committee for the service in its area. It framed its own budget, subject to ratification by the Health and Finance Committees (at the time of this study the budget for Division 5 amounted to over £250,000 a year); it was responsible for certain staff appointments and could sanction expenditure (within the approved estimates) up to £1,000 in any one case, and reported quarterly to the Health Committee on the action taken under delegated powers. The Divisional Committee was also empowered to consider any of the services within its jurisdiction, and report to the Health Committee on them.

The Divisional Medical Officer directed the services in his Division and was assisted by three senior officers: the Divisional Administrative Officer, the Divisional Nursing Officer and the Divisional Treatment Organizer. Their work entailed frequent communication with professional and administrative staff in County Hall. The central office provided guidance on matters of policy, and advice and information flowed both ways between those in the Divisional Office and their opposite numbers in County Hall. General responsibility for the Home

Help service lay with the Divisional Medical Officer, but the Divisional Administrative and Nursing Officers and their staff carried out most of the work done at the Divisional Office in connection with this service—the latter being concerned with particular problems arising in connection with illness and the visiting of recipients of the service, and with the 'special home help service' to be described later.

The Division was split into three districts for the purpose of this service: North (Bethnal Green, the City and part of Stepney). East (Poplar and part of Stepney) and South (most of Stepney). Each district had its own office run by a Home Help Organizer. At the time of this study the Organizers each had one full-time Assistant Organizer, one full-time clerk, and (in Poplar and Stepney only) a part-time Assistant Organizer. The organizer was responsible for the recruitment and briefing of her home helps. She visited new clients to assess the amount of help needed, and made the initial assessment of the charges (if any) which they were to pay. She allotted and supervised the work of the helps. Monthly returns on the work of the office were made to the Divisional Medical Officer, and the Organizer gave estimates of the service's cost which were used in drawing up the Divisional budget.

The three Organizers attended bi-monthly meetings on the Home Help service with the DMO, the Administrative Officer and the Nursing Officer. They also attended the Divisional Co-ordinating Committee on the fairly infrequent occasions when one of their cases was being discussed. This Committee consisted of social workers and others from statutory and voluntary agencies who met regularly to consider particularly difficult cases. The DMO was its chairman but frequently left the Area Children's Officer—its vice-chairman—to conduct the proceedings. The Treatment Organizer was secretary to this committee—the main capacity in which she had contact with the Home Help Organizers.

Twice yearly a meeting was held at County Hall which was attended by all Organizers in the County, and the Principal Clerk and other officers of the Central office Division responsible for the Home Help service (and much else besides). The meetings were chaired by the Chief Administrative Officer of the Public Health Department, and covered a wide range of general topics concerning the service given and the recruitment and training of its staff. Home Help Organizers also attended the periodic, informal meetings arranged between social workers in voluntary and statutory agencies in the various Boroughs. In Division 5, as was usual, they were members of the Old People's Welfare Committees for each Borough.

The structure we have described had changed very little since it was first established by the County in 1948. The development of the Home Help service over the previous decade can now be traced.

The Development of the Service

Before the National Health Service Act came into force, each of the three Boroughs making up Division 5 had employed a few home helps who had worked with maternity cases, under the direction of the Borough's Superintendent Health Visitors. Bethnal Green had 5 part-time helps, Poplar 1 full-time and 6 part-time helps. Stepney had been helping 'general' cases as well, and employed altogether 7 full-time and 53 part-time workers. The City, which is also included in Division 5, had had a small home help service run by its Welfare Officer, who was invited by the LCC to carry on with the service. But she did not wish to organize a service for which the clients might have to pay, and it was therefore agreed that she would continue to deal with old people's cases in the City (since these were not likely to involve any charge), and all others would go to the Bethnal Green office. There were very few of the latter—perhaps four in a year. The division of work between the County and the City appeared to operate very well; co-operation between the two services was good, and they had been able to help each other out during difficult periods. Owing to this arrangement the City does not feature significantly in the following account.

The three Borough services were taken over by the new Division in 1948 and plans were made to combine and extend them. During the next twelve months an Organizer was appointed to each of the three district offices and given the assistance of one clerk. They faced a difficult task, having to build up a new service whose dimensions and precise functions were unclear, evolving their own methods of working, recruiting and training staff, and at the same time trying to meet heavy demands with inadequate resources and experience. The Public Health Department as a whole was then in the throes of major re-organization and expansion as a result of the National Health Service Act, and the Home Help service, having a comparatively minor part to play, was left to develop along its own lines without interference or precise guidance. A Departmental committee, set up in October 1948 to inquire into this rapidly developing service, made a number of recommendations concerning its organization, but it was decided to allow the service to gain experience and establish itself before making any changes.

The Bethnal Green office in Division 5 was set up at the beginning of 1949 by a young woman who was still in charge there at the time of this study. She had received in-service training in a neighbouring Division where the borough service had been fairly well developed. She had a clerk, but no assistant. Recruitment was exceedingly difficult, and although the Ministry had urged organizers to conduct intensive campaigns, most were too overburdened to use more elaborate tools than the Employment Exchange and notices in local shops. Many of the early recruits seem to have been unreliable; some disappeared without ever doing any work at all (having merely gone through the motions of job-hunting in order to satisfy the Labour Exchange), some falsified their time-sheets or skimped their work if not closely supervised, others gave notice after experiencing the squalid circumstances or uncertain tempers of some of those they were asked to help. The work was heavy and the strain of travelling round the district could be serious. As the service became better known and more effective, unreliable workers became comparatively rare but the other factors continued to produce a wastage rate of 50 per cent over a full year.[1]

The other two district offices experienced similar difficulties, but those of Stepney were even greater. This was partly because the larger heritage to be assimilated from the pre-1948 services presented considerable problems, and partly because the proximity of the City provided a ready source of easier, better paid cleaning work for potential home helps. But the main difficulties seem to have arisen from the nature of the area—poor, congested, housing many nationalities and religions with widely varying standards, customs and attitudes. Stepney had a larger population, producing more cases, more difficult cases, and relatively fewer workers to help them. In July 1950 the Division re-drew the boundaries of the districts, transferring part of Stepney to the other two in order to distribute the work more evenly.

When the LCC took over the service the demand for it was expected to increase, though to what extent and in what ways could not be foreseen. From the initial response of hospitals and general practi-

---

[1] We made enquiries among three large office cleaning contractors and two University institutions employing cleaning staff. Office cleaners work different hours from home helps and are required to do less travelling (usually confining their work to one building). Turnover rates vary widely, but an annual figure of 50 per cent does not appear to be abnormal among large agencies employing staff of this kind.

tioners when the service was proposed it could be inferred that there would be many more chronic sick and elderly clients. In 1949 the Health Committee approved the following order of priorities for the types of cases then appearing: (1) confinement, (2) acute or chronic illness, (3) the aged, infirm or blind, (4) households including a mentally deficient person or large numbers of children under school leaving age. It was made clear, however, that this order should not be too rigidly applied. During the early stages, the demand for help greatly exceeded the supply available. Maternity cases, with first priority, were always helped, but the Medical Officer's annual reports on the whole County give high figures for 'other' cases refused—3,500 in 1949, 1,560 in 1950. But in Division 5 it is claimed that no one who was entirely without other sources of help has ever been refused, although occasionally there has been some delay in giving service, and the amount given may frequently be less than is required. We made no attempt to verify this claim by enquiring elsewhere.

Two changes arising from the operation of the National Health Service were soon reflected in the caseload of the Home Help service. The first and lesser of these was the preference shown by mothers for hospital confinement. Although help can be given to the families of women confined in hospital as well as to those confined at home, and also to expectant mothers during difficult pregnancies, the proportion of help devoted to maternity cases declined during the first four years, and remained low thereafter. Of the 500 households helped during the second half of 1948, 14 per cent were maternity cases. This proportion fell to 3 per cent of the 2,254 cases dealt with in 1952. Since then the proportion of maternity cases had not changed, but the total number of cases helped each year had risen to over 3,000 by the time of this study.

The second influence concerned the aged and chronic sick. Until July 1948, they had been cared for in two ways. The chronic sick—that is, those who are bed-ridden or virtually so, needing daily and continuous medical treatment, 'and also extremely aged persons who although suffering from no specific disease, are confined to bed on account of extreme weakness'[1]—had been admitted to local authority hospitals. These hospitals were now administered by the Regional Hospital Boards and were struggling to care for much larger numbers of acute cases with many near-acute cases waiting for admission.

[1] Definition taken from a report to the Council made on October 21, 1952, by the Special Committee on the Welfare of Old People (Minutes, p. 506).

F

There was a shortage of nursing staff, and among physicians geriatrics was a much neglected speciality, with the result that a 'chronic case' once admitted was likely to occupy a hospital bed for years. Even when the patient was fit enough, discharge was difficult unless relatives were willing to provide a home, for housing was scarce and accommodation in old people's homes was at least as scarce as that in hospitals. Until 1948 old and infirm people had been cared for in Poor Law Institutions; these 'homes' were now run by the Welfare Department and debarred by law from accommodating those in need of constant medical care. They were full, with waiting lists—a situation aggravated by the acute housing shortage—and since the hospital chronic wards were so congested, many were driven to maintain 'illegal' wards for chronically sick residents who could not be transferred to hospital.

In this situation a good deal of the strain was taken by the home nurses and home helps. During the first quarter of 1949 the Public Health Department examined a sample of nearly 11,000 patients treated by district nurses and found that 30 per cent of them should have been in hospital—most of them elderly people suffering from respiratory, heart or artery diseases. At the end of the same quarter over 6,700 non-maternity cases were receiving home help in the LCC area; some 3,900 of them were chronic sick cases and 780 were having home nursing care as well. As the care of the aged and chronic sick became the subject of increasing public and professional interest, it was accepted that domiciliary services were essential, not merely to eke out inadequate institutional care or to deal with crises, but because many old and sick people preferred to remain in their own homes as long as possible, and should be helped to do so. This view was endorsed in a Ministry circular of January 1950 which called on local authorities to co-operate with voluntary bodies in extending such services. At this time the LCC made a survey of the care of the aged chronic sick, asked Divisions to provide additional domiciliary services where possible (washing, shopping and chiropody services, for example) and urged them to make the maximum use of existing home nursing and home help services. In the autumn of 1952 the Committee approved a scheme to provide night attendants for households where elderly sick people were cared for by relatives, to enable the family to have two nights uninterrupted sleep per week. Division 5 was able to introduce the scheme with volunteers from the existing staff of home helps. This service has never been drawn on heavily—normally, none of the Districts carries more than one or two such cases—but it is of great value to those who do use it.

This was the only deliberate extension of the scope of the service during its first five years. The number of home helps in Division 5 (expressed as an approximate measure of their 'full-time equivalent') rose from 90 in 1949 to 145 in 1953. Numbers continued to increase until 1955 (with a full-time equivalent of 162), fell off slightly in 1956, and then rose again considerably in 1958 (to a figure of 191). Over this period the population in the Division fell steadily from 240,000 in 1948 to 216,000 in 1958, but the numbers of old people were probably increasing. (Figures are not available for the Division, but in the County as a whole the population fell during this decade while the numbers in the pensionable age groups increased).

In Division 5, unlike the rest of the country and some parts of London, the factor limiting expansion of the service was not its cost but the scarcity of home helps. This was particularly true of Stepney. Although the numbers employed in Division 5 were below the establishment permitted, the Division nevertheless helped more cases per thousand of the population than the London average. As time went on, help was refused or postponed in fewer cases, and each year more long-term cases remained on the books.

The cost of the service rose steeply, though income from the charges made for it remained at a low level. The Department, making a random check on information supplied by applicants, was shocked to discover how many people understated their incomes. A check made in 1950 on 36 per cent of the applications arising during one year throughout the County showed that 48 per cent of applicants understated their incomes. After that all statements of income were verified, usually direct from employers.

The information needed for assessment was gathered on the initial visit which was usually made by the Home Help Organizer herself. The assessments were done either by her or by her clerk, and were checked by a member of the Divisional Administrative Officer's staff. The assessment scales were complicated. They depended on the joint income of husband and wife, plus whatever was paid for household expenses by children, lodgers, or other non-dependants. Allowances were made and living expenses deducted at rates used by the NAB, and a proportion of the remaining income was regarded as available for payments—one-third of the first pound, one-half of the second and two-thirds of the remainder. In cases of prolonged illness the weekly payment could be reduced to one-third of the first pound and half of the remainder. In addition the hourly charge varied according to the amount of service given; for example, the charge for the first ten hours was 1s 6d per hour, but the cost of twenty hours' service was one guinea. In 1959 the maximum charge was 3s per hour (though the home helps' wage alone was 3s 5d per hour at this time) and there were always some people who preferred to pay the full amount rather than have their incomes investigated. Those receiving national assistance were automatically given free service.

By the beginning of 1954 the Home Help service was well-established and its value recognized by other branches of the health services. It then entered a period of expansion to meet new, specialist demands made upon it by other services, and its administrative structure was overhauled. The special schemes will be described first.

The County Children's Department was set up in 1948, and its activities soon reflected the growing belief that every effort should be made to enable families to care for their own children before removing them from home. During 1952 these problems were discussed among officers and committees of the Children's and Health services and it was suggested that home helps might have a part to play in this connection. Divisional Medical Officers were consulted and their opinions (based on discussions with their Home Help Organizers) reported to the Health Committee, together with those of the Children's Officer. The Committee approved the scheme suggested and it came into operation on December 1, 1953, for an experimental year.

This scheme provided for 'child helps' to be sent to families referred by the Area Children's Officers, although direct application to Divisional Medical Officers has since been encouraged. The families catered for were those in which two or more children under school-leaving age were temporarily deprived of care at home and likely to be received into the Council's care if this help was not available (for example, children with mothers in hospital, and fathers working away from home or on night-shift). The child help would live in, sleeping in the home at night and generally taking the place of the parents. It was found at the same time that in some cases the father or a relative could sleep in at night, but that help was still required to get the children off to school and care for them on their return until the father finished work in the evening; this need could be met by ordinary home helps provided outside the usual hours—from 7.00 a.m. to 9.00 a.m. and from 5.00 p.m. to 7.00 p.m. for example—and this 'early morning and evening help' scheme thus grew as an off-shoot of 'child help'.

Morning and evening help was found to be extremely effective in the cases where it could be used, but Division 5 scarcely ever supplied residential helps, and after the experimental year annual figures for residential helps in the whole County did not exceed five. It was also realized that in a number of cases home helps working on 'general' cases were instrumental in preventing families breaking up. As early as November 1954 the Ministry of Health issued a circular (27/54) commending the child help service—which then operated only in London and one or two other areas—and encouraging all health authorities to follow suit. After receiving reports on the first full year, the Health Committee accepted the scheme as a permanent and integral part of the home help service in June 1955. A few amendments were made—families with only one child became eligible for help and the helps no longer had to be drawn from the normal staff; thus, if a friend or relative of the client were prepared to give up a paid job in order to do the work they could be employed by the Division for that purpose.

In the following year a further step was taken. Ministry of Health circular 27/54 had mentioned the need to prevent 'problem families' breaking up, and suggested the use of home helps to teach housecraft to mothers of these families. 'Problem families' were a source of concern to the Health and Children's Departments at this time, and in March 1956, after consulting the Divisions, the Health Committee approved a scheme whereby a small number of 'special home helps' from each Division would receive training for work with these families. The first group, including ten from Division 5, took a five-day course of instruction in simple home management, cookery, child care, and teaching methods. The families to whom they were sent were referred by health visitors and social workers who continued to work with them, while the Home Help Organizer retained full responsibility for service matters. The special home help attended monthly meetings with the Home Help Organizer, the health visitor and other social workers concerned with the family. This scheme demanded the closest co-operation between all those involved. The Health Committee did not alter the order of priorities established in 1949, but left the allocation of these cases to the discretion of the Organizers. Ten cases were dealt with in the first six months of the scheme. The Division claimed that five showed clear improvement, and some improvement took place in three others. The special service continued and further groups of helps joined it. They were chosen by the Divisional Medical Officer on the recommendation of the Home Help Organizers and the Divisional Nursing Officer. The Nursing Officer reported that the service would be much more extensively used but for the difficulty of winning the co-operation of the families. Comment from other agencies suggested that the location of this and other home help services in the

Health Department may have encouraged families and the social workers serving them to assume that they were designed only for 'health cases', thus discouraging applications from people who might have benefited. But we have no other evidence that this was the case, and the Department did its best (in the LCC's 'Directory of Social Services', for example) to publicize the full range of needs dealt with by the home helps. On several occasions a special home help from this Division worked in close collaboration with the local Family Service Unit—a voluntary organization working intensively with a small number of 'problem families'.

These developments brought no reduction in the numbers of old people assisted by home helps. The number of 'special' cases always remained very small, and the aged and chronic sick continued to take much the largest proportion of the service. The aged and chronic sick were not distinguished from other non-maternity cases in the Division's statistics until 1953, when they accounted for 86 per cent of all cases—a proportion maintained until the time of this study. A Ministry survey made in 1954–5 (The Boucher Report)[1] stressed the importance of local authority domiciliary services, including home helps, and even suggested they might mask deficiencies in the hospital services—though the Organizers in Division 5 did not believe this was happening there at the time of our study. The Ministry's circular issued after the publication of the Report urged local authorities to extend their services for old people and to encourage voluntary activity in this field.

While the special schemes were evolving, the arrangements for the service came under scrutiny. During 1954 and 1955 the Organization and Methods Branch of the LCC Clerk's Department carried out a thorough survey of the work of the Public Health Department and the report made by its Reviewing Committee to the Health Committee suggested that the Home Help Service in the County had developed in a way that led to considerable variations in working methods and standards of service. It also remarked on the rapidly increasing cost of the service. Whereas in the first nine months the total cost of the service was £200,340 and in 1955–6 it had risen to £756,635, income from clients over the same period had only risen from £26,670 to £44,740. These comments were referred to a Departmental working party under the chairmanship of the Administrative Officer and including the Principal Clerk of the relevant Central Office Division,

[1] Ministry of Health Reports on Public Health and Medical Subjects No. 98. *Survey of Services Available to the Chronic Sick and Elderly*, 1954–5.

one Divisional Medical Officer, one Divisional Administrative Officer, one Divisional Nursing Officer and two Home Help Organizers. The working party was appointed in May 1956, and presented a detailed report to the Health Committee in February 1957.

The Reviewing Committee had suggested that variations in standards within the County arose through confused lines of supervision both within the Divisions, and between the Divisions and County Hall. As far as the Divisions were concerned, the working party found it was not clear whether the Divisional Medical Officer's responsibility for the home help service should be channelled through the Divisional Administrative Officer or the Divisional Nursing Officer—the arrangement within any Division depending rather on the amount of interest shown by the officers concerned. The working party decided for a 'tripartite administration', with the Divisional Medical Officer at the head of the service, and the two other officers responsible for supervision of those parts of the service connected with their work. This decision made no significant change in the organization of Division 5. The working party urged that regular meetings be held between the Home Help Organizers and the senior officers of the Division, with the result that the periodic meetings hitherto held in Division 5 were now arranged on a formal, bi-monthly basis. The problem of the Home Help Organizers' isolation from the central office was tackled, not by the appointment of a County Organizer as suggested by the Reviewing Committee and the Organizers themselves, but by arranging twice-yearly meetings between the Organizers and administrative officers at County Hall which enabled the Organizers to give their views to Headquarters more directly. These meetings also afforded a useful opportunity for contact between the Organizers themselves, who tended only to be acquainted with colleagues working in neighbouring areas.

When considering the uneven distribution of service between one area and another, the working party showed that during the previous three years there had been increasing uniformity in the amount of service given, but pointed out that local variations in need—as between a relatively scattered residential area like Eltham and a congested area like Stepney, for example—would inevitably lead to variations in service. The working party agreed that major economies could not be made without a fundamental change in policy which would be a matter for the Council to decide, and that an increase in cost was to be expected if the service was to form an effective complement to other health and welfare services.

Much of the working party's time was devoted to the detail of organization and changes were recommended which would simplify and standardize administrative routines, so reducing confusion and making it easier to transfer staff from one Division to another. They also provided for a much more detailed system of statistical recording in order to make closer supervision of the service's development possible. The earlier, simpler forms of record keeping had not shown changes in the Division's work in any detail.

Schemes of training were recommended for Assistant Home Help Organizers—post-entry training under the supervision of selected Organizers, and a more theoretical course, possibly leading to a formal qualification, to be arranged after consultation with the Institute of Home Help Organizers. The Institute was not officially represented on the working party, but one of its chief officers was a member in her capacity as a Home Help Organizer.

The Institute of Home Help Organizers had its origins in a small group of London and Home Counties Organizers who in 1948 created an informal association which met to discuss ways of raising the standards of training and performance among Organizers then being appointed. By 1954 the association was incorporated as the Institute of Home Help Organizers (affiliated to the National Association of Local Government Officers) and had established good contacts with similar bodies in other countries. In 1959 the Institute claimed a membership of over 300, organized in eleven regional branches, and its International Secretary (an LCC Organizer) had been elected first President of the International Council of Home Help Services—a body formed that year with the approval of the governments concerned.

During the previous two years the Institute had been instrumental in persuading some authorities to set up in-service training for Organizers and in 1958 the LCC began a course of in-service training for newly appointed Assistant Organizers. The Institute also had plans for a brief training for home helps along the lines of the courses for 'special' home helps, and a more ambitious plan for a six-month postal course leading to an examination that would confer a certificate on Home Help Organizers. This plan had been approved by the Chairman of the Society of Medical Officers of Health and it was hoped that local authorities would give it their support. Thus the Organizers, originally a group of women chosen (often rather haphazardly and with little or no training) for a harassing and scarcely understood job, were beginning to emerge as a recognized body, concerned with their professional standards and reputation.

Conclusion

This is the story of a new service, created from a patchwork of schemes taken over in 1948 and developed into something more comprehensive and much bigger than had ever been envisaged before. It was several years before the scope and purpose of the service emerged clearly. Then there was a phase of reorganization: administrative procedures were standardized, specialist branches were identified and developed, regular statistics were prepared, links with other services were forged, a new professional group took shape, and training was begun. By the time of this study the service had settled down into recognized routines; the numbers of cases helped continued to rise slowly, but the distribution of help between different types of case had remained remarkably stable for the previous seven years. The service was still experimenting but fresh developments now appeared as modifications of a well established pattern.

Before 1948 the service had in most places been a rudimentary affair, designed for the purpose of helping families in which the housewife was temporarily incapacitated. Then three major changes took place. The County authority was given powers to provide domestic help to meet a much wider variety of needs. It was accepted that the service could not succeed without a competent staff of organizers. And it was recognized—more slowly—that the home helps were neither an independent, self-sufficient service nor a frill upon the fabric of the welfare state, but an essential ancillary to the hospitals, the domiciliary health services, the old people's welfare services and the child care service. Thereafter the growth of the service depended mainly on the number of home helps who could be recruited and kept on the job.

What the principal functions of the service would be was still an open question—but not for long. Priority was always given to the family in which there was confinement or serious illness, and the aged and chronic sick were not separately identified in the statistics for five years. But it is clear that the old took the lion's share of resources from the beginning. Maternity cases fell steadily from 14 per cent to 3 per cent of all cases. After 1953 the aged and chronic sick constituted 86 or 87 per cent of the caseload each year, and all other types of case continued to provide the remaining 10 per cent of the caseload. These figures understate the importance of the maternity cases, each of which demanded more hours of service per week than were required by other cases, but the trend is clear. This pattern of work is typical of that found in other LCC Divisions and many other local authorities.

The principal factors shaping the course of this development lay outside the service: the growing demand for home help among the aged and chronic sick arose from the growing proportion of elderly people in the local population, the growing numbers in this group who were able to continue living in their own homes, and the scarcity of accommodation for them in hospitals and residential institutions. This demand was directed and supported by hospitals, general practitioners and the welfare services whose patients and clients needed the service. Being based in a Public Health Department, the service is likely to have been particularly attuned to the demands of the chronic sick and particularly responsive to the pleas of medical authorities. Priority was accorded to young families, but the growing proportion of mothers having their babies in hospital provided an alternative means of meeting their needs. Meanwhile the system of charges (although it was exceedingly complex, and raised only a small fraction of the total cost of the service) demanded relatively high payments from households with a full-time wage earner needing several hours' help each day, and negligible payments from households with no wage earner needing only a few hours' help each week. Thus the aged and infirm may have been more willing to seek help than were mothers with young children. Moreover the provision of occasional help for elderly people, many of whom lived alone, must have entailed a more easily sustained pattern of personal relationships (for helper and helped alike) than the provision of more intensive help in a family of young children.

The Council, its Health Committee and senior staff gave the Home Help Organizers great freedom to develop the service in response to the demands made upon it, and subsequently devoted their attention to the development of special branches of the service and the general improvement of its administrative structure and procedures. The pattern that eventually took shape in response to the demands of clients and the social services assisting them was accepted and confirmed, rather than initiated, by those ultimately responsible for the direction of the service.

DISCUSSION

The previous studies in this series dealt with tasks that formed a part of a longer or larger administrative process. But this one deals with the origins and subsequent development of a particular local branch of the social services. It therefore provides an exceptional opportunity for studying the manner in which the functions of such a service take shape. Our discussion of the case will be restricted to a few general features of this process which reappear in later studies of similar developments.

Many attempts had been made to establish a service of this kind since the government first gave its blessing to such schemes during the first world war. But it was not until the National Health Service was introduced in 1948 that the appointment of full-time organizers provided a corps of junior administrators who were wholly devoted to the development of the service and backed by a local authority prepared to provide the financial resources it would require. Despite initial difficulties and a continuing scarcity of labour, the staff of the service was rapidly built up in the area studied, and ideas which had been discussed for close on fifty years became viable at last.

Nevertheless the functions of this service, derived from disparate needs and traditions, were not specified at all precisely in the National Health Service Act or in the initial directives issued by the County Health Department. Its eventual extent and scope and the priority to be accorded to different needs were uncertain. This uncertainty, and the freedom given to the Organizers to develop the services in their own way, were increased by the overwhelming urgency of other tasks which engrossed the attention of the Committee and its senior officials at the time.

The influence of other bodies which made demands on the Health Department, referred clients to the Home Help service, and provided general support for its growth at central and local levels of government constituted one group of factors that played a part in shaping the development. A service of this kind cannot develop without spending money and recruiting staff, but these must be secured in competition with other potential users of the same resources. To compete successfully for resources the service must convince those who control them that it does—or will do—valuable work. The people to be convinced are not themselves directly responsible for the service but their support for it is crucial. In this case the service required the initial backing of the Ministry of Health and the Ministry of Labour, and the sustained support of general practitioners, the hospitals, the medical services represented on the Divisional Committee, the County Welfare Department and the Children's Department. Its functions were partly shaped by the needs and expectations of these bodies.

A second major influence shaping the service was provided by the increasingly confident and coherent group of Organizers managing it. Within the broad limits assigned to them, it was they who interviewed applicants and determined how much help they should have and how soon they should have it; it was they who selected home helps and assigned them to households, drew up budgets and distributed resources. In a perfect world it would no doubt have been recognized from the start that those responsible for these complicated and onerous tasks required some training, adequate assistant staff and opportunities for regular consultation with each other and with senior officials. But in real life a group of workers must struggle to gain recognition for such needs, first among themselves and then at more senior levels of the services in which they operate. Hence it took time—and the creation of national and international associations—for the Organizers to secure these things and to ask for further developments, such as the appointment of a County Home Help Organizer with direct and permanent access to senior staff in the central office, which had not been achieved at the time of this study. From the start, individual Organizers played an important part in shaping the service; in future their professional association and the climate of opinion it creates may play an increasing part in this process; though its operations will doubtless be guided by the more influential administrative and professional interests (represented by the chairman of the Society of Medical Officers of Health, for example) whose support it requires.

It has been suggested that the number and character of the applicants coming to ask for the service played the most important part of all in shaping its development. But these demands are a complex phenomenon depending on the motives and behaviour of people on both sides of the counter, and the relationships between them. We have only examined one side of that process. But it seems likely that demographic changes, the general climate of opinion affecting the growth and function of services for people living in their own homes, the growing interest in the needs of old people, scarcity of alternative social services and the home helps' close links with the whole system of health services, all played a part in determining the volume and types of applications received and the priorities accorded to each of them. Unlike the charges made for Legal Aid, dealt with in the previous study, the charges made for the Home Help service were entirely under the control of those providing the service itself, and the assessments were to a considerable extent designed to accord with the priorities laid down for the service. We have no reliable evidence about the effects of this system of charges (and neither had the LCC)

but it seems likely that these effects were appreciable and partly unforeseen, producing a larger proportion of elderly and infirm applicants
than would have been expected had the service been provided free.

This brief outline of the principal features of the development may
be summarized in the form of hypotheses to be tested in subsequent
studies. The creation of a service calls for considerable resources
which can only be secured with the agreement of influential bodies
outside the group responsible for providing it. The variety of these
bodies and the diversity of their interests may partly account for the
broad and ill-defined terms of reference with which the service begins.
To secure the growing volume of resources it needs, those providing
the service are compelled to enter into general, if ill-defined, commitments that command the approval of those whose support they require
in competing with other potential users of these resources. The staff
directly responsible for managing the service find they have common
problems and common interests in their daily work of dealing with
their clients, their subordinates and seniors. They formulate general
principles for their own guidance and for the training of their successors, and they seek direct access to more senior officials and greater
influence over the development of the service. Meanwhile staff providing the service can exert considerable influence on the character and
volume of the demands made on it by the public, through selection
procedures, deliberate or accidental, and through the reputation they
create for it. But to develop extensively, the service must go a long
way towards meeting the needs expressed by its clients and by those
who play a part in directing clients to it.

In conclusion it may be noted that the principal relationships in this
simplified model—particularly those between the people providing
the service, their clientele, and the external 'backers' controlling the
resources they require—are not unlike those to be seen in the development of industrial and commercial institutions. The price mechanism
plays a smaller (though by no means a negligible) part in the transactions of the social services; but, although money may not be the
principal medium of exchange employed, the relationships between the
parties to these transactions are similar in many ways to those which
are to be seen in the market. In order to grow, the service must both
meet a demand and maintain its creditworthiness among those controlling the resources it needs.

———————

CHAPTER 8

THE DEVELOPMENT OF CASEWORK IN A CHILDREN'S DEPARTMENT

This study, like the previous one, deals with the first decade of a new social service, but it is restricted to selected developments within the organization. As before, the scope and objectives of the service were initially unclear. They were gradually worked out by the staff providing the service, through successive adaptations which had to be reconciled with the expectations of external interests controlling the growing volume of resources required. The 'vagueness' of the service's objectives appears to have been a necessary condition for successful evolution. As the work developed, changes occurred in the structure of the organization, affecting the relationships between those working in it. But considerable differences in outlook could be tolerated, provided new developments went some way towards satisfying the aspirations of all concerned.

THIS report deals with Area 5 of the London County Council's Children's Department—the same geographical area as that served by Division 5 of the Health Department which formed the subject of the previous study. When asked to select the most important developments that had taken place in the work of her office during recent years, the Area Children's Officer chose two: first, and most important, a reorganization which delegated responsibility for casework with children in the Council's care to whichever Area Office received the children into care and dealt with their families; secondly, an experiment in 'intensive' casework which had been made in this and one other Area Office. The Home Area Scheme was introduced in October 1953, and the first intensive caseworker was appointed in January 1955. Since each formed a part of the same general evolution of the service, this study deals with both of them. It was carried out in 1957 and 1958.

Neither of these innovations can be understood without some account of the structure and history of the whole Department. Our report therefore begins with an outline of the Department's origins and early growth. The development of the Home Area Scheme and the intensive casework service are then traced in turn. In both these sections of the report the description of developments at County Hall generally precedes the description of developments in the Area Office, but it is the work of the Area Office which forms the focal point of the Study. After a summary of the situation as it was in 1957, the report closes with some general conclusions.

The main sources for this account were the people who took leading parts in the developments described—the Chairman of the Children's Committee and about ten of the Council's staff, including the (then acting) Children's Officer, the Area Children's Officer of Area 5 and her predecessor. The Department also provided a report on its work made by the Organization and Methods branch of the Clerk's Department and a number of other reports and directives. Three cautions should be borne in mind while reading this study. The Area Office chosen for the study was not typical of the other eight in London County, for although all followed the same general principles each was free to develop its work in response to local needs and problems. Considerable further growth and change took place in this Area shortly after the completion of the study, but although a note on these later developments appears at the conclusion of this report we have not attempted to bring the story up to date. The term 'casework', frequently used in this report, can have several meanings: here it refers simply to 'work on cases' carried out by child care officers and others in the Area Children's Office—which is the sense in which the phrase was normally employed in the Department.

The Establishment of the Department

The administrative structure to be described originated in the Children Act of 1948 which amended and extended the responsibilities of Local Authorities for deprived children. The Act provided for the creation of new departments to carry out these functions and those imposed on Local Authorities under Parts III and IV of the Children and Young Persons Act 1933, the Adoption of Children (Regulation) Act 1939, and (in the case of the LCC) Part XIII of the Public Health (London) Act, 1936. Among their responsibilities were the reception into care of children orphaned, deserted or for other reasons deprived of proper care in their own families (including those committed to the Authority's care by the courts under 'fit person' orders) and the provision of foster homes or other residential establishments for them. For children in their care they were also given wide powers in the field of adoption, and enabled in certain circumstances to assume the rights and duties of parents. The Children's Authorities also have other duties—those under Child Life Protection Regulations, for example —which are not elaborated here as they played no part in the developments to be described.

In November 1948 the London County Council appointed its Children's Committee to which all this work was referred, and the Department itself came into being in the following year. Many of its functions were inherited from other Departments; hitherto the Social Welfare Department had been responsible for decisions about the reception of children into care, the form of care to be provided for them, and the assumption of parental rights; it also assessed and collected parental contributions. Of the children received into care and placed in institutions, those under two years had been put into residential nurseries run by the Public Health Department, and those over two years had gone to residential nursery schools, residential schools and homes run by the Education Department. The latter Department was also responsible for selecting foster homes, placing and supervising the children who went into them, providing after-care, and generally implementing the decisions made by the Welfare Department. Along with these functions, 32 residential establishments were transferred to the new Department, and 1,440 staff, of whom 70 worked 'in the field', 140 were in office grades, and the remaining 1,230 were in residential homes and schools. Field workers and residential staff were transferred *en bloc*, but when a new service is carved out of existing departments in this way, it is natural for the parent departments to endeavour to retain their most efficient office staff.

The administrative centre of the new Department was at County Hall, but work on individual cases was decentralized to nine offices set up in Areas corresponding to the Divisions already existing in the Education and Public Health Departments, each Area covering about three Metropolitan Boroughs. Most of the records, field workers and office staff were transferred to these offices.

The Department was thus faced with multiple problems, having not only to build up a new service, but also to assimilate and modify a patchwork of inherited functions, attitudes, staff and records. The Area Offices were undermanned, and contained many people trained under the Poor Law or in the Education Department who had been uprooted from their accustomed settings. The Department had to begin by creating a new set of loyalties and a clear understanding of its enlarged responsibilities throughout this heterogeneous team. Moreover the legislation establishing it had been directly prompted by popular concern about the fate of children in public care, and no provision had been made for helping children still living in their own homes. Placed like an ambulance at the foot of a cliff, the service had no power to prevent the casualties it awaited. This restriction could not be maintained indefinitely.

Up to this time residential institutions had been accepted as the normal and desirable means of caring for children, but the Children's Act required the new Department to use foster care whenever possible. This was in accordance with recently developed ideas on child care, but was also made necessary by the acute shortage of space in residential establishments. This was the most important change made during the first few years. The Department had its work cut out to get the new service going, and there was no time to spare for other tasks.[1]

The Department in 1953

The beginning of 1953 forms a convenient starting point for this study. The numbers of children in care had by then risen from 5,681 (in 1949) to 8,027; the numbers in foster homes had almost doubled, raising the proportion boarded out from 18 per cent to 25 per cent.

The Children's Committee was responsible to the Council for all questions of policy and for interpreting the work of the Department to the Council. It met monthly and had twenty-one members, some of whom were co-opted. Members sat on the managing committees of residential homes and schools, and visited these establishments from time to time. The duties, membership and procedures of these managing committees still remained largely unchanged, but the establishments to which they were attached were henceforth to play a less predominant part in the service than they had done previously.

At County Hall the Children's Department consisted of four Divisions. Two of them, responsible respectively for child care and work on individual cases, and for the management of residential establishments, came under the Chief Assistant Children's Officer. The other two Divisions—one dealing with staff and the other with finance and the general organization of the Department—came under the Department's Administrative and Establishments Officer. All four Divisions were staffed by administrative and clerical officers. In the course of time three Inspectors of Child Care were appointed to

[1] For an account of the early development of this Department, see Donald Ford, *The Deprived Child and the Community*. London, Constable, 1955.

supervise the residential establishments and to advise on child care generally.

The Area Offices handled direct relations with the public, receiving children into care, and finding and filling foster homes. Each was responsible for liaison with a particular group of residential homes and schools, principally for the purpose of boarding out children from them, and they were gradually expected to extend their 'casework' as far as their limited resources allowed. In January 1953 Area 5 had a staff of seventeen, ten of whom were social workers. The Area Children's Officer was responsible for both the administrative and casework aspects of the Area's work and, like all Area Children's Officers appointed before 1955, she was graded as a Senior Assistant in the administrative class of officers (though we have included her among the social workers numbered above). She had started her career in residential work at the time local authorities first took over children's homes from the Boards of Guardians. During the war she ran special schools for evacuees, and in 1944 jointed the LCC Education Department as a boarding out officer. She was responsive to new ideas and enjoyed experimenting. Moreover her experience had given her great respect for the advantages a child can gain from his own home, and considerable reluctance to place children in institutions whenever this could be avoided. She was supported by a staff that was anxious to use opportunities for innovation. Like all but two of the Area Children's Officers, she had had little administrative experience. Like some of the others, she had come from the Education Department which had established standards of boarding out work widely considered to be in advance of anything comparable at that time.

There were nine child welfare officers in the Area. Three of them were 'special duties' officers dealing only with court cases, including adoption, for which they undertook the work of 'guardians *ad litem*'. Each of the others was responsible for liaison with one or more establishments, and two of them also undertook 'aftercare'—that is, the supervision of children in care who had left school. The three 'special duties' officers and one other had worked for the Council for many years but had no paper qualifications. The remaining five held University Social Science Certificates, and two of them held a professional qualification—the Home Office Certificate in Child Care— as well.

The administrative staff of the Area consisted of one Administrative Assistant, two male clerical officers who dealt with new applications for children in need of care, another who assessed parental contributions, and two general clerical officers, one of whom did some local visiting as well as clerical work. Much of this would have been regarded as social work, even at that time; thus there was no clear distinction between the activities of administrative staff and social workers.

The methods employed by the Department at that time were still based on those used before 1948. All establishments and the allocation of vacancies in them were controlled from County Hall. Applicants coming to the Area Office in Bethnal Green Road were interviewed by a clerical officer—a former relieving officer, experienced in record-keeping and in dealing with 'difficult' clients. If a child was to be received into care he collected the information needed to fill up the application form, and telephoned to County Hall for a place appropriate to the age, sex and special needs (religion, length of stay, etc.) of the child. The child was only accepted into care if an appropriate vacancy could be found or created. In practice about one in four seem to have been accepted—the desperate shortage of places meant there was room for the most urgent cases only, and the rest had to be placed on a waiting list. It was generally felt that places went to whoever put in most applications and pushed hardest, and the staff tended to react accordingly. The procedure placed a great strain on everyone. Thus the clerk responsible for this work in the Vacancies Section at County Hall was at one time christened 'Molotov' by staff in the Area Office. But when child welfare officers were brought into County Hall for a short period to take over these duties the position was just as bad. All concerned were the victims of a system devised years before which could no longer cope with the increased demands being made on the new service.

Social workers in the Area Office took no part in this procedure, for child welfare officers assumed no responsibility for children until they had been placed in care. Children were sent to establishments in all parts of the County and far beyond, and they then became the responsibility of the Area Offices to which the establishments were attached, while any dealings with their families and with children returning to their homes were the concern of the Areas in which their parents lived. Often several children from one family were placed in different establishments, and two or more Area offices dealt with a single family. Satisfactory liaison between Areas was difficult, and mountainous paperwork resulted.

In 1952 the extension of boarding out came to a halt, and for the next five years there were fewer children in foster homes. Most foster parents wanted a child of a specified age and sex, free from close ties with his own family. Few would take children for short periods, few would take more than one child (and the Department's policy was to keep brothers and sisters together) boys were harder to place than girls, Roman Catholic foster parents were always scarce, and children with behaviour problems had to be cared for in the Department's establishments. Foster parents resembled hesitant adopters and were treated as such.

Meanwhile the rising numbers of children in care and the larger staff required was making the service increasingly expensive. Although officers in the Areas recognized these financial problems, they were primarily the worry of those in County Hall who stood nearer to the Committee. The Area Children's Officers' main complaint was that the system for placing children was cumbersome; some felt that if they themselves controlled the vacancies they would be able to develop a better policy for reception into care. As early as 1951 a few of the leading members of the central office had come to believe not only that it was cumbersome and expensive, but that more stress should be placed on the welfare of children in their own homes, and relatively less on the 'child minding' aspects of the service. At County Hall the principal advocates of this approach were found in the Child Care Division and the inspectorate. But several other senior administrators felt that if Area Children's Officers controlled reception they would bring much greater numbers of children into care, and cause a calamitous drain on the Department's inadequate resources. The Children's Officer himself was reluctant to subject a newly established Department to the radical change implied by such a step. It was a heavy responsibility to justify such trouble and expense to his Committee and the Council.

The Home Area Scheme

Plans for the new system originated in the Child Care Division at County Hall, and the details were thrashed out in informal discussions. After two months or so the Area Children's Officers were brought into the talks. At first it was not clear whether the proposed scheme was to be regarded as a change in administration (and therefore to be left to the officers of the Department) or as a change in policy (and therefore subject to the Committee's approval). The officials took the view that it was an administrative change; the plans were discussed with the Chairman of the Committee, and after long debates within the Department in September 1953 the Children's Officer issued a directive outlining two plans: the 'Home Area Scheme' for regrouping Area offices and establishments and the 'decentralization of vacancies', both to come into force on October 1, 1953. The nine Areas and their outcounty regions were grouped into four 'Sectors'. Area 5, with Area 6 and their contiguous outcounty regions constituted Sector C, and they were given control of vacancies in the group of homes and schools in that Sector. But since these two Areas were divided by the Thames they agreed to operate autonomously, each using the establishments in its own outcounty region; Area 5 was therefore able to work as a more or less independent unit. Responsibility for cases and the allocation of children to establishments was to be settled by the Areas amongst themselves—County Hall declined to act as arbitrator over the details of individual cases, and only consented to receive appeals on questions of exceptional difficulty. The central office remained responsible for providing and running establishments, for negotiations with other local authorities, and for authorizing the use of private and voluntary establishments. The immediate aim was for children to be placed within their own 'home' Sector, though a few big specialist establishments were to be temporarily available to all Areas. It was intended that the officer making the initial contact with a family should be in charge right through a child's time in care, and that the child *and his family* should be regarded as the 'child care unit' for which the service was provided. 'Anticipated results' of the scheme, outlined in the Children's Officer's directive, included a speedier and more elastic procedure requiring less paper work, and a greater sense of personal responsibility among officers; child welfare officers would be brought into close touch with reception work, and there would be closer contacts both between children, parents and the service, and between Area offices and establishments. Finally, it was hoped by some that there would be opportunities to begin 'preventive work', leading to the growth of a casework service dealing as much with families as with children. The directive added that 'All officers will be aware of the long term child care principles and aims underlying the scheme'.

Differing views of the new situation were found in different parts of the Department. In practical terms what had happened was that the Vacancies Section at County Hall had disappeared. Instead there was an informal grouping of the nine Areas and their outcounty regions into four Sectors, and each Area had been allotted space in a group of homes, schools and so on; within Sectors, each child had become the responsibility of its receiving Area (which potentially at least, was also the establishment Area), and families were no longer split between several Areas. Ultimately the effect of these changes would be that the children in any group of establishments, together with those boarded out in the same Sector, would (with a few inevitable exceptions) be those received into care by the Area offices of the Sector. Each of the four Sectors would then form a self-contained unit.

But in October 1953 this scheme had hardly begun to take shape. The children from one Area's territory were still scattered throughout the four Sectors since it had been decided that none would be transferred simply for the sake of administrative convenience. Two years later, when the pattern had begun to grow clearer, further complication was caused by the creation of three subcommittees of the Children's Committee, known as District Committees, which substituted a three-part division for the original four-part system. Another continuing source of untidiness remained in the reception and assessment centre at Poplar, a short-stay home in Wandsworth, after-care hostels, and a large home named Wood Vale: these were still used as 'all-London' establishments and small homes for disturbed children were added later to this group since it was not possible to make every new experiment in triplicate.

The Committee seems to have been most concerned with the redistribution of children brought about by the Home Area scheme, laying less stress on the reallocation of responsibilities between County Hall and the Areas, and between individual Areas. Caseworkers recognized the importance of these administrative changes, but more important to many of them was the fact that this development held out hopes of making the 'long-term principles of child care' a reality. The Areas had been given considerable freedom in interpreting their new powers, and Area 5 was particularly responsive to the opportunity offered. Before the Home Area scheme was introduced it had already given its child welfare officers the task of dealing with applications for admission to care. Developments in this Area were worked out in staff meetings which were frequent, though at that time irregular and unrecorded. These meetings included all members of the staff—clerical and administrative officers and social workers. The Area Children's Officer commented that the plans discussed were to alter the policy and procedure of the whole office, and it was therefore important that everyone should accept the new methods and contribute to them.

At these meetings it was decided that reception into care should be the responsibility of social workers rather than administrators, and that something more than a formal interview was required if the needs of a family were to be understood. That is, all stages of the work—

not merely boarding out and aftercare, but also reception and eventually 'preventive' work—should be conducted by those experienced in applying 'the principles of child care'. The first step had been taken when a woman clerical officer, originally a Welfare Department worker who had done local visiting, took over reception interviewing, while each application was followed up by a home visit from a child welfare officer. In order to share this extra work and to economize on travelling time, the Area was divided into 'patches', and one child welfare officer made responsible for all investigations in each. Child welfare officers began to gain effective control over reception policy in June 1953 when the clerical officer was withdrawn from reception work altogether and a new division of duties was made: all preliminary visits of investigation were undertaken by one half-time child welfare officer; all short-stay and rehabilitation cases were allocated to another, and the remainder of the child welfare officers undertook reception interviewing for one-week periods on a rota system, in addition to their work with the establishments.

This system for dealing with applications for care created new problems, but visits to applicants and the discharge of short-term cases were handled more quickly, and social work criteria could be brought to bear on the crucial decision to receive children into care. The introduction of the Home Area Scheme completed the picture. Within the limits determined by the policy, powers and resources of the department, the Area now had full control of residential placements, and reception into care depended on social workers' assessments of the needs of children and their families. It also became administratively feasible to make one social worker responsible for a family and for any of its children that might be in care.

The Area then had to assimilate its new functions and deal with the snags in its reception system. These snags were in part a reflection of the large case loads and inadequate staffing the Department had always had to contend with. Developments were therefore determined as much by the peculiarities of the staffing position as by deliberate policy. (The Council's Organization and Methods Branch made a study of the Department in 1955 and found the situation bad enough to call for an interim report recommending the appointment to the Department of twenty additional child welfare officers, bringing their total numbers to 108.) The solution reached in Area 5 was partly due to administrative reorganization and partly a reflection of changed thinking about the functions of social work within the service.

The 'patch' system had the disadvantage that decisions were delayed whenever the officer responsible for one of the patches was absent; moreover it was not easy to demarcate boundary lines. In September 1954 the Area was divided into three 'sections' within which were grouped more clearly defined patches. (These Area 'sections' must not be confused with the four Sectors into which London's nine Areas were grouped. They will be escorted by inverted commas to mark the difference.) Officers still worked their own patch as before, but in addition had an overall responsibility for a whole 'section' and thus could more easily deputize for each other. A clerical officer was assigned to work for each 'section'.

Meanwhile, interviewing by rota had given rise to serious difficulties, for there was no uniformity or continuity of treatment. This created difficulties for the visiting officer and caused confusion and frustration for social workers elsewhere—almoners, for example, who might have to deal with different reception officers on different days of the week. The public was also affected, and some people were quick to spot the idiosyncrasies of different officers and vary their tactics accordingly. It was not unknown for parents to put their heads round the door, say 'Oh, it's you!' and come back another day.

It was decided that all reception interviewing must be done by one child welfare officer, and the job was given to a new member of staff who was slightly lame and therefore unable to do much visiting. (She had more positive qualifications too, being a trained and experienced social worker.) This arrangement smoothed the internal and external relations of the office, but continuity and uniformity had still to be achieved, for office interviews and home visits were handled by different workers. The staff continued to discuss the whole problem. Then in July 1955 the interviewing officer left unexpectedly, and in the emergency the Area reverted to the rota system of interviewing, while a half-time officer took over all visits of investigation.

Finally it was agreed that a permanent team of officers should be responsible for initial interviews and the home visits that followed. But it was felt that short-stay cases should not be transferred to other officers for the few days or weeks while such children remained in care, and the team ought not to be limited to reception work. But who was to draw the line between 'short-term' and 'long-term' cases?

An opportunity for reorganization came in February 1956 when two more child welfare officers were appointed to Area 5—one half-time and one full-time. The Area's three geographical 'sections' were retained to deal with long-term cases, and a fourth 'section' created: 'section 4', consisted of two (later three) child welfare officers who took over all reception interviewing, investigation visits, and short-stay cases. 'Section 4' officers collaborated with those in the other 'sections' and could consult the appropriate workers at a very early stage in any case that seemed likely to present long-term problems. The precise moment of transfer from one officer to another was decided between them. That is, the demarcation of officers' responsibilities—which might well have been regarded as a purely administrative question— had become a 'casework' decision, left to the two officers directly concerned. This system was felt to work well, and had not been changed up to the time of this study (though it has since been abandoned).

'Intensive' Casework

The second development to be described is the experiment in 'intensive' casework. We have seen how the social workers extended their sphere of work 'backwards' from the supervision of children already in care to the investigation of new applications and the selection of those to be accepted. But concern for the welfare of children could not be halted there. Throughout this period child welfare officers became increasingly interested in the cases in which it seemed that intensive work might forestall the breakdown of normal family life or in other ways prevent children coming into public care. The seeds of this development had already been set when the first changes in reception procedure were made, and after the introduction of the Home Area Scheme one officer began to give special attention to this kind of work. But though all child welfare officers had done fairly intensive work with some families, heavy case loads prevented them from devoting much time to it.

The Child Care Division at County Hall had already recognized the whole family as the proper focus for preventive and rehabilitative work, and those responsible for the preparation of budgets acceptable to the Council had pressing reasons for supporting any measure that would reduce the number of children in care. The interest of the Chairman of the Children's Committee was sharpened by conferences and discussions, including a paper read at a conference of children's workers on the unit experimenting with intensive casework in Oxfordshire. The example of the Family Service Units, which had for long been developing intensive work with specially difficult cases, must also have been in the minds of many people. In the spring of 1954 the Chairman and the Senior Inspector of Child Care visited the Oxfordshire unit, and in July a report was presented to the Committee suggesting that two people should be appointed to attempt similar work in London. The scheme was submitted to the Director of Establish-ments—a chief officer of the Council to whom proposals for new staff positions in all LCC Departments were referred at that time.[1] He advised the Committee that the project lay outside the scope of their work: the Children Act provided no basis for it. But he suggested that comment be invited from the recently formed Joint Special Sub-committee on Children Neglected or Ill-treated in their own Homes. This Sub-committee consisted of the Chairmen of the Public Health, Education, Housing, Welfare and Children's Committees, together with other representative members, and was attended by the chief officers serving these Committees. It was appointed to investigate the co-ordination of services for neglected children. If it reported favour-ably on the plan (which it did) the Director of Establishments said he would have 'no further observations to offer'. The Chairman of the Children's Committee (who was also Chairman of the Joint Special Sub-committee) had a special interest in the project and was able to do a good deal to put the idea over. It was arguable not only that the scheme was good child care, but also that it would save more money than the amount required for additional salaries.

At a meeting in July 1954, the Children's Committee approved the experimental appointment of two intensive caseworkers for one year. The scheme was then sanctioned in turn by the Establishment Com-mittee, the Finance Committee and the Council. Areas 5 and 8 were asked to take part in the experiment, but since the worker in Area 8 withdrew after a very short time the experiment was in effect confined to Area 5.

There the intensive caseworker took up her appointment on January 1, 1955. She was fiftyish, extremely alert and brisk. She had no paper qualifications, but plenty of relevant experience, having worked in a county children's department, helped in the founding of Spofforth Hall,[2] and run what she called a 'spare-time, private FSU'.[3] At the outset she was given a case load consisting mainly of well-known 'hard-core' cases, and was left free to develop her work as she chose. Monthly case reports were submitted to the Child Care Division

[1] This office was concerned with the Council's general staffing policies, not with the Children's Departments residential 'establishment' previously referred to. It was later abolished and at the time of this study its duties were carried out by the Clerk's Department.

[2] A residential institution which provided rest and re-education for mothers and children from families with very low standards of house-keeping and mothercraft.

[3] The Family Service Units work with small numbers of families needing the most intensive help. There were three operating in London at that time (later four), one of which worked in Area 5.

in County Hall and a full report was presented to the Committee at the end of the year. It was soon discovered that it was a mistake to take on so many 'hard-core' cases, when other families in difficulties were able to respond more quickly to a comparatively short period of intensive help. It is remarkable that the worker achieved as many 'successes' as she did: the report on her first year's work claimed that out of 24 cases, 5 had been satisfactorily closed, 5 still needed 'close supervision and support', 4 'less frequent supervision', and the remaining 10 were making 'slow progress'. Financially, too, the experiment proved successful; the Area Children's Officer estimated that a net saving of nearly £1,000 had been made in the first year. These results gave general satisfaction, although it was realized that twelve months was too short a period in which to assess the real effectiveness of such work.

During the year an interim report of the Joint Special Sub-Committee had given warm support to this work, and the Public Health Department was ready to start a similar venture. As a result there were extensive inter-departmental discussions, and the formal decision by Council to maintain and extend the Children's Department's experiment had to be delayed until the end of 1956, although the worker in Area 5 was in fact able to continue with her duties during this interval. Two intensive caseworkers were then appointed to Area 8, and a second one to Area 5. The latter joined the Area in July 1957. She had a Social Science Certificate and had worked in the Education Department until 1948, when she transferred to a county children's department and there worked closely with its 'Part III accommodation unit' for homeless families. These two workers appeared to form a largely independent unit within the Area office. Potential cases were passed by 'section 4' (the reception officers) to the Area Children's Officer who decided whether or not they might be suitable for intensive help. It was then left to the intensive caseworkers to decide which families to work with. Much of their work was devoted to families who might be enabled to take back children already in the Council's care. They kept their caseloads down to twelve families each, and considered anything beyond fifteen would be unwise. The Area Children's Officer called case conferences to discuss these families with outside agencies when necessary. Monthly case reports were still prepared for the Child Care Division, and a more general report was made to the Committee each year, for the work was still regarded as experimental.

General Development of the Department

Area 5's experience was only a small part of the developments that were taking place over the same period in the Department as a whole. Many of these arose from the report made in 1955 by the newly created Organization and Methods Branch of the Clerk's Department. The Children's Department was chosen for the first o & m investigation conducted outside the Clerk's Department because it was the youngest Department and expanding rapidly. The report distinguished two aspects of the Department's work: administration and casework. The latter was described as a specialized function with a policy derived from professional and administrative considerations. It was the casework aspect of the work that was found to be in need of strengthening. The report also drew attention to the lack of effective links between Areas and County Hall. All the main recommendations were based on these two points.

The Chief Assistant Children's Officer and his two Divisions were replaced by a Senior Child Care Officer (replacing the Senior Inspector) who was to advise on child care and run a Policy and Casework Division with the assistance of an administrative officer. This new Division was the former Child Care Division, shorn of its routine administrative responsibilities which were transferred to the Department's Administrative and Establishment Officer who now supervised three Divisions: Finance, Staff, and General Administration. The Senior Child Care Officer, and the Administrative and Establishment Officer were to be of equal rank, but it was the former who would deputize for the Children's Officer in his absence. The inspectorate was increased, with one Inspector to work in each of the new Districts.

The LCC region, including the out county zones, was divided into three Districts, with new District Offices (situated in County Hall) responsible for each. The o & m report had accepted the existing informal four-fold division into Sectors as the basis for the new system, but the Children's Committee had for some time been considering a decentralized committee structure that would enable Councillors to maintain closer contact with local units of the Department. The three-part division proposed in the Committee's plans was eventually adopted.

With the help of District Administrative Officers the new District Committees took over some of the functions hitherto exercised by the central committee, notably the provision and maintenance of establishments and certain general responsibilities for children in them. The District Committees consisted of members of the Children's Committee and co-opted members. Most members also chaired House Committees attached to the establishments. They carried as much responsibility as could be delegated without threatening the main Committee's overall responsibility for the service.

It was decided that Area Children's Officers should henceforth be classified as Social Workers and not as Assistants in the administrative class. Each Area was to have one Administrative Assistant, who would deputize for the Area Children's Officer in administrative matters only —a point which had not been clarified before. It had been found that in practice one child welfare officer tended to act as deputy in child care matters, and this situation was given official recognition by creating the post of Senior Child Welfare Officer with this responsibility. No ruling was made about the officer who should act for the Area Children's Officer in the latter's absence, though it would not have been surprising if practice tended to follow the precedent set in County Hall where the Senior Child Care Officer was the Children's Officer's deputy.

By the end of 1957 a child welfare officer who first joined Area 5 in 1950 had become the Area Children's Officer. She had taken a Social Science Certificate at the University of London and had some experience in the probation service. Most of the other eighteen social workers on her staff had University qualifications in the social sciences, but only six had any formal professional training for social work. On the Administrative side the Area Children's Officer's deputy was graded as an 'Assistant I (a)'. After resort to arbitration, the salary scale for Senior Child Welfare Officers had recently been raised to £815-£1,140, placing them slightly above the I (a)s' £815-£1,090, and this was assumed by some to establish the Senior cwo's authority to act for the Area Children's Officer in her absence. (In fact the increase was granted in order to relate Senior Child Welfare Officers' salaries to those of other social workers. When the I (a)s sought, unsuccessfully, to regain parity, the Council specifically stated that there was no relation between the scales for administrators and social workers— hence differences in salary were not to be taken as an indication of differences in status). A clerical officer was attached to each of the four 'sections', and five others dealt with parental contributions, statistics, a case review system and other matters. Thus there were 19 social workers and 10 administrative and clerical officers in the Area, responsible for 992 children. In 1953 there had been 10 social workers and 6 administrative and clerical officers responsible for over 1,100 children.

Conclusions

The two innovations traced in this study were but a part of a more general development of the whole service: a Department originally formed to care for children without adequate homes of their own was beginning to provide more general forms of help (of which child care still formed by far the major part) for families having difficulty in caring for their children. The family, rather than the child, had become the focus of the service, and from a child care service there had emerged the beginnings of a general social work service.

The extent of these changes should not be exaggerated, nor should they be visualized as a continuous and precisely planned development. It was a gradual shift of emphasis that took place. Three changes of emphasis were in fact discernible, bringing about redistributions of influence and status—from County Hall to the Area offices, from the residential establishments to the Area offices, and from administrators to social workers. In 1949 it was inevitable that the new Department should rely mainly on its central office, its residential establishments and its inherited administrative patterns: the Area Office's job was simply to deal with the public. But as the Areas gained experience, skill and staff, more and more powers were delegated to them. This decentralization began at once. By the following year the Areas had already been given responsibility for administering holiday grants, and grants for children with special abilities and disabilities. Soon they were responsible for parental contributions (their collection and assessment, including discretion to waive claims) and for boarding out allowances paid to foster parents. They made recommendations to the courts on the necessity for 'fit person' orders, and they were empowered to prosecute or take other action necessary in the rare cases of cruelty or neglect. The decentralization of vacancies formed an important part of this trend. Interwoven with this was the development of casework and the growth of a professional child care 'interest' within the Department. Before 1948, child care was provided and administered by three different Departments; it was a relatively minor feature of the education, public health and poor law services. The attitudes and expectations that arose from this system were not changed overnight by the creation of the Children's Department. But gradually it was accepted—within the Department at least—that casework in child care was a service in its own right, for which special skills and training were required. An important contribution to this development was made by the group of administrative officers within the Policy and Casework Division—the former Child Care Division. These 'administrators of case work' became a source of information and guidance on the legal and administrative aspects of the Department's work. They interpreted Committee decisions about casework to the Area Offices, they explained to the Committee the implications of central government policies, circulars and reports dealing with child care; they kept in touch with the Children's Department of the Home Office, and briefed the Council's spokesmen in Parliament when child care legislation was to be debated. Meanwhile the District Officers did similar work for their District Committees. These activities were carried on as a side-line by the old Child Care Division, but the reorganization that followed the O & M report enabled the new Policy and Casework Division to devote itself entirely to such work. This new Division only consisted of four administrative and two clerical officers, but it performed a vital co-ordinating function, interpreting the principles of child care and casework in workable administrative terms. An important part was also played by the so-called Inspectors, who were given rather loosely defined duties and acted as casework consultants: they urged the delegation of powers to Area offices, and stressed the need to make the family the focus of the service—a policy which implied a corresponding stress on Area offices within the structure of the Department.

Within Area 5, too, the balance of power between social workers and administrators was altered. Child welfare officers became more numerous and tended to have rather more formal training: in 1958 thirteen out of nineteen held a University Social Science Certificate or comparable qualification, compared with five out of ten in 1953, but the proportion having further professional training for child care remained more or less the same. A growing discrepancy appeared between the responsibilities they carried and their official status. They took on reception, preventive casework and other duties, yet the status of their chief was still an administrative one, and her sole official deputy was an administrative officer. The O & M report found, however, that in Area offices generally the administrative officers received comparatively little attention and consequently tended to lack enthusiasm. The reorganization following that report was designed to relieve difficulties arising from these shifts of emphasis and responsibility within County Hall and the Area offices. By regrading officers and by reorganizing the central department the growing importance of the social workers was recognized, the casework side of the work was strengthened, and responsibilities were clarified. The District Committees were formed to enable Children's Committee members to keep in closer touch with the new work going on in the Area offices from which they had felt increasingly remote.

For Area 5 the crucial steps in the story were the withdrawal of clerical officers from reception work, the creation first of the three geographical 'sections' and then of 'section 4', and the agreement to take part in the intensive casework experiment. These developments were long debated, but their character and timing were in large part determined by the exigencies of the staffing position. The final separation of short-term from long-term casework came about almost as a last resort—indeed, the Area Children's Officer felt at the time that her decision was taken in defiance of 'sound casework principles'. The intensive casework experiment formalized and accelerated a trend that had developed during the previous twelve months from a growing awareness of the problems posed by certain families and the difficulty of providing adequate help for these families owing to staff shortages and heavy caseloads. The attempt to develop preventive work had been germinating for several years and naturally suggested further development in the directions leading towards a family casework service.

The main decisions taken at County Hall (about the Home Area scheme, the intensive casework experiment, and the steps arising from the O & M recommendations) emanated from a policy-making unit and were formulated in directives to the whole Department, though the long-term implications of these developments were not made very explicit—often for diplomatic reasons.

These changes were often interpreted differently by the various groups involved. The Home Area Scheme was seen by many of the administrators as a redistribution of responsibility between offices; Committee members tended to regard it as a redistribution of children over the region, and among social workers, the inspectors and the administrators in the Policy and Casework Division it was seen as an avenue to a new and more comprehensive approach to child care. Similarly the intensive casework experiment was for some Committee members an exciting new departure, for the Policy and Casework Division and some of the social workers it represented a step in a long term and much-discussed development of the Department's work, while for some of the administrative officers and for various groups outside the Department it was a doubtfully relevant innovation.

Nevertheless, all those favouring these schemes felt not merely that they accorded with their own ideas but that they originated directly from their own efforts.

No attempt has been made here to evaluate the services of the Department or the success of the developments studied. Indeed, until recently there would scarcely have been sufficient agreement about the functions of the service to form a basis for evaluation. What *is* evidence of success in such a service? Higher numbers of children in care, or lower numbers, or an increase in the proportion boarded out? The speed at which the children are returned to their own homes, or the number of children enabled to remain in their own homes? If children are kept out of care is this being achieved by a 'goal-keeping' technique or by skilled casework? How should the costs of the service be measured; and how important is it that the service be understood and accepted by public opinion—even if important developments may be delayed as a result? The Committee and its staff attempted to reconcile these considerations and create a policy from them. The Department was aware that more information was needed before much progress could be achieved, and attempts were made to collect and analyse relevant statistics, particularly at Area level—research had begun, for example, on new applications to Area Offices in an effort to determine what criteria should be used in evaluating the Department's policy and allocating its resources.

Some of the pressures making for change emerge fairly clearly from this account. The limited resources of the Department were at once restrictive and stimulating. The very size and complexity of a London-scale service meant that extensive delegation of powers was necessary, and indeed such a tradition had already been established by the Public Health, Education and other Departments. The Committee and the central office were willing, once the teething stages were over, to allow Area Children's Officers to develop what amounted almost to their own departments. Individual attitudes and experience and the outlook fostered among the staff of each office thus became very important and produced marked differences between Areas. When the first Children's Officer of Area 5 moved to another Area Office she commented that it was hard to believe she was in the same service, administering the same Acts of Parliament.

The early growth of boarding out came to a halt because of the scarcity of appropriate foster homes. With larger numbers in residential homes and schools the cost of the service increased, and the building programme of the LCC could not provide sufficient new, small homes for children requiring institutional care. The Department was thus forced to pay more attention to the prevention of family breakdown, and the rehabilitation of families whose children might return home from the Council's care. Meanwhile, Area offices had to search for any redistribution of duties that would ameliorate the effects of staff shortage by making better use of the available social workers and improving liaison with outside agencies such as the courts and hospitals.

Underlying these changes was the development of new ideas about children and social work, expressed by an increasingly numerous and confident group of social workers within the Department, and supported by a more widely disseminated climate of opinion. 'We were aware of Bowlby, "A Two-Year-Old Goes to Hospital", the Oxfordshire experiment, and the general swing to family casework,' said the Area Children's Officer. Meanwhile, many of the staff attended conferences and refresher courses which helped to crystallize and circulate ideas first formulated a little hazily on the job, and students from new professional training courses in the University came to the Area for field training, and some of their superiors attended seminars at the University.

Subsequent developments in the Department, many of them beginning in this Area office, show that the events traced in this study were the forerunners of much further change involving a reappraisal of rules and procedures, large increases in staff, and the introduction of further intensive caseworkers and a new grade of supervisors within the Area offices. New factors played a part in these developments, including a study of the Department made by the Home Office inspectorate, changes in senior staff, and a renewed increase in the numbers of children coming into the Department's care, due partly to growing stresses in the London housing situation. But most of these later trends flow directly from the developments to be seen in this study.

DISCUSSION

The services taken over and incorporated in the new Children's Department were more extensive and had a longer history than those that formed the basis of the Home Help scheme considered in the previous study. But the terms of reference the Council approved for the Department and the terms of the Children Act that established it were again of the most general kind, leaving plenty of scope for interpretation—particularly in the work of the Area Offices which formed the subject of this study. The 1948 Act and the Government Reports from which it sprang offered scant guidance for the development of this work; they only provided a basis for experiment—and until the new legislation of 1963 many regarded this as a very slender basis for the edifice erected upon it.

The Children's Departments were new and small. The services they provided were of the most vital kind, but in the Area studied the number of families served was less than a third of the number served by the home helps who themselves provided only a small fraction of the Health Department's services. In the years immediately following the war the London County Council gave first priority to housing and education and the new Department—viewed with some suspicion by neighbouring empires out of which it had been carved—could not expect a generous share of the County's resources. The resources it secured depended on the backing of Council members on the Children's Committee and on the support of other sections of County Hall, the Clerk's Department, the Health Department and the O & M Branch, for example. The latter gave decisive support for increases in Area office staff in its 1955 report, and the consent of the Director of Establishments and of members and officers representing the Health, Housing, Education and Welfare Departments was eventually secured for the appointment of intensive caseworkers.

The Home Office appears to have exerted little influence on these developments—partly because it was more wary of intervening in the affairs of the LCC than in those of smaller authorities, but largely because the Act provided a flimsy legal basis for preventive social work. Such work could be justified by arguing that reception into care under Section I of the Act called for considerable investigation of the family situation before decisions could be taken; and later the Children and Young Persons (Amendment) Act of 1953 provided further scope for it. But until the new legislation of 1963 the Home Office was frequently aware that a benevolent silence was its most helpful contribution to the efforts of Children's Departments to make good the omissions in the original Act.

Increases in staff—particularly social work staff—were crucial at every stage in the development of the Area office; many of the most important changes in procedure and in the work these procedures permitted sprang directly from the gain or loss of one or two workers. Some of the additional resources secured by the office were provided for the fulfilment of existing legal commitments for the supervision of foster children. Others were secured by entering into new commitments; the appointment of intensive caseworkers, for example, was justified on the grounds that they would cover their costs by reducing the numbers of children in care, and procedures were devised to ascertain whether this claim had been justified. But on the whole, the Area office's objectives retained their general character, providing ample scope for subsequent interpretation in the light of experience. Within the Department, the realization of 'long term child care principles and aims' was one of several phrases used to indicate general objectives without clarifying these too precisely. Though the lack of precision about objectives was partly an unavoidable aspect of the kind of work the Department was doing and the uncertain legal basis for doing it, this was also a necessary tactical device for sustaining continued expansion of the service without provoking dissension inside and outside the Department. Some vagueness about objectives is often an essential means of maintaining consent and collaboration among a large and varied team of people.

Objectives were gradually, though never completely, clarified in the practical day-by-day work of the Area office. The participants approached common problems from different points of view and defined them in different ways, according to their past experience and training, and their current status and duties within the organization. Thus different people ascribed differing meanings and significance to the developments brought about. This, too, is a recurring feature of administrative studies, but there may be special reasons for it in units employing new and developing professions.

The gradual growth of a distinctive professional group in the Area office, supported by some members of the central office, made an important contribution to the developments studied—as it did in the previous case. Initially these staff had little training, and although later arrivals had rather more preparation many were young women and there was a considerable turnover among them—as in nearly all Children's Departments. In this situation people may have a special need to isolate and identify the tasks, skills, attitudes and principles which distinguish them and their work from other people and other work to be seen all round them. It would not be surprising if a professional group tended during this stage of its development to overemphasize its distinctive characteristics and to neglect general administrative work that does not have a distinctly professional content. If so, this stage should be succeeded by a phase of reintegration during which the profession achieves closer collaboration—a rapprochement —with others engaged in providing the service.

The principal developments studied were accepted or welcomed by people who differed considerably in outlook and aims. Many of these people—Council members, senior administrators and social workers —not only participated in these developments but subsequently claimed in discussion with the authors that they themselves had played a major part in conceiving and initiating the schemes studied. This, too, was a feature of other studies in this series. It suggests that different objectives derived from different frames of reference—even extreme diversity, amounting to mutual incomprehension—need cause no serious conflict or administrative breakdown, provided the objectives of all concerned can be reconciled, and provided many are left with the conviction that the achievements of the service are in some sense their own.

Nevertheless, the development of an organization usually imposes stresses of some kind since its benefits are seldom evenly distributed. The Area office doubled its staff and reduced its caseload in five years. At the end of that time it was not simply doing the same job more efficiently or with less effort; it had assumed duties previously performed in County Hall, embarked on entirely new tasks, and modified and extended its work—or at least its objectives. In the course of these developments the social workers who did the bulk of the new work had gained greater influence in the affairs of the office, just as those concerned with casework had gained greater influence in County Hall. Meanwhile administrative and clerical staff, despite increases in salary, were feeling neglected and 'lacked enthusiasm', the Children's Committee became increasingly isolated from the work of the Area offices, and communications between Area offices and County Hall were weakened. The o & m report proposed means for easing these stresses, but there could be no return to the roles or the balance of power of previous years. It will be shown again in later studies that additional resources cannot for long be treated simply as an improvement in the means available for performing unchanged tasks. They often lead to changes in the tasks themselves—changes in the character and scope of the work done—and these in turn bring about changes in relationships, communications and status amongst the people concerned— changes, that is to say, in the structure of administrative organization.

The smooth progress of such developments depends heavily on those responsible for communication with, and supervision of, the groups with divergent and potentially conflicting interests and attitudes. It is they who have to reconcile these differences or suffer the consequences. In the first case examined, a Deputy Town Clerk bore these responsibilities. In this case the small Casework and Policy Division and their predecessors in the Child Care Division clearly did the same. They, and others at similar levels, exercised great influence in advising senior officers and members, consulting officials in neighbouring Departments, preparing memoranda for submission to those with the formal authority to make decisions and subsequently preparing explanations interpreting the meaning of these decisions, besides generally directing and filtering the flow of communications.

One further point deserves comment at this stage. We argued in an earlier chapter that distinctions between the work of 'policy-making', assumed to take place amongst senior officials, and the 'implementation' of policies that is assumed to take place at humbler levels, tend to be misleading—and particularly so in an organization conferring considerable discretionary powers on the staff actually providing the service for which it is designed. What could appear more trivial than the selection of the people to sit at the reception desk in the Area office, the arrangement of their rotas of work, and the invention of procedures to determine when a short term case should be regarded as a long term case? Yet it was decisions on such issues that brought about some of the main developments in the work of the Area offices and called for a reappraisal of the objectives of this work. An approximate distinction can be made between 'more important' and 'less important' decisions: it rests on the implications of the decision—particularly on its long-term and irrevocable implications. But it may be difficult to predict precisely where the important decisions will be made, and the policy and character of a service is not determined by such decisions alone.

The features of this case we have chosen to comment on may be briefly summarized. Many will already be familiar from previous cases. The purpose of the Area office was initially ill-defined. The struggle for the resources such offices required in order to develop their work could only succeed with the support or consent of senior officials in other services and, ultimately, of Council members. To convince 'outsiders' of the justice of their cause, staff in the Children's Department had to commit themselves to certain objectives approved by members and officers responsible for neighbouring services. Nevertheless the objectives of the Area office remained unexplicit and capable of being interpreted in different ways.

This 'unexplicitness', or vagueness, was a necessary feature, enabling the Department to maintain unity within its own ranks, to avoid conflict with other bodies and to preserve opportunities for (and a choice of) future developments. Differing objectives and interpretations persisted within the Department, but could generally be reconciled without the necessity for disruptive choices. The formulation of the Area office's aims and methods was worked out gradually and empirically in day-by-day discussion and modification of working procedures. The growth of professional loyalties and working principles among the increasingly numerous and influential group of social workers played an important part in this process. This group derived some of its ideas and aspirations from association with wider professional and academic circles. The development of the Area office's work and the acquisition of the resources required for it also depended heavily on administrators—mainly without specialist training—at the 'upper middle' levels of the heirarchy. These officials needed a thorough understanding of the interests and aspirations of elected members, of staff in neighbouring Departments and of their own professional staff, and the ability to reconcile these aspirations and render them administratively and politically viable. Thus the growth of resources led to gradual but important changes in the objectives and character of the service, bringing about simultaneous changes in the structure of the organization. In the Area office and in County Hall the policies of the service took shape in the course of changes in the deployment and management of these resources. Thus the structure and functions of the service—its management and policy—could not be understood in isolation from each other, but were closely related aspects of the same general process of development.

CHAPTER 9

HIGH FLATS IN FINSBURY[1]

The next study is the only one in this series which deals with a construction project—the building of some Council flats in central London. Many organizations, public and private, have to collaborate in the process, and some of them have little or no interest in the project for its own sake. Their participation has to be organized through prolonged discussion and bargaining, and occasional resort to arbitration and coercion. Formal decisions required at various stages in the development have to wait on the outcome of these informal negotiations. The architect acting as the Council's principal professional adviser bears most of the responsibility for the management of the whole process and he needs a sensitive grasp of the timing and phasing of the decisions required. But decisions that call primarily for an assessment of risks remain the responsibility of the Council.

A FEATURE of the first study in this series which particularly interested us was the major part played by firms of private architects in the management of a public housing programme. We therefore resolved to take a firm of architects engaged on public housing programmes as the starting point for one of these studies. The firm of Emberton, Franck and Tardrew provided this opportunity and they suggested we examine one of the most important of their recently completed projects—the building of 240 flats for the Metropolitan Borough of Finsbury. The Borough agreed to participate in the study which was eventually carried out in 1963, two years after the completion of the flats. In the early stages of the project the firm consisted of three senior architects and four assistants, specializing in large-scale developments with high flats, mainly built for local authorities. They normally had about four projects in hand—typically one under negotiation, one going to tender, one under construction and one on the point of completion—amounting to a little over a million pounds'

---

[1] The study presented in this chapter was carried out by Michael Meacher and Angela Sears, and the account presented here is a shortened version of a report they prepared.

worth of building each year. Over the preceding decade much of this work had been done for the Borough of Finsbury. The data for the study were provided by the architect in charge of the project, officials and members of the Borough Council, officials of the London County Council and the Ministry of Housing and Local Government, the Secretary of the Guinness Trust and the caretaker of a Trust estate adjoining the site. Further evidence was gathered from the reports, correspondence and working papers prepared in the course of the project, and from a number of published articles dealing with it.[1] We also had the benefit of a thoughtful analysis of our report prepared by staff at the Building Research Station who are making studies of the administration of urban planning.

The study traces the principal stages of the development in chronological order. The first of these led to the acquisition of the site under compulsory powers; this could well have formed an independent study in its own right, but the brief account presented here is only designed to explain some of the problems arising later when rebuilding began. Next we deal with the preparation of detailed site plans, negotiations for securing the approval of the London County Council for the height and layout of buildings, and negotiations with the Ministry leading to the provision of subsidies and permission for the Borough to raise the necessary loans. The progress of building operations and the resolution of problems arising in the course of building are then described, and the study concludes with a brief account of the completed scheme. Its purpose is to trace the principal decisions that had to be made in the course of building of these flats, and to analyse the criteria and the evidence brought to bear on these decisions.

Finsbury lies near the centre of London, immediately north of the City. It was the smallest of the Metropolitan Boroughs, except for the adjoining Holborn, and the population of its 587 acres had fallen from an estimated 57,000 in 1939 to 33,000 in 1961. But its daytime population was estimated at 150,000, for this is one of the most highly industrialized areas of London. Its eighteenth-century dependence on the manufacture of clocks and watches had almost been abandoned, but Finsbury can still claim pre-eminence in clock repairing and in the supply of parts and tools for the trade. Manufacturing and repairing opticians and jewellers are also common, and the Borough's numerous other trades include light engineering, machine and other tool dealers,

[1] Articles by Dr C. Franck in the *Architect and Building News* (December 31, 1958, and August 17, 1960), *Official Architecture and Planning* (April 1959), and *Interbuild* (January 1963).

silver, electro and chromium dealers, and the production and distribution of surgical and scientific instruments, ladies' and children's garments, radio accessories, tobacco pipes, printing, process engraving, bookbinding and stationery. During the war Finsbury lost many offices, warehouses and factories, most of which have now been replaced by new buildings. The area's commercial and industrial future is assured since it lies near London's northern railway termini, adjacent to the City, and not far from the docks. Wartime losses of housing were also extensive, but the Council had carried out an extensive rebuilding programme, helped by the LCC. In the first fifteen years after the war, nearly 3,000 flats had been built in the Borough, in 24 different projects of varying sizes. The Borough itself owned about 2,600 dwellings, consisting of 600 built before the war, 180 acquired from the City Corporation at a very high density of 500 persons to the acre, 440 in miscellaneous property due for demolition and 1,400 postwar flats. At the beginning of 1963 plans had been prepared for the building of another thousand dwellings.

Administrative Procedures

When a development scheme is taken in hand there is no single national set of rules to be followed by the authorities involved. The procedure varies according to the type of development and the location and powers of the housing authority. As in many fields, the regulations applying to London differed slightly from those for the rest of the country. At the time in question the administrative procedures for a scheme of slum clearance and redevelopment fell into five distinct but over-lapping stages:

(a) First of all, the local authority applied to the London County Council for *planning permission*. The density and type of development proposed in this request would accord with the general intentions of the current London Development Plan. This plan, revised by the County Council every five years after consultation with the Boroughs, included the areas to be designated for clearance and redevelopment. Although it delegated certain powers to the Boroughs, the County, as planning authority, was responsible for final decisions on the development plan which had then to be approved by the Minister of Housing and Local Government who might consider any objections made by the Boroughs.

(b) Once outline planning permission had been granted by the LCC, proceedings for *compulsory purchase orders* were set in motion, and at the same time the architect's first detailed site layout schemes were drawn up. A compulsory purchase order must be submitted to the Ministry with details of the properties involved and their status—'fit' or 'unfit'—as decided by the Borough's Medical Officer of Health. Once the order had been submitted to the Ministry, the Borough was required to give public notice in the local press and to every owner, mortgagee or tenant involved. Objections against the order might then be lodged with the Ministry. The Ministry is bound to hold an inquiry if there appears to be substance in any of these complaints. The most frequent objection is that properties have been wrongly classified as 'unfit' and in such cases a final assessment is made by government inspectors. Site plans were usually provided by the Borough at such enquiries to refute suggestions that no development would take place if compulsory purchase were permitted. These negotiations normally took at least six months.

(c) Meanwhile, the *detailed site plan* would be in preparation. Certain features of the plan are pre-determined by the shape of the site, its surrounding landscape, and the proximity, character and height of adjacent buildings. The final scheme was the outcome of influences exerted by the Borough Housing Committee, the LCC Planning Department and the Ministry. Conflict might arise if these authorities employed divergent criteria in judging the architect's plans. The original brief from the Borough Council normally included the types of dwellings required and the costs likely to be allowed by the Ministry. The latter would be based on the Council's experience and the advice of the Borough Surveyor, the Engineer or the architect. The architect then outlined successive schemes for the site as a whole. The Housing Committee might ask for changes in the size of flats, the numbers of rooms or other features of the plan, relying mainly on its Housing Manager for such suggestions. Before the Borough could apply to the Ministry for loan sanction, approval of the detailed plans had to be granted by the LCC which would be mainly concerned with density, appearance and layout. Even then, the Ministry would only permit the Borough to raise the necessary loans if the final detailed plans conformed with certain standards and expenditure limits evolved by their own planning staff. Constant informal consultation was therefore necessary between the architect and the three public authorities at each stage in the development of his plans, so that a compromise might be reached which would satisfy all concerned.

(d) When the final scheme had been drawn up, further permission was required for *buildings over 100 feet in height*. Consent was given provisionally in accordance with the London Building Act of 1930, and then public notification was posted at specified points on the site boundary and in other places. Notice was usually sent to all neighbouring owners and tenants within a radius specified by the LCC. Objections had to be made within twenty-one days of the issuing of provisional consent and they were considered by a Tribunal of Appeal where, if they were upheld, provisional permission for buildings over 100 feet would be withdrawn and the plans would have to be reconsidered. Normally, however, the LCC would reject most complaints as untenable, and the more substantial objections would be referred to the Borough Council in the hope that some compromise might be achieved to appease objectors.

(e) When these steps had been completed *invitations to tender* were issued. Once a tender had been accepted, application could be made to the Ministry for *subsidy and loan sanction*. This request was accompanied by the Borough's formal resolution specifying the tender to be accepted, enclosing a copy of the planning permission, the district valuer's report, and certificates relating to land ownership. If reductions in tender price were required by the Ministry, satisfactory modifications were usually arranged without much delay and loan sanction was given for the whole capital expenditure, including fees for the architect, quantity surveyor and consulting engineer, and the cost of site clearance which might already have begun. The loan was normally repaid over a period of sixty years. An Exchequer subsidy was provided according to graduated scales designed to meet the additional costs of high buildings and expensive sites. But the Ministry's anxiety to restrict expenditure to a minimum led to administrative pressures intended to counteract the encouragement for high buildings exerted by the subsidy system.

Certain features of these procedures should be noted before we examine their application in this case. Each stage of the development hinges on the attainment of some specific agreement between the Borough and other bodies. Many of these agreements take a very simple form, and their original intentions were often equally uncomplicated. But they have become the fulcrum on which the authorities concerned can exercise a much more extensive leverage, influencing the Borough's policies in their own interests and in the light of wider considerations of regional and national policy. Thus the central government, which is responsible in the last resort for the solvency of local authorities, must ensure that these authorities do not borrow more than they can repay. But the procedure for granting loan sanctions, originally introduced 130 years ago for this purpose, is now employed as a means of restricting the inflation of building prices, standardizing the character of local housing policies, controlling the overall rate of public investment, and for other general purposes. Meanwhile each of its building projects is an integral part of the local authority's whole housing programme. Each may be held up by factors outside the local authority's control—by technical snags, labour shortages or bad weather for example. Any delay will upset the timetable for other projects which cannot proceed until housing is available for those whose homes are to be demolished in subsequent schemes. An authority the size of Finsbury has no buffer stock of vacant accommodation to absorb the effect of such delays, and it must often accept compromises over particular projects in order to keep its whole programme moving in an orderly fashion. Thus the right to object to some aspect of one project confers on the individuals and authorities prepared to use it a formidable bargaining power. The objector's principal concern may not be the detail objected to but the advantages to be secured from compromises on other points which the authority can be induced to accept as a price for the withdrawal of the objection and the avoidance of the delays it might cause.

The Galway Street Project

The housing project to be studied was built on the Pleydell Estate covering three and two-thirds acres on both sides of Galway Street. The area is densely packed with commercial, industrial and tenement buildings—mainly old and without aesthetic or architectural distinction. The scheme arose from the bombing of the French Hospital which occupied part of this site. Other areas to the south and west of the site were considered for slum clearance in 1949, but agreement was not reached with the County Medical Officer of Health, although they were included in plans for development made at that time. Galway Street was included later, however, and by 1955 planning permission for redevelopment on this site had been secured from the County Council.

In June 1955 the compulsory purchase order was submitted to the Ministry. It included 157 'pink' (unfit) houses with 685 occupants, two 'grey' (fit) houses with ten occupants and five other buildings, including a public house. After thirteen objections had been received, a public local enquiry was held in October, at which the Borough Council pleaded that the houses were unfit and that demolition was the best means of dealing with conditions in the area. Objections were lodged mainly against the Council's assessment of 'fitness', and on the grounds that certain properties were not houses but business premises. 'Unfit' property is purchased at the value of the cleared site, whilst 'fit' property is bought at its full market value for such purposes. Disagreement was rendered more acute because the terms for compulsory purchase at that time (since amended) were regarded by many as providing inadequate compensation for property owners. Hardship was argued by persons who had bought their properties within the preceding three or four years and still had mortgages outstanding. Thus a Trust complained that they had bought property consisting of 106 premises in 1951 with an unexpired lease of 765 years, after enquiries which revealed that the Council had no intention to acquire at that time. The Trust expected to lose about £10,000 in capital value, and had still to repay an outstanding mortgage of £28,000. The Ministry's inspector, however, recommended that the compulsory purchase order be confirmed with modifications to exclude a Methodist Mission Hall which was being acquired more economically by private agreement, and he asked for only one 'well-maintained payment' for a house classed as unfit. Most of the properties belonged to the Corporation of the City of London who made no objection. The order was accordingly confirmed in January 1956, after which the Council applied successfully for loan sanction of £110,240 to enable them to acquire the site. A further loan sanction for purchase of the Mission Hall by agreement was granted later in the year.

Soon after the compulsory purchase order was submitted, and before the public enquiry of October 1955, the architect had begun his designs for a layout scheme for the site. The working relationship between the architect and the Council varies in different boroughs. In Finsbury the same firm of architects had been working for the Borough since the early post-war period and the arrangement had become traditional. Negotiations between the architect, the Council and its Housing Committee were more direct here than in many London Boroughs. The architect did not negotiate through the Surveyor, a Borough Architect or other intermediaries, but himself carried many of the responsibilities such officers would bear, preparing papers for the Council and discussing them with the Housing Committee. This encouraged the growth of mutual confidence between him and the elected representatives, since he knew that the arguments for any proposal had been adequately presented and understood, even if the Committee chose to reject them. Criticism of the architect's schemes could be offered by an architect in the Borough Engineer's Department, but the latter played no part in project design and was concerned mainly with estate maintenance. The Housing Manager also had an opportunity to comment on the plans, but this was a recent development: one of her main responsibilities was to tell the architect how many flats of various sizes, ranging from one to four rooms, were needed within a total determined by a specified density ratio. These proportions alter with changes in the types of households to be catered for. In this case the architect provided flexibility in design that permitted a redistribution of rooms between neighbouring flats, both during building and (with minor modifications) after completion. An incidental contribution of the Housing Manager was the idea of using the basements of demolished houses as a sunken playground.

Two problems confronted the architect on the Galway Street site. (See plan.) The first was the need to take full advantage of a permanent open space to the south of the west side of the site. The existence of this space clearly meant that as many units as possible should face in that direction, provided that there were not so many 'slab' blocks as to cut down the light and air between them. The need to avoid this latter danger was reinforced by the LCC's insistence on safeguarding the entry of light and air to Guinness Trust buildings adjoining the site to the north. The second problem was the need for compactness to leave room for adequate neighbourhood facilities such as play areas, parking space, service roads, pathways, access for fire engines, tree and flower landscaping, and a certain amount of open space for the residents' general use. This difficulty was accentuated by the high density for the area laid down in the London Development Plan, already approved by the Minister. In the case of Finsbury, 200 persons per acre had been decided on—London's highest planned density—and this, with a site area of 3·63 acres, permitted 726 persons to be rehoused. On the basis of the standard LCC figure of 1·1 persons per room, the total number of rooms was thus fixed at 660. The combination of the need to allow enough free ground space and the need to reach the total required density inevitably called for tall blocks of flats.

In October 1955 the architect set about preparing layout schemes

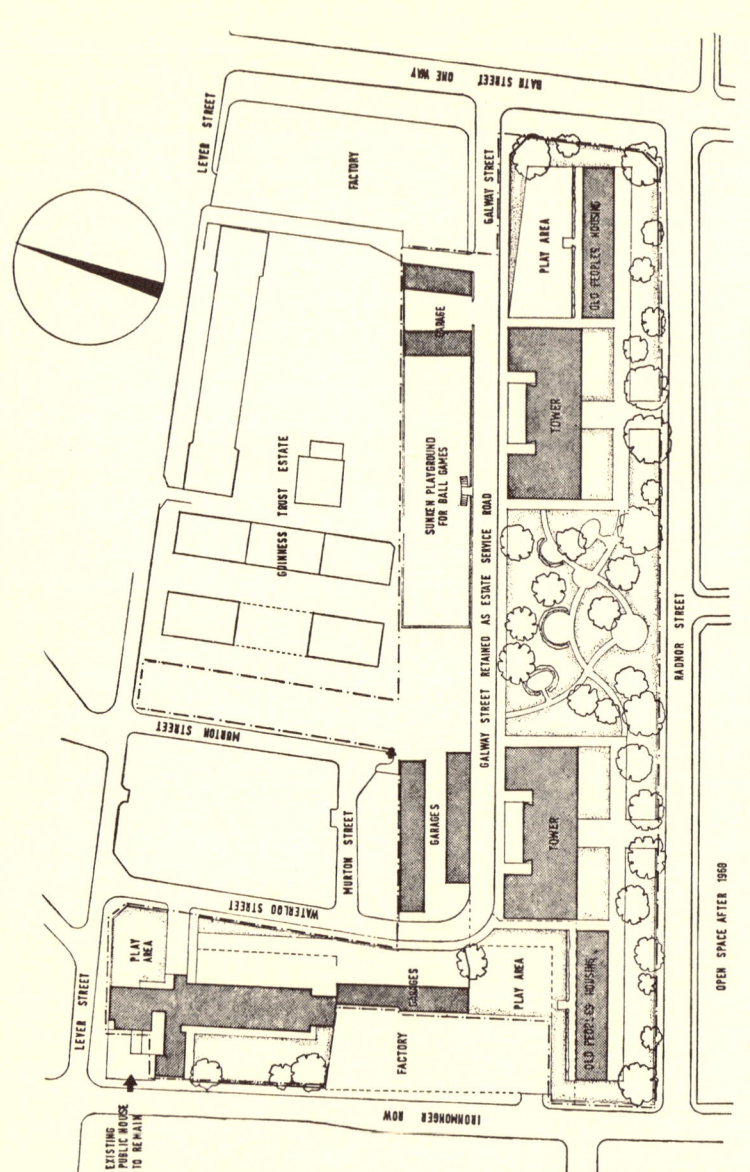

GALWAY STREET HOUSING SCHEME, FINSBURY—SITE LAYOUT

From a plan prepared by Emberton, Franck & Tardrew, Architects

for the site. During the next twelve months three successive plans were prepared and modified in the light of discussions with officials in the County Planning Department. These discussions dealt mainly with the arrangement of blocks, the amenities to be provided in the area surrounding them, the heights of buildings (with an eye to the need for subsequent LCC permission for buildings over 100 feet), the appearance of the buildings, the provision of access and circulation space for vehicles and pedestrians, the obstruction of light and air, and the relation of the project to adjoining buildings. Officials in the County Planning Department could only offer their advice, and the architect constantly met different planners who might disagree with each other or change their minds. Nevertheless it was essential to prepare a plan likely to be acceptable to the Council's Planning Committee whose decisions would depend mainly on the recommendations of these officers. In the event of disagreement it would be open to the Borough to appeal to the Minister—assuming the uncertainty of the outcome and the delay of six to nine months that this would involve could be tolerated—but Finsbury had never done this. If necessary, discussions could also be initiated between the elected members of both Councils. The majorities in each were drawn from the Labour Party, some of their leading figures had known each other for many years, and Finsbury had the advantage of particularly forceful and experienced leadership. But that avenue was not tried in this case. The fact that an intervention of this kind was to be used to the full shortly afterwards in another Finsbury project may have restricted the scope for personal interventions at member level in this project. Informal agreement was finally reached over a layout based on three 'point' blocks (which the LCC's officers preferred to longer 'slab' blocks) having four flats on each floor and restricted to seventeen storeys in height. These towers would be linked by single-storey housing for old people, with garages, playgrounds and planted open space in the surrounding area. The Housing Committee then resolved to apply formally for planning permission and the Town Clerk made arrangements for the Borough to take possession of the housing that had been compulsorarily purchased.

At this point, in November 1956, the architect in charge of the firm died. His two senior colleagues took over as partners by agreement with his executors and one of them assumed responsibility for the Galway Street project. He immediately made contact with the Ministry to ensure informal approval for the cost of the scheme before the LCC gave its planning permission. This move, which had hitherto been neglected, was in accordance with the policies of the Ministry which has since issued a circular (61/58) stressing the desirability of early consultation between a local authority's professional representatives and Ministry officials at the sketch layout stage, before either the layout or the detailed designs have been settled. The suggestions of the Ministry's architects do not necessarily prejudice the future acceptance of a scheme though their criticisms obviously carry weight when the plan is formally submitted. Ministry approval is required at all stages which require Government expenditure, and the Galway Street project was eligible for a subsidy as a slum clearance scheme. Subsidies consisted of a fixed sum, paid per dwelling according to the number of storeys comprising the block. Under section 3 of the Housing Subsidies Act, 1956, which was operative during the negotiations with the Ministry, dwellings other than a block of flats of four or more storeys qualified for an annual exchequer subsidy of £22 1s for sixty years, blocks of flats of four storeys for £32 per annum per dwelling, five storeys for £38, six or more for £50, increased by £1 15s for each storey by which the block exceeded six storeys. Since the additional costs of steelwork, lifts and other high-building devices heavily increase expenditures at high levels there was a strong incentive for local authorities either to keep their buildings low or to raise them so high as to recoup their losses from the very large subsidies available as the twentieth floor was approached: at seventeen storeys the subsidy was very nearly £70 per annum per dwelling. This incentive to build tower blocks clearly worked in opposition to the Ministry's desire to limit its expenditure by keeping heights down. The Ministry did not oppose high building on principle: the circular quoted above states that 'sometimes a limited amount of really high building will produce a saving of expenditure on the scheme as a whole, while in other cases the extra cost of high building may be well worth-while to preserve gardens and trees or to make the most of an open prospect. The aim in all cases must be to get value for money'. Thus the criteria employed by the Ministry in considering a scheme for loan sanction were that it be judged 'technically sound' and 'reasonable as to cost'. Architects coming at an informal stage for consultation were generally diverted to the Ministry's architects who provided them with a ceiling target figure of costs at which to aim. The Ministry has ceiling costs which are constantly readjusted in the light of different schemes being presented for approval, though the exact amounts vary from one region to another and are not made known to the architects. If at a later stage the Ministry feels that costs may be reduced in any part of the scheme they do not criticize particular items too specifically but merely suggest general areas where expenses may be cut.

When the architect approached the Ministry for discussions in January 1957, he was received by their Principal Regional Architect and a Senior Architect responsible for an area including Finsbury. The latter was the main representative of the Ministry in the negotiations. He stated that they were greatly disturbed by the rising costs of flats in tall blocks and that a tendency was growing to reduce expenditure by building more flats per staircase—six flats instead of the four favoured by the LCC's planners. This arrangement would cut down costs considerably by greatly reducing the area of perimeter walling. He therefore strongly advised the floor plans recommended by the Ministry, with a long interior corridor to a staircase and lifts at either end. The Finsbury architect, however, claimed that these corridors developed in practice into badly ventilated, dark and noisy tunnels which were liable to be treated as football pitches by the children. As to lay-out, the Ministry architects objected to three seventeen-storey blocks with single-storey old people's flats between them on the grounds that this would prejudice future redevelopment to the north. They proposed two seventeen-storey blocks at new angles and made several other suggestions about the old people's housing, the contrast between high and low buildings, the service road and pedestrian access. The architect then returned to discuss the Ministry's recommendations with the Housing Committee at two meetings on successive days. Some, but not all, of these modifications were accepted, and he set about drawing revised plans in January 1957.

During January and February the quantity surveyor was engaged in working out estimates for comparison between the costs of the Ministry scheme or its revision, and that which had been submitted by Finsbury's appointed architect. The Ministry's version was found to be more expensive and the quantity surveyor's comparative estimates were sent to Whitehall. This result was taken to provide grounds for intervention by leading members of the Finsbury Council to discuss the scheme with members of the administrative staff at the Ministry. At this stage the procedure was for administrators to put their Ministry's case and point out the reasons why, on the advice of their own professional staff, they did not consider the expense of the scheme to be justified. The Town Clerk was the equivalent in the local authority organization of the administrative officers at the Ministry, and he would advise his Council. If the Council did not agree with the Ministry's decision, then they might have access to the Minister himself who would be advised by his administrators on the main points involved and the principles at stake, and by his professional staff on technical matters. On this basis he would make the final decision.

In this case the Ministry's divisional Senior Architect brought in the administrative section at an early point in the negotiations. This was quite usual when the professionals felt that complications were likely to obstruct progress when tenders were called for later, for costs would then have to be estimated accurately and loan sanction passed as quickly as possible. The Senior Architect, together with the Assistant Secretary in charge of London housing, a Principal and another administrator met the Chairman of the Finsbury Council, the Vice-Chairman of the Housing Committee, the Town Clerk, the Borough Engineer, the Housing Manager and the architect in March 1957. This meeting, amounting to a head-on clash, was called at the request of the architect. Finsbury asked for the acceptance of the three point blocks in their plan on the grounds that the criterion of cost employed by the Ministry to reject their scheme ran counter to the Ministry's wish to reduce expenditure by introducing six flats per storey instead of four. But the Ministry's representatives again stressed the importance of opening up the site, they again objected to the number of single-storey old people's flats and they practically rejected three tower blocks. (The discussion also dealt with the visual effect of three tower blocks standing not far from St. Paul's Cathedral, but this hardly constituted a decisive point of difference between the Borough and the Ministry since the latter were asking for two broader towers of the same height.) Finsbury still defended their scheme, but it was made clear that loan sanction would not be granted if three tower blocks were retained in the plans. The Ministry did agree at this meeting, however, that they would regard the site as a single unit. This was crucial because it meant that the single-storey old people's dwellings would not be treated separately, and a more generous 'expensive site' subsidy could be offered.

Two days later, Finsbury's Housing Committee rejected the Ministry's first revised scheme and a compromise scheme was submitted by the architect and approved by the Committee. The Ministry's demand for six flats per floor was accepted but the defects of an internal corridor structure were avoided by a novel disposition of the flats. The Ministry's objection to three tower blocks was also accepted and other changes were made, but resistance to various features of the new plan was still expected from the Ministry.

Later in the month informal discussions were held with the LCC's planners to discover their reaction to the revised scheme. These talks exposed a basic disagreement between the LCC and the Ministry over the point blocks. The Ministry disliked tall thin blocks because it wanted to restrict costs, while the LCC disliked highly directional slab blocks because they fitted less easily into the landscape, were less likely to produce satisfactory aspects from all directions, and were liable to obstruct light and air in the surrounding neighbourhood. Various other problems were discussed, but the LCC refused to permit an increase in height to nineteen storeys which—with six flats per floor—would have accommodated all the housing required except for twelve single-storey old people's dwellings. This restriction on height was relaxed shortly afterwards when the architect gained the County's approval for nineteen storeys on another project, and still higher flats have been built since then. But at the time of the Galway Street project the planners would not go higher than seventeen storeys.

Meanwhile, at the end of March 1957, permission was received by Finsbury from the LCC Planning Committee for the plans submitted in October 1956 before an approach was made to the Ministry. In its accompanying comments the LCC suggested the reduction or redistribution of play areas to avoid noise nuisance, and also the reduction of the large expanse of hard-paved areas between and along the old people's dwellings. The block in the north-west corner of the site was excluded from planning permission so that new designs might be made for the better inclusion of the public house standing there. Adjustments had also to be made to the fire escapes and it was stipulated that the site had to be cleared and the buildings erected in a single operation.

This consent was acknowledged by the architect but at the same time he submitted the revised scheme, explaining the Ministry's refusal to accept three tower blocks, and arguing that changes introduced under pressure from the Ministry did not materially affect the LCC's planning requirements. He also included a shadow diagram which showed that in summer almost no shadow fell on adjoining properties and what fell on the site itself touched only the least important parts of it such as the car park and the playground for ball games.

The architect then made a first trial of the Ministry's views about costs. In May 1957 he wrote to the Senior Architect there and presented information about the costs of foundations and dwellings. These were examined by the Ministry's quantity surveyor, who found one of the lower blocks to be extremely expensive. He estimated that the accommodation could be provided in a four-storey block at a saving of about £1,000 per dwelling, since such a height would obviate the need for lifts and certain structural strengthening devices. This conclusion was passed on to the Finsbury architect who was told that the disputed block was too costly in its present form and he therefore agreed to redesign it. But this block remained expensive, owing to its brick dressing and other items, and the whole scheme came within the Ministry's cost ceiling only because of the economy derived from the unusual structural design of the tower blocks.

Having informally discovered both the LCC's and the Ministry's opinions of the latest plan, based on their different criteria, the architect finally submitted a revised application for formal planning permission to the LCC Planning Committee in May 1957. With this request he included the suggestion of closing Galway Street, which ran through the middle of the site, and using it as an access road. He also asked for a waiver of the ruling that permanent ventilation must be provided since at seventeen storeys this would render the modest degree of central heating ineffective.

The LCC were clearly disposed to accept the plan except for their crucial disagreement with the Ministry over the desirability of point blocks as opposed to slab blocks. They accordingly consulted representatives of the Ministry about this. (Such informal contacts between the Ministry and the County became more frequent later, to avoid situations in which Boroughs played off one against the other. Meetings of this kind had nevertheless to be regarded as confidential to avoid suggestions of collusion, since if local authorities resort ultimately to appeals against LCC decisions the Ministry has to arbitrate and must preserve an impartial status.) Various points were made at the meeting, held in July 1957, but the crucial one was again the prohibitive cost of the three 'point' blocks and the saving to be achieved by substitution of 'wing' blocks with six flats per storey. The LCC's aesthetic preference for non-directional tall blocks was finally overruled.

After this encounter with the Ministry the LCC granted planning permission for the final scheme in July 1957. Discussion of the siting of the children's playground was requested, and attention was drawn to the new ruling, published two months previously by the Metropolitan Standing Joint Committee for Parking, which required provision of one garage for every two flats. The architect responded to this by asking that parking space be increased only to the sixty-three-car maximum which the Borough Council regarded as the highest permissible number (about half the proportion recommended) and this permission was granted in February 1958.

Permission had also to be gained for extinguishment of rights of way and for the construction of buildings over 100 feet high, though the procedure was different in the two cases. For the former, all objections had to be heard *before* permission was considered; in the latter, provisional consent was given first, and only then were objections invited. Objections against proposed building heights must be made within twenty-one days, though this period was often extended until the actual day of the hearing. Petitions were lodged with the Tribunal of Appeal. Under section 52 of the London Building Act all owners and lessees within a radius of 100 yards of the proposed building (or whatever other distance is specified by the LCC) had the right of appeal. They were notified of the proposal, a similar notice was published in *The Times*, two notices were posted in public view, and the LCC notified all tenants affected. If objections were raised—usually concerning light, access or outlook—it was essential that some compromise be reached to the satisfaction of the complainant, for if the case were pursued to a public enquiry, a delay of over six weeks might arise which could be very damaging now that preparations were being made for the start of building operations. The notices mentioned stated that copies of the detailed site plans were available for inspection at County Hall. Thus objectors were able, and entitled, to object to any feature of these plans, not only to building heights and rights of way.

Seven complaints were received. The first batch came from the factory at the north-east corner of the site, the insurance company who were the head lessees for the factory, and the Church Commissioners who were its ground landlords. The Commissioners sought further information. The insurance company complained about obstruction of light, and they and the factory complained about the closure of Galway Street and the difficulty that this would entail for the loading and unloading of the factory's lorries. This objection was pushed to an extreme at a later stage in the negotiations. Another firm, situated on the western boundary of the site, were more favourable and after requesting information did not raise any complaint except about access to their loading bay. A third firm protested about the obstruction of light and raised questions about the possibility of the Borough buying their property. A further objection came from the

Church Commissioners, this time in connection with their property interests in yet another factory; it was claimed that a restriction on height had been agreed in 1891 with the French Hospital (destroyed during the war) which limited the height of any building on the south-eastern fringe of the site to 44 feet. This light and air agreement was attested to be binding on the French Hospital, their successors, lessees and tenants. The final complaint was made by a tenant living on the top floor of one of the Guinness Trust blocks adjoining the site to the north, again on the grounds of the barring of light. It was true that one of the proposed buildings, 148 feet high, would overshadow part of the Guinness block at 9.0 a.m. (summer time). The objector's daughter was secretary of the Guinness Trust Tenants' Association, a body which first became active about this time, mainly for the purpose of securing a badly needed supply of electricity in the Trust flats: they felt that as ratepayers they could not reasonably be asked to contribute to expensive redevelopment when the basic amenities of their existing dwellings were neglected.

The Tribunal of Appeal disallowed all objections about light obstruction except the one from the Guinness Trust tenants, though this too, on investigation, proved to be too weak to uphold. As for the French Hospital's agreement, this was felt to be a matter for personal settlement between the Borough Council and the factory involved. Thus by the time that official permission was received for buildings over 100 feet in October 1957, all objections had been dismissed except those of the two firms appealing, for different reasons, against the closure of Galway Street. The actual application for extinguishment of rights of way was sent off by the Council in November for approval by the Ministry.

The objection by the factory on the western boundary of the site was that the inclusion within the redevelopment site of a strip of road 14 × 60 feet in area meant that their lorries had insufficient space to manoeuvre at their loading bay. The factory on the north-east, on the other hand, complained that the closure involved the inconvenience to them that their lorries, instead of being able to use the shorter route through the middle of the site from their unloading to their loading bay, would have to drive round the outside of the whole site. Finsbury was notified of these two objections by the LCC in January 1958, in the hope of some satisfactory settlement. This was made all the more urgent, if the Council was to avoid disastrous delays, by the vehemence and perseverance with which the management of the factory to the north-east pursued their case. They made representations to the

Ministry, who referred the inquiry to the LCC, who in turn referred the objectors to the highway authority for the area (the Borough). Finally, by March 1958, the company approached the Guinness Trust and the Council with a proposal that if the former allow them right of way through the existing access road to the Trust estate, then the Council should make up at their own expense an exit road to the south to connect with Galway Street (see plan). Thus the Borough would provide the Company with a new road, partly on Guinness Trust property, linking existing streets and extending right round the factory building. This agreement was extorted from a reluctant Council, and accepted by the Secretary of the Guinness Trust to help out the Council. Co-operation between the Trust and the Council over the exchange of tenants and other matters had been excellent for some years. It was this tradition which induced the Guinness Trust to concede right of way to the objector in the interests of the Council. But at the same time the Trust insisted that the right of way be fenced off, with a gate offering access for fire engines to their site. Further, the Secretary of the Trust arranged privately with the objecting firm that their lorries only use the road at certain stated hours of the day, so as to minimize the consequent noise and disturbance. As an additional check against unnecessary use, the firm and the caretaker of the Trust estate were each given possession of three keys to the gates at both ends of the access road over Trust property. On the Council's side, discussions in May 1958 showed that, apart from the construction of the end of the access road, the objector's requirements could be met by closing a small additional part of Galway Street that was not covered by the Council's previous resolution about extinguishment of rights of way. Permission for the change of plan, with right of way over Guinness Trust property, was granted by the LCC in July 1958. The factory on the western side of the site was sold the 14 × 60-foot strip of land they required so that it might be incorporated in their loading yard. By October 1958, Finsbury's Town Clerk was able to report to his Council that both objections to the extinguishment of public rights of way and to the height of the proposed buildings had been withdrawn. Next month both companies withdrew their requests for payment of costs and fees incurred in the arrangements made with them to secure withdrawal of their objections. However, the company securing the new road over Guinness Trust property never made use of it. The significance of the road to them had been its value as parking space for their employees, though this was partly frustrated because the Trust caretaker retained keys of the gates at both ends of the section of road on Trust property. Nevertheless the company gained permission in March 1959 to park in the unenclosed cul-de-sac at the south end of the road until site operations were completed in September 1960.

Meanwhile, on the assumption that negotiations with objectors would be successfully concluded, preparations for the start of building operations had gone ahead. The District Surveyor and the Metropolitan Water Board had to be consulted before building could begin. District Surveyors, appointed by the LCC in each Borough, were responsible for ensuring the structural safety of all new building. In this case the Surveyor's requirements caused some delay at a later stage in the project. The Metropolitan Water Board interprets and enforces by-laws in its field—by-laws which required, for example, two huge water storage tanks at the top of each tower block and a small tank in every flat. Again, demands made by the Board at a later stage in construction resulted in prolonged argument.

The consultant engineer collaborating with the architect had to be satisfied that the ground would support blocks of the necessary height without subsidence. At Galway Street trial borings were originally estimated for at a cost of £175, but in October 1957, they had to be made in the roadways at a cost of £630 because demolition had not yet started and further delay had to be avoided. In July 1958, however, the architect was obliged to inform the Housing Committee that the trial borings showed very variable ground, and the consultant engineer now wished to sink eleven additional holes. These were accordingly approved provided the cost did not exceed £1,200.

Arrangements had also to be made with the London Electricity Board and the South-Eastern Gas Board for the supply of fuel and power to the flats. In another of the Borough's recent housing projects the flats had been equipped with gas water-heating except for one floor which was supplied with electricity. Later the tenants were asked for their comments and all favoured electricity. This was discovered at a time when gas ducts were already being installed in Galway Street. These ducts were required for gas water-heating in the kitchen, and had been chosen partly as a favour to the Gas Board who were anxious to experiment with them on tower blocks since they had previously been used only to a height of six storeys. Meanwhile the Council resolved in March 1958 to approve the terms of the Electricity Board for electricity supply; these involved an additional service charge of £2,400 for electricity mains and meters if the proposed installation did not conform with certain 'standard requirements' (agreed between the

Board and the Metropolitan Boroughs Standing Joint Committee) which excluded the use of gas planned for these flats. Thus the charge had to be paid before the Board would start installation, though the possibility of further negotiations about the charge was kept open. Meanwhile, a sixty-year lease for an electricity transformer station was granted by the Council to the Electricity Board at a nominal rent of £1 per annum.

Once informal approval had been given for the detailed layout scheme by the LCC and the Ministry, the Borough Council set about obtaining loan sanction. In November 1957, the architect reported to the Housing Committee that typical ground-floor plan working drawings for the main blocks and for the one-storey old people's flatlets had been completed and handed over to the quantity surveyor. Within six months the bills of quantity had been despatched and tenders were delivered by July 1958. The lowest tender, at a price of £669,331, was accepted, with the time of completion given as ninety weeks. This selection was based on a competition between some eight or ten large companies. Invitations to tender were not made public. These firms were recommended by the architect and chosen to ensure they could cope with the size and building methods of the scheme. But before tenders were actually invited, the architect had taken the precaution of informally contacting the Senior Architect at the Ministry in May 1958, to check that the cost of the seventeen-storey blocks would be acceptable. Their economic structural design would offset their height and might also offset the expensive smaller block. This economy was a considerable achievement. Having thus gained informal approval from the Ministry for the cost, the official application for loan sanction was made by the Council in August 1958, for two seventeen-storey blocks of 201 dwellings, one six-storey block and one three-storey block, together providing 29 dwellings, and two single-storey rows of flatlets providing 10 dwellings—240 in all. With this application were sent the usual documents required by the Ministry—notice of the tender to be accepted, a copy of the planning permission, the district valuer's report, and certificates showing that the local authority owned the land. The tender figures were examined by the Ministry's architects, who recommended that they should be accepted. Decisions to pass loan sanctions are made by the executive grade without reference to administrative officers, when no questions of policy are involved. The Minister is only called upon to play a part when the case is unprecedented. The Finsbury Council received a formal reply in September 1958, from a Principal on behalf of the

Minister to say that he had no objection to the Council's acceptance of the tender; he also gave consent for the provision and maintenance at the site of forty-six lock-up garages.

The Exchequer subsidy for high building was requested in May 1960.[1] Finsbury was asked to show how many families had been displaced from unfit properties and how many houses had been built to rehouse them. At the end of the month a formal letter on behalf of the Minister was written to the Council approving 240 dwellings to be provided for the purposes of the Housing (General Purposes) Act, 1958, and stating how much subsidy was payable for each dwelling. The application for 'expensive site subsidy' under section 7 of the Act was dealt with separately. The Regional Architect at the Ministry considered the application for the payment of £45,579 and approved this figure as reasonable. The application was then considered by the specialist division dealing with subsidies, and in a letter of July 1960, the Council was told that the cost of the site as developed had been provisionally determined at between £40,000 and £41,000 per acre. On behalf of the Minister it was agreed to pay an Exchequer subsidy of £4,661 per annum for sixty years.

Meanwhile building had begun on January 1, 1959, but not before an additional appointment had been made to the construction team. The engineer and the quantity surveyor had been appointed in January 1957, the sub-contractors were nominated by the Borough Engineer in November 1957, the main contractors were appointed in July 1958, and then, in October 1958, the engineer recommended that his company be permitted to appoint a resident engineer to assist him. The reason for this suggestion was that the reinforced concrete structure designed according to the specifications of experts allowed considerable savings in steel and concrete, but required a high degree of precision in construction. It was claimed that the additional cost of about £1,800 would be more than offset by the saving effected. The Council accordingly made an application to the Ministry for loan sanction for this amount, and after the Regional Architect had been consulted this was granted in December. The appointment was a fortunate one as the consultant engineer died that month and was not replaced till June 1959.

Tenders from a large number of sub-contractors for specific items were received during the last few months of 1958. These items included lifts, plumbing, electrical work, lightning conductors, heating, ventilation, pram lockers, external railings and gates, roof railings, kitchen

[1] The rates of subsidy at that time are explained in Ministry Circular No. 33/1956.

fittings, timber doors, metal door frames, metal windows, door fittings and piled foundations.

Work on the site proceeded slowly at first. The contractor dealing with the 'stage one' demolitions did not satisfy the Council with the progress made, and so, in the negotiations with the Regional Architect in March 1959, it was explained that the Council were not accepting the lowest tender for future demolition work. Consequently, loan sanction was given by the Ministry for acceptance of the second lowest tender. The danger of such failures is always inherent in the tendering system. The advantage of working for considerable periods with the same architect who knew the needs and procedures of his clients was sacrificed in the case of the contractors. Building also began rather slowly, largely because of lack of experience in handling and fixing prefabricated parts. But after initial trouble with the construction procedure had been overcome and erection teams had been trained, a considerable saving in building time was achieved. The thirty-six prefabricated units, excluding edge beams, of the first floor built on the Galway Street site took three weeks to complete. Later this time was reduced to 5½ days, including the construction of floors; the teams were able to cut down the fixing of one unit from forty-five to eight minutes.

Changes in the sizes of flats were requested by the Housing Manager in March 1960. By comparison with the schedule of accommodation fixed when the LCC approved the final lay-out scheme in July 1957, forty fewer three-roomed flats were now needed and more four- and two-roomed flats were wanted instead. Changes in the distribution of rooms were easily achieved on this site since the construction techniques employed permitted considerable flexibility. The system was based on staircases and lift shafts forming central load-bearing cores which, with concrete gable walls at the end of each block, provided structural stability and wind-bracing. The perimeter of the building consisted of load-bearing columns set in the external walls, and a floor slab 6½ inches thick spanned the area from the perimeter to the structural core. This large span of 23 feet, without structural cross-beams, provided an uninterrupted space enclosed by a concrete shell which made possible a wide variety of layouts. After completion of the flats further modifications remained possible through the provision of bedrooms with doorways opening into the corridors of two flats, and movable insulating and sound-proofing panels that could easily be fixed to the door not in use.

This system provided some badly needed elbow room for the

Housing Manager whose selection of tenants for the flats available was complicated not only by normal changes in requirements arising during the period of five years that usually elapsed between the preparation of building plans and the occupation of the flats, but also by the tendency for people to move into an area as soon as it was known to be due for demolition. Under the terms of compulsory purchase orders the authority was bound to rehouse all who were living in the area when the order was made. Since the order may take nine months or more before it is confirmed by the Ministry, this gives ample opportunity for a considerable influx of relatives and friends and there is no legal means of preventing this. Even after the order is made, the local authority can only control the entry of tenants to privately rented property by taking out a 'notice of entry' which entitles them to take over the leaseholds from landlords of residential property. But this procedure has its drawbacks too, since the local authority then collects the rents and must compensate landlords fairly generously until the property is finally acquired from them. Some landlords realize that it would profit them to hold up negotiations for the compensation settlement so that they may continue to draw these payments, and compensation may not be settled for months or even years.

The final selection of tenants was made by the General Purposes Sub-committee of the Housing Committee after detailed study of the circumstances of individual households. Within the limits imposed by the Council's slum clearance requirements, the most important criterion governing the allocation of flats was the financial capacity of prospective tenants who must be capable of maintaining their rent payments. If they could not afford the higher rents that some of the newer blocks required, or if in general they were not felt to be suitable for new accommodation, then they were rehoused in older buildings at lower rents. Previous housing conditions were not a relevant factor; in any case, all the houses had been in bad structural condition. The process of selection began when the General Purposes Sub-committee were given lists of all those to be rehoused, stating their present rents, the amounts they said they were able to afford, the sizes of their families and their occupations. Prospective tenants were seen by the Housing Manager and her staff, who gave them details of the rents and flats, and finally they were interviewed by the Sub-committee who then made the selection. This was decided for most of the flats at Galway Street in May 1960, though further tenants continued to be chosen as late as October 1960, and January 1961, as more flats became available.

Rents came up for discussion at the time that changes in the sizes of flats were being considered. Council members who are also Council tenants are normally excluded from this discussion, but since about half Finsbury's Housing Committee lived in Council property this bar—but not the prohibition on voting—was waived, with the approval of the Ministry, as is normal in such cases. Finally the Committee recommended to the Council that the rents be calculated at two-thirds of the gross value assessed for rating purposes. This meant rents of £2 3s 1d, £1 17s 0d, £1 11s 6d and £1 3s 6d for 4-, 3- 2- and 1-room flats respectively. The blocks were then named and in May a caretaker was appointed.

The progress of work on the site was interrupted early in 1960 owing to technical difficulties. When the flats were half-finished, the Metropolitan Water Board insisted that the over-flow pipe from each storage tank, which projected through the bathroom walls over the bath waste pipe, must be diverted the whole way round the wall to discharge over the 'head' end of the bath. This, they said, would ensure that tenants reported faults in the tank stop cocks promptly, for if the stop cocks failed cold water would fall on their heads and not on their feet! After weeks of argument the Board was persuaded to drop this unsightly and expensive requirement.

Further delays led to a meeting on the site between members of the Housing Committee's 'Progress of Site Sub-committee', Borough officials, the architect and contractors in June 1960. The reasons given for the delay were: compliance with the District Surveyor's requirements, difficulty in obtaining bricks, modifications to the top floor of one block, the break enforced by winter frost in January, and the scarcity of plasterers. The contractors agreed to seek more men and to prepare a revised progress chart for the architect.

But the most serious challenge to the administration came from the association of tenants in the neighbouring Guinness Trust property who united to form a Social and Welfare Committee, composed of about twelve people. Their principal motivation still appeared to be resentment at not having an electricity supply. They had already raised an objection against the height of the new buildings in May 1957. At the end of 1958 they protested over the facilities provided by the Council for the factory alongside the Guinness property which was given a new service road. The contractors had entered the site, six weeks before building operations began, to construct this access road to the rear of the factory. In December 1958, a deputation from the tenants made the first of many protests to the Council about the road.

The tenants' association took their complaint to the Ministry in April 1959, after the completion of the road, claiming that it was dangerous because it was used as an access walk to the Guinness Trust estate, and also that it was not subject to permission granted under the town planning layout scheme which had been officially approved. The LCC knew of the proposed revision of the plans and gave formal approval for the road that month. The Ministry, however, offered to take the matter up with the Borough Council. Meanwhile, after the road had been built and despite the fact that it appears virtually never to have been used by the factory, the tenants' association complained that the lorry drivers could see into their bathrooms and that the lorries would disturb them. The Guinness Trust had arranged for use of the road only at stated times, and the Trust caretaker had keys to the gates at either end of the right of way which would prevent disturbance by car parking. Of the thirty-six windows overlooking the site, six were in bathrooms. The Council followed a policy of appeasement, and part of the fence dividing the road from the Guinness estate was replaced by a brick wall which was constructed in the latter part of 1959. The wall was intended to be 6 feet high and up to this height no planning permission would be needed for this change. But a request that the wall be raised to a height of 8 feet was made by the caretaker of the Guinness Trust to prevent children climbing over it. (Not that it ever did.) This request was granted but the necessity for planning permission was overlooked by the architect at this point. Meanwhile the tenants' association, having gained their wall, began to protest about its cost. They were helped, when their protests proved ineffective, by a Communist opponent of the Labour council. A QC was briefed and an appeal was fixed against the Council's action for July 1960. The architect therefore hastened to arrange a meeting with planning officers of the LCC in May to discuss whether planning permission had covered the building of the wall on part of Guinness Trust property. It was they who drew his attention to the height of the wall and pointed out that no consent had been sought. The architect apologized, saying that the increase in height had been made to keep on good terms with the Guinness Trust, and he at once applied for retrospective permission under the London Building Act which was soon granted and formally confirmed. At the public enquiry in July, held before the District Auditor, the Guinness Trust tenants objected on three scores. Their main one was that money had been spent on providing facilities for the neighbouring factory and that this expenditure was not in the ratepayers' interests, and that, therefore, the councillors should be surcharged £3,000—the full cost of the wall and the access road. This was a serious matter: a surcharge of this amount would have disqualified councillors from standing for re-election. But the District Auditor, the presiding Ministry representative, dismissed the charge that the expenditure was illegal and no negligence was found. Nor was the attempt to isolate the wall and the gate as impermissible expenditure successful, for they had always been intended as part of the access road provision. A further objection, raised by Guinness Trust tenants, was that fumes from trucks would cause sickness, that the noise would create a disturbance and the trucks would endanger the children. But the Medical Officer of Health did not agree that any detrimental effects on health would result. The one ground of appeal which succeeded, however, was the discovery by the QC on the tenants' side that permission had not been obtained at the proper time for the 8-foot wall and the architect was criticized by the Auditor on this score. But thanks to the retrospective permission given by the LCC, the councillors and officers concerned were released from the obligation of paying a surcharge of £831—the cost of the wall. This protracted and detailed hearing, which involved the Town Clerk, the Borough Engineer, the architect, the Housing Manager and Medical Officer of Health for three days, therefore had no effect. Building operations continued and the Council was exonerated. The tenants' association lost its momentum after this and the movement ceased a little while later when they obtained an electricity supply.

The final request for planning permission on the site was made in September 1960, and concerned play areas. The LCC replied in October that no planning permission was required, as this item had already been covered in previous grants of approval but they assumed that contact had been made with the District Surveyor to seek his advice under the Building Act. They had no comment to make on the equipment provided, but noted that both the smaller play areas were partly overshadowed by old people's flats and that they might therefore be better placed to obtain an unobstructed southern outlook.

At the scheduled date for completion, in October 1960, the contractors were six weeks behind on site progress. Attempts were made to speed up the work but the lack of plasterers delayed the recently increased force of painters. By February 1961, however, instead of an official opening ceremony, a show flat furnished free by a local company was used to celebrate the public opening of the estate. Two blocks and the old people's flatlets were occupied in March and the others were taken over soon afterwards.

The completed project cost £35,000 less than was originally estimated. Both the principal problems of the site had been satisfactorily resolved. The longest boundary to the south overlooks an area scheduled to become an open park, and the blocks have been planned so that twelve out of the eighteen living rooms at each floor level have a southern aspect. The need for compact spacing to permit adequate neighbourhood amenities on the ground has been met by building six flats per floor and by enabling the perimeter of the blocks to be used as living space; for the core of lifts, stairs, wc's, bathrooms and ducts are grouped at the centre on each floor.

The areas around and between each block were planted and laid out with paths. A play area for small children was sited next to each block to make supervision easier. On the other side of the estate service road from the point blocks there is a large playground sunk four feet below street level to make use of existing basements, which is suitable for ball games. In the same area, with access from the service road, are forty-six lock-up garages with further open parking space for at least another sixteen cars. The finish and fittings of the blocks themselves are of high quality. Each flat has a gas water-heater and drying-cabinet which are ventilated into internal ducts. There is oil-fired central heating, with radiators in the two main rooms of each flat, giving a temperature of 65 degrees in the living rooms and 55 degrees in the halls. The roof, which is finished in asphalt, holds the lift motors and plant rooms, which have been housed in brick with a curving concrete canopy. Part of the roof can be used by residents as a sun terrace at the discretion of the Housing Manager, and a 5-foot close-meshed railing was built round it. Each flat has its own balcony. There are no inter-connecting passages or corridors and the only covered space for circulation is provided by two open, well-lit lobbies on each floor between the lift and the staircase. Fittings included floor finishes of thermoplastic tiles, tiled window sills, special safety catches on all windows, generous tiling round baths, 'eating kitchens' seating up to five persons, plentiful power points, built-in electric wall fires, a built-in TV aerial, and special baths for old people. Much of the equipment was in fact specially made, for many of the advantages of large-scale production can be derived from a development of this size.

But ground floor storage appears inadequate and many tenants have to bring prams up in the lift; the lifts take one minute from bottom to top, and prams can barely be parked inside the flats. The two rows of old people's flatlets are rather exposed to the street. Though each flatlet has its own front garden and sun terrace, they have no private or even semi-screened open space. The balcony walls in the flat are too high and solid for children to see over and this may tempt children to climb on them. No lighting was installed in the sunken play-ground, and at the time of this study the cost of providing this, at £700, seemed likely to prove prohibitive.

The Architect in this case made unusual efforts to follow up his past work and assess its faults. When a scheme was completed, he made a point of visiting the caretaker each year for about three years to see what difficulties had appeared in running the buildings. He said, 'You must remember, that 75 per cent of your reputation is made in the kitchen. That's where the housewife spends her time, and it's her opinion that counts—and she may be on the Council.' Several of the points we have criticized were corrected in the next project built for the Borough of Finsbury by this firm of architects.

DISCUSSION

This study differs from the rest in this series in dealing with a specific and concrete piece of capital investment. Though it formed a part of a continuing, long term housing programme, this project had restricted and fairly well defined objectives. Thus the story has a beginning and an end.

The case clearly illustrates the distinction between studies which deal with the work of a particular administrative unit, and studies (like our own) which deal with the management of a particular task or the progress of a particular development. The participants in this development did not form a single administrative unit or group, and did not have any overriding common aims or any continuing relationship to each other. Indeed, many of them were unaware of the existence of others participating in the story. This kind of situation is typical of many that confront the more senior administrator. Moreover it has serious implications for the future housing policies of this country. It took twenty-six months to build 240 flats, from the start of demolition to the rehousing of the new tenants. But four years elapsed after the first planning permission given by the LCC before demolition could begin. The only delays in this process that might have been avoided arose from the postponement of informal consultations with the Ministry about the design and cost of the scheme, and the negotiations that led to the building of the access road for a neighbouring factory. The building industry appears to be capable of the greatly enlarged schemes of urban redevelopment now envisaged for the future, but whether our administrative system is capable of sustaining such a programme remains an open question.

The Borough and its architect were subject to controls of various types imposed by the County Council and the Ministry. Placed in the thick of central London, its housing project brought about the movement—outwards, then inwards—of well over a thousand people, and it called for widespread changes in land use and ownership, the closing of streets, the diversion of traffic and the disturbance of many long established patterns of life. The individuals and groups involved—in the Ministry, the County Council, the Gas Board, the Water Board, and among local land owners, commercial organizations and residents —had all to participate in the scheme before the Borough's flats could be completed. Their interests were diverse and for most purposes they were subject to no common authority. Securing their participation was therefore a 'political' task—a matter of using, reconciling or defeating potentially conflicting powers—not simply a matter of organizing available resources for generally agreed ends.

Such tasks call for the discussion and exploration of the interests of those concerned in an attempt to establish common objectives, and (where unity of aim is lacking) a process of bargaining designed to arrive at mutually satisfactory solutions, or (where even that proves impossible) a process for determining the balance of power. To the Ministry and the County Council the Borough could offer a contribution to the national housing programme and the relief of housing needs in London; from them it received subsidies, technical advice and authorization for certain actions. To others the Borough could offer money, or special advantages of various kinds—space for parking or loading, an exchange of tenants, an opportunity for experimenting with gas services, a site for a transformer station, or a more attractive view. In return it received land, technical services and agreements to participate without causing undue delay. Where land uses are concerned, democratic rights have a cash value, and the objector's power to delay and disorganize a complex and costly programme sometimes constituted a crucial bargaining counter in the negotiations. The formal authorizations required at each stage of the project from the Ministry and the County Council frequently constituted the seal placed on a much more complex bargaining process covering issues, important or trivial, many of which had no statutory place in the proceedings. Similar processes of bargaining and arbitration operated elsewhere in this series of studies, but frequently in an informal manner, more difficult to discern. In this case the Ministry and the County planning authority were specifically required by the legislation to arbitrate between contending interests at many points: authorizations for action on building plans, building heights, closure of rights of way and the borrowing of money formally established the outcome of these arbitrations. Such discussions had therefore to be preceded by lengthy negotiations to determine the views, interests and bargaining strengths of all concerned. Even when different departments of government were responsible for assisting progress on the same project, their frames of reference—the Ministry's coloured by a concern for economy, the LCC's by a concern for the visual amenities of London, for example—overlapped but did not coincide. Thus there were important differences in the criteria they employed and the evidence they regarded as relevant for the decisions to be made.

In negotiations subject to arbitration or decision by official bodies it was often found that criteria which could be specified in numerical terms proved easiest to establish and apply—the density of rooms per acre, the heights of buildings, the obstruction of light (as measured in shadow diagrams), volumes of water storage and waste disposal, fire escapes and access for fire engines, the cost of buildings, the floor area of rooms and flats, for example. Some of these criteria were based on technical requirements that were liable to be rendered obsolete by further technical development; rules for water storage and the height and capacity of fire escapes, for example, appeared to reflect technical assumptions that might no longer be justifiable. Questions for which there were no quantifiable criteria often proved harder to settle—questions such as the choice between 'slab' and 'point' blocks, the 'preservation of the London skyline' and the disturbance of privacy among Guinness Trust tenants had eventually to be resolved by overriding legal authority. Issues over which the Borough had to satisfy two or more potentially conflicting interests also presented special problems. The prolonged conflict between the County Council's and the Ministry's views has already been mentioned, but such disagreements cannot always be foreseen so easily: the Borough's attempt to appease one objector by providing him with a road led to time-consuming and potentially damaging objections from the neighbouring tenants' association which probably originated from other discontents of which the Borough had no direct knowledge.

While most of the requirements which the Borough had to meet in the course of the project were established for good technical or political reasons, it should not be concluded that all relevant needs were therefore taken into account. Indeed, the impression was gained at times that the interests of the authorities responsible for technical services, subsidies, land uses and other matters were so precisely quantified and so effectively represented that little scope was left to attend to the general needs of the people who would live in the flats. If the share of a fixed total of resources which must be devoted to fire escapes, water storage, and other technical requirements is expanded beyond a certain point, the share left for the general purposes of living may be unduly restricted. More recent developments in housing policy, following the publication of the Parker Morris Report,[1] have gone some way to improve this situation.

The person principally engaged in reconciling all these interests, co-ordinating the resources they controlled and creating a habitable environment out of them was the architect. He was manager as well as professional adviser to the Council. To perform his task he required a thorough and sensitive understanding of the administrative system, and the play of human nature and political and commercial interests within it—an understanding that was as essential a part of his pro-fessional equipment as his more specialized technical skills. The Housing Committee could advise him about the needs of tenants—half of them were Council tenants themselves—and the Housing Manager could also give useful guidance, though (extraordinarily enough) she had only recently been accorded the right to comment on building plans. Nevertheless a heavy social responsibility remained with the architect for envisaging and meeting the needs of those who would live in his buildings—and regulations about the size and equip-ment of flats, layout, access and many other matters left him scant elbow room for responding to it. The traditions of professional training in this and many other fields were originally based on the assumption that the architect—like the lawyer, the doctor and others —was clearly and primarily responsible to an individual 'client'. In this case the client was the Borough Council, but the value of the project will depend on its success in meeting the needs of present and future tenants. Somewhat similar problems arise in other cases we have considered. (Are child welfare officers working primarily for children, for parents, or for the Council employing them?) These questions have major implications for research on the development of social policies and for professional education which we return to later in this book.

[1] Ministry of Housing and Local Government, *Houses for Today and Tomorrow* London, HMSO, 1961.

The 'timing' of each step in the project was a crucial feature of its management. Not only had each phase of the project to be completed in appropriate sequence, but many decisions could only be made when the necessary preliminaries of the bargaining process had been completed and the 'balance of power' clarified. Thus negotiations had to be started soon enough but could not be completed too hastily. The LCC's devotion to point blocks could be surmounted as soon as it became clear that it would preclude subsidies from the Ministry, but delay in ascertaining the Ministry's point of view postponed the resolution of this conflict. Meanwhile, once this decision was accepted, the Ministry agreed to make useful concessions on other points in return. The administrator's need for a good sense of timing is a question that emerges again in later studies.

But important though the architect was, owing to his central role in the network of communications and the phasing of decisions, it should not be forgotten that the project was the Borough Council's, not his. At critical points in the story it was the Council or its Housing Committee which had to decide—in the light of many other commitments—whether to compromise and when to do this, whether to resist and when to muster delegations capable of presenting their views. They relied on the architect and their chief officers to advise them on such occasions, but once armed with this advice, the weighing of risks, potential delays and alternative costs was their responsibility, not their advisers'. Likewise, the architect had always to know how far the Council was prepared to go in supporting him before undertaking negotiations on their behalf. Thus he consulted the Committee and its senior officials and assured himself of their support at every stage of the project.

CHAPTER 10

CRISIS IN A CANADIAN SERVICE FOR CHILDREN

This study deals with a period in the history of a voluntary agency. Important developments were initiated by new members of the agency's staff, but additional resources required to sustain these innovations were not forthcoming in sufficient quantity. The financial crisis that followed compelled a reappraisal of aims and methods which revealed differing perceptions of the situation and precipitated a conflict in which a widening circle of people was embroiled. The phases of this conflict, and the character and timing of the intervention which eventually resolved it may prove instructive.

THE study of a Children's Department, presented in Chapter 8, posed a number of problems which had appeared in some earlier research carried out in a similar agency in Canada. The opportunity for an international comparison and the inherent interest of the Canadian story led us to add this study to the London cases. It deals with developments in a local Children's Aid Society which took place between 1952 and 1954, and the research was done during the following months, in the course of a broader study of the social services of Brockville, Ontario.[1] These social services and the legislation on which they were based have undergone major changes since then, but no attempt has been made to bring the account up to date. The Society's Board and staff and other members of the community gave generous help in the study, and we are most grateful for their willingness to let us use what was at times a painful experience for the purposes of this research.

All those working for the Society agreed that the growing emphasis laid on 'protection services', or preventive casework, constituted the most important recent development in their agency. This is the aspect of their work that we deal with. Since the Society and its environment

[1] See D. V. Donnison, *Welfare Services in a Canadian Community*, Toronto University Press, 1957.

will be unfamiliar to many readers, this report begins with two intro-
ductory sections: an outline of the responsibilities of Ontario's
Children's Aid Societies and the way in which they are administered,
followed by a brief sketch of the town and surrounding district that
form the setting for the events to be described in the third section.
The story ends with an appraisal of the changes that occurred, followed
as usual by a discussion of more general issues.

Children's Aid Societies

At the time of this study there were fifty-three Children's Aid
Societies in the Province of Ontario. Most of their work fell under
five headings: (i) the guardianship of children committed to their care
by the courts; (ii) the provision of a social work service for families
that have difficulty in bringing up their children; (iii) the arrangement
of adoptions, including the placing of children with prospective
adopters, the supervision of these homes during a trial year, and the
provision of a report for the court that made the legal adoption;
(iv) the selection of foster parents and adopting parents; (v) the
provision of help for unmarried mothers. The Societies did a number
of other things besides. They called on parents who were seeking a
divorce whenever there were children under the age of sixteen in the
family, and they presented reports to the provincial Supreme Court
to help it decide who should have custody of the children. They made
investigations for the Department of National Health and Welfare
when the Department received complaints that people drawing family
allowances were not spending the allowances on their children, or were
failing to send their children to school. In the few places where there
was no probation service (and the area studied was at that time one
of them) the Societies were informed of all children due to appear in
court and they provided the courts with reports on the home surround-
ings of these children. They might also be asked to supervise those
found guilty.

The administration of these services was a complex business, for the
Children's Aid Societies retained many of the characteristics of a
voluntary organization, yet from their beginnings in the last decade of
the nineteenth century they had always had certain statutory duties for
which they were responsible to the Provincial government. Their
incomes which were drawn partly from voluntary sources and partly
from three different levels of government, their accounting problems,
their public relations—in fact all their work—reflected this dual
statutory-voluntary constitution.

The Children's Aid Society studied was typical in having a Board of not more than twenty members elected at an annual general meeting to which were entitled to come all who paid a subscription of at least one dollar a year or a life membership fee of fifty dollars. The membership of the Board was in practice decided by the Board's own nominating committee which was called upon each year to prepare a list of names for the approval of the general meeting. The Board's principal members were the President—normally serving for about three years —a Vice-President, a Secretary and a Treasurer. All of them were unpaid. There was also an Honorary President—a distinguished member of the community who occasionally presided on formal occasions.

At the time of this study the Society's paid staff consisted of an executive Director, seven case workers, an office manager, three clerical workers and a cleaner.

A Children's Aid Society only received children into its care when they had been committed to its wardship by a Juvenile and Family Court. Committal was made on grounds of neglect,[1] and might be 'temporary' (for one year at a time) or 'permanent'—which meant that the Society assumed full parental rights and duties unless wardship was brought to an end by a resolution of the Board confirmed by the Provincial government's Director of Child Welfare.[2] In practice, children were seldom brought to court for proceedings leading to temporary or permanent wardship unless the Society had already spent some time in attempting to help the parents fulfil their responsibilities. Once committed to a Society's care, children were in nearly every case placed in foster homes and supervised by the Society's workers. The costs of caring for a Society's wards were met by the municipal authorities in whose areas the children previously lived, but 25 per cent of these contributions were refunded to the municipalities by the Provincial government. The court might also

[1] The legal definition of 'neglect' inevitably left ample scope for interpretation. According to the Provincial Child Welfare Act of 1954, which slightly extended the definition given in the earlier Children's Protection Act, neglected children included those with no one to look after them, those whose parents or guardians were unable or unwilling to care for them properly, those whose parents or guardians permitted or encouraged them to break the law, those who associated with thieves, drunkards, prostitutes and other undesirable people, and those judged by qualified psychiatrists to be rejected or deprived of affection to a degree sufficient to endanger their emotional or mental development.

[2] At the time of the study a new Act came into force, limiting the period of temporary wardship to a total of two years and permitted Societies to terminate permanent wardship any time by bringing wards to court for the magistrate to determine whether 'the welfare of the child might best be served by the termination of . . . permanent commitment'. *Child Welfare Act* of Ontario, 1954, S.16 (13) and S.16 (14).

order parents to contribute to the maintenance of their children. The sum to be paid to Societies for the maintenance of their wards was a fixed 'per diem rate', determined by the local magistrate or judge. At the time of this study it was the responsibility of Boards to apply to the courts when necessary for revisions of their per diem rates.[1]

The work of caring for children took by far the largest share of the Societies' resources of time and money. They were responsible for this work to the Director of Child Welfare, the head of the Child Welfare Branch of Ontario's Department of Public Welfare. They sent monthly reports to the Branch, and the Branch issued regulations, set standards and inspected each Society at least once a year.

The Societies' 'preventive casework', directed at children living in their own homes, had always been encouraged by the Provincial authorities. As early as 1897 the Provincial Superintendent of Neglected and Dependant Children (later called the Director of Child Welfare) wrote in his annual report that 'In all child-protection and philanthropic work generally the true aim should be the conservation of family home life . . . It is true that the removal of children from the control of vicious parents is advocated, but this is only as a last resort, and when all reasonable likelihood of securing better training for the child in its own home has been given up.'[2] (An outlook that was in some ways in advance of our own Children Act of 1948.)

But in contrast to child care services, for which responsibilities and standards had long been precisely defined, preventive work had largely been left to the Societies to develop according to their own lights and resources, with some guidance and encouragement from the Child Welfare Branch's Inspectors. The Societies' Boards had to finance this work from voluntary contributions—through subscriptions, bequests, flag days and house-to-house campaigns—to which the Provincial government added two grants: a sum equal to 25 per cent of the money raised from voluntary sources, and an annual grant (which at the time of this study had been temporarily fixed according to a formula that in effect gave most to those Societies judged in the past to have been most efficient). Municipal authorities were also allowed to make grants to the Societies, and a few Societies had been able to secure generous help from this source, arguing that local authorities could save themselves the costs of child care by enabling the Societies to prevent families breaking up.

[1] Subsequent legislation required the courts to re-consider the rates annually, and provided for a standard code, drawn up by the Director of Child Welfare, for the estimation of these rates. (Child Welfare Act, 1954, S.24.)

[2] *Neglected and Dependant Children.* Ontario, Report of Superintendent, 1897, p. 6.

With some modifications, the Societies' adoption work followed a pattern similar to that found in adoption agencies in England, but the probationary period, when children are fostered without payment with prospective adopters, lasted a year, the Societies were not required to secure the consent of parents when arranging for the adoption of their permanent wards, and there was no 'guardian *ad litem*'. The Societies, when presenting their reports to the County Courts, acted—legally speaking—as advisers to the Director of Child Welfare whose responsibility it was to provide much of the evidence required by these courts when considering adoption applications.

The selection of foster homes and adoption homes also followed a familiar pattern, except that foster care and adoption were both pursued on a much larger scale than would be considered possible by most English Children's Departments. Thus the Society studied had some 250 children in its care, of whom 9 per cent were in 'adoption probation homes' (thirty-one adoptions had been completed during the previous year). All but 8 per cent of these 250 wards had been boarded out, the few exceptions being children placed in mental hospitals, boarded out by other Societies or otherwise provided for. The provision of foster care as the normal—indeed, the almost universal—method of child care demanded skill and organization on a scale that is not required in agencies whose foster care is restricted to a smaller number of foster parents who are relied on to look after a minority of children specially selected from those in the agency's care. In the larger Societies the finding of foster homes was often handled by a separate department, but this work was administratively and financially a part of their child care service.

Societies encouraged unmarried mothers to seek help early in their pregnancy, but their first contact with these clients usually arose when the Child Welfare Branch (to which the provincial Registrar-General reported all illegitimate births) passed on information about the birth to the appropriate Society whose duty it was to write to the mother offering to help her gain her legal rights and make plans for her future and the future of her child. Unmarried mothers might then call on the Society or ignore the letter. In this work, which was closely related to their child care and adoption services, the Societies again acted as the agents of the Director of Child Welfare.

This outline of the functions of Children's Aid Societies presents a simplified and somewhat unreal picture. The Societies and the problems they face vary widely. At one extreme are complex organizations, found in two or three big cities, with a large professionally trained staff, working in collaboration with family casework services, health services, public housing authorities, a probation service, child guidance clinics, children's homes of many kinds, and other agencies. At the other extreme are small Societies, thankful if one member of their staff of three or four has relevant training of some sort; these workers may be called upon to cover a sparsely populated territory of several hundred square miles—much of it impassable in the depth of winter—with the support of an equally small public health unit, a few welfare or relieving officers (typically part-timers) and no other public services except the schools, the churches and the police.

The links the Societies were called upon to sustain with other institutions should be borne in mind. They drew family allowances from the *Federal government* for all their wards and made investigations on behalf of the Department of National Health and Welfare at Ottawa. They could only be set up with the approval of the *Provincial government*, and were legally responsible to that government for much of their child care, adoption and unmarried parents' services; they sent monthly reports to the Provincial authorities in Toronto, and received regular guidance, inspection and grants of money in return. Moreover, if they failed in their duties the Provincial government had power to dissolve a Society, take over its property and direct its chief officer to carry on its statutory services. They relied on the *municipal councils* in their districts for the bulk of their incomes (in the form of payments for the maintenance of wards) and they could receive further grants from these local authorities. The councils were frequently represented on the Societies' Boards but at the time of this study there was no effective requirement that this be arranged. The Societies often appeared in *Juvenile* and *Family Courts* seeking wardship of children, and they made occasional applications to these courts for changes in their *per diem* rates; unless there was mutual trust between the Societies and the magistrates (who were professional lawyers, appointed to full-time, permanent posts by the Provincial government) neither of these procedures would work smoothly. The Societies also had frequent contact with the *County Courts* (whose judges were appointed by the Federal government and therefore tended at the time of this study to differ from the magistrates in their political allegiances). In these courts they presented evidence in adoption and affiliation proceedings.

The Societies also had to maintain sound relations with the *public*—or rather with many 'publics': with adopters who tended to come from the professional and business sections of the community, with foster parents who were more likely to be lower-middle and solid working class people, with contributors drawn from all sections of the community, with Board members and others who held leading positions in voluntary and statutory welfare services, with clients who were predominantly unskilled and poorer people, and with clients' relatives and neighbours and the various professional workers (doctors, teachers, ministers, etc.) who often provided the channels through which a Society first heard of those whom it helped.

The Setting

The Society that forms the subject of this study served Brockville, with a population of about 14,000, two smaller towns each with about 4,000 people, and the two counties surrounding them—the whole area containing some 60,000 people spread over a rectangle about fifty miles long and thirty miles wide, divided between five municipal authorities. All three towns lay on the main highway that runs along Lake Ontario and the St Lawrence between Toronto and Montreal; smaller villages had grown up around road and rail intersections in the rocky or gently rolling farming country to the north. The Society's headquarters was in Brockville; other services which covered much of this area also operated from the town—the labour exchange, the Public Health Unit, the Red Cross and the Canadian Legion, for instance.

Brockville is the main shopping and marketing centre of the region, an old town that grew from settlements established by United Empire Loyalists who sought refuge here after the American revolution. By the middle of the last century it had become a railway junction, a market town and a small but busy centre of industry. Later the place became famous for the great wealth of a few of its citizens—most of it earned in big cities across the American border—and for its beauty, its respectability and its tendency to stagnation. In 1906 a local journalist described the town thus:

... while the Creator of the Universe did much in preparing a superb location for Brockville, the people whom he has honoured by sending them here to live have done and are still doing their share. It is true there is no mad, boom rush in the old town and never has been, but, like the handsome structures which grace its streets, Brockville's mercantile and business interests are mostly on a solid foundation, and unmoved by those fluctuations in trade that invariably drive to the wall the financial weaklings. Brockville's business men are neither splurgers nor plungers, nor yet are they plodders . . .

After the second world war a new highway, the St Lawrence seaway, and the gathering pace of Canada's industrial growth brought new factories, new people and new enterprise to the district. The local 'aristocracy' was still accorded the respect due to public service and inherited wealth, but a new class of managers, business and professional men and their wives had taken over leadership of most of Brockville's institutions. Of those in proprietary, managerial, professional, commercial or clerical jobs, little more than a half had lived in the town for ten years; those holding the chief positions in the town's welfare services included an even larger proportion of newcomers. Of those doing manual work, about three-quarters had lived in the town for more than ten years.[1]

Life was comfortable by British standards, but no better than Canada's average. A quarter of the town's households lived in flats and apartments, and most of the rest lived in owner-occupied, detached houses. Practically every house had its own garden. At the time of the 1951 census, nine out of ten households had their own bath or shower, and the great majority had a washing machine, refrigerator, telephone and vacuum cleaner. There was one car for every four people. Living standards in the surrounding countryside were somewhat lower and even in the towns there were a few families living in houses scarcely better than shacks.

The district contained a few Roman Catholics and small groups of Dutch immigrants, but the population was mainly protestant and of British origin. The Loyal Orange Lodge, the Freemasons and other 'fraternal orders' still flourished.

People came and went frequently, there was no local accent and most of the adults were not born in the districts where they had come to live. Nevertheless there were strong local loyalties and a thriving local social life: people read the local newspaper (founded in 1820) and listened to local radio stations, and they turned out to performances of their operatic, film and concert societies in numbers that would put any British community of similar size to shame. They complained they were overrun with strangers and no longer knew their neighbours, yet even in Brockville people noted new faces and kept track of their neighbours' affairs. Thus at the time of this study the new Director of the Children's Aid Society was favourably commented upon—not because he was a good social worker or a sound administrator, but because 'he takes his (own) children to the right shows'. In the smaller

[1] See *Welfare Services in a Canadian Community.*

towns and villages everyone seemed to know everyone. Local services were provided by a rudimentary but reasonably effective profusion of nominated and elected *ad hoc* authorities (for health, housing,
protestant schools, Roman Catholic schools, recreation, etc.) and by
voluntary organizations. The hierarchy of social classes was less
obtrusive than England's and these distinctions were overlaid by
others not of a hierarchical kind—distinctions between newcomers and
local boys, between the smart set and those with more modest, frugal
and sober habits, between Liberals and Conservatives, between the
young and the middle-aged, and between thriving religious denomina-
tions of a dozen different kinds.

The Development of 'Preventive Casework' in the Children's Aid Society

The local Children's Aid Society was founded in 1894 when a public
meeting resolved 'to bring the matter before the official member of
each church in town . . . requesting them to name two gentlemen and
two ladies to act as directors on the board of the proposed corporation'.
Three years later the Society extended its work to the two neighbouring Counties. In 1901 the Provincial authorities urged its Board to
provide a shelter for homeless and neglected children, but it was not
until 1912 that the shelter was found—through the generosity of one
of the town's leading families. In 1914 the Society appointed a paid
agent for the first time—a part-timer who was also the local YMCA
'boys' work secretary'. Children were cared for in the shelter, but
little was done to find foster homes for them or to help the families
from which they came. In 1916 the agent left to join the army.

The Society was put on its feet in 1934 when it appointed as its
first full-time executive Director (or Superintendent as he was then
called) a man who had for many years played a leading part on its
Board. He had been the local director of an immigration society which
brought children over from Britain and placed them on farms throughout the district, and his long experience of foster care revolutionized the
Children's Aid Society. The shelter was transformed into a reception
and training centre (in the face of considerable opposition from local
benefactors who had founded and supported it) and more children
were boarded out—many of them in 'free' or 'wage' homes where they
received board and lodging in return for personal service or a part of
their wages. Attention was then given to the prevention of neglect and
more staff had to be found. In 1935 the Society's first trained social

worker was appointed—a graduate of the University of Toronto's School of Social Work. She worked with the Society until 1953 and became widely known and respected in the district. She and the Director were helped from time to time by untrained, temporary workers who were called 'case-aides'. From about 1936 onwards an appeal was made for voluntary contributions nearly every year.

The war brought new demands. The armed forces and new departments of government asked for investigation and supervision of soldiers' families and asked the Society to help with the administration of allowances paid to them. A special worker was appointed to give her full time to these duties. In a report prepared by the Director in 1944 the Society was described as 'a private organization which could logically develop its services to a much further degree and form the backbone, particularly in rural areas, of an adequate family welfare service . . .' By 1947 the superintendent had a staff of two trained social workers, two case aides and three clerical workers. Next year the shelter was closed. Soon after, the Society's 'Women's Auxiliary', which had devoted itself to caring for the shelter and the children who lived in it, was also brought to an end.

In September 1952 two more trained workers were appointed—two men who had just graduated from the Toronto School. They came with a firm conviction that children lost more when removed from affectionate parents than they could ever gain from the orderly and healthy conditions of a foster home, and they looked upon child care as one aspect of a wider service designed to enable families to cope with their problems and take charge of their own affairs. In their casework they were less willing than some of their colleagues to seek or use the advice of relieving officers, ministers and other 'lay' people, they refused to divulge information about their clients to people with whom these things had previously been shared, whenever possible they attempted to make appointments before calling on their clients, and they tended to use a technical language—a jargon, some people called it—largely derived from psychoanalytic sources. Both were married men in their early thirties, both had had fairly wide experience before entering social work and both had some private income. In the small and rather conservative communities of the district, their new methods and attitudes were a potentially explosive intrusion.

By this time the Director had four full-time trained caseworkers, another trained man working part-time, and two workers without professional training. The trained workers were given very wide discretion to develop their own methods.

F

The Director was an active but reserved man, with a strong sense of duty. He had lived in the town for about forty years and had invested some money in rented houses bought during the depression. His friends were few but loyal. He was due to retire in three years' time.

A year or two earlier the Society had acquired a new President. She was the wife of a factory manager who had come to the town about five years before. She had been a Board member for several years and had already taken the lead in establishing and running a number of voluntary organizations in the district. She was an intelligent, loquacious and compelling woman with tremendous drive and a tendency to inspire admiration or enmity among those with whom she came in contact. She was in her late forties and had a Ph.D in Sociology.

In March 1949 the Society had 305 children in its care and was working with 51 unmarried mothers and 84 'protection' cases involving children living in their own homes. Its income, which had exceeded its expenditure by only 803 dollars during the previous year, was drawn from the following sources:

Income of the Society in 1948–9

	$	$
Provincial and municipal payments for maintenance of wards*	50,486	
Municipal grants	3,493	
Provincial grants	1,500	
Payments for services to Federal government departments	732	
Family allowances for wards*	10,957	
Total from public sources		67,168
Donations, subscriptions and bequests	4,319	
Revenue from investments	189	
Contributions from parents for maintenance of wards*	7,630	
Miscellaneous	126	
Total from private sources		12,264
TOTAL INCOME		$79,432
Surplus of income over expenditure		$803

* Items directly related to number of wards in the Society's care.

During the next few years the numbers of children in care rose slightly, but increases in income (due to larger payments from Provincial and municipal authorities) failed to keep pace with rising expenditure, and by 1952 the Society was drawing on its reserves to the extent of some $4,000 a year.

The arrival of the new men precipitated a crisis. Fewer children were committed to the Society's care, and larger numbers were returned to their own homes. This struck at all the main sources of the Society's income—maintenance payments from Provincial and municipal governments, family allowances, and parental contributions. No compensating economies were made; indeed more workers were being employed, the costs of preventive casework had increased, and foster parents were being given a freer hand in clothing and equipping foster children. A comparison with figures for 1953, presented below, shows that the proportion of income directly related to the numbers of wards in the Society's care remained unchanged (at 87 per cent of the total) during a period when the Society's resources were being increasingly turned to other work.

By 1953 the Society was going bankrupt. During the last nine months of the year[1] the Society was overspending by more than $1,000 a month. All available investments had already been sold and the bank was becoming restive about the Society's mounting overdraft. Its manager was a member of the Board. Appeals for grants were made to the municipal councils in the Society's area, but without success. The annual financial campaign for voluntary contributions was a failure, either through bad organization or through lack of public confidence in the Society.

Meanwhile relations amongst the staff deteriorated and their disagreements were reflected among Board members. The President and some of her colleagues were convinced they should press on with the development of preventive casework, even if the resources for it were not immediately available. Her determination to back the new element in the Society and to be available to any of the staff who wished to express their views to the Board led its members to intervene in the daily work of the agency to an unusual extent; on at least one occasion the President asked a caseworker to visit a family that was already being helped by another worker. The Provincial authorities were aware of these difficulties and Supervisors from the Child Welfare Branch came down twice to discuss the situation, but little was achieved.

---

[1] The Society's accounting year was at this point altered to coincide with the calendar year; hence the shorter period covered by these figures.

Income of the Society, April-December 1953

	$	$
Provincial and municipal payments for maintenance of wards*	49,113	
Municipal grants	1,987	
Provincial grants	2,582	
Payments for services to Federal government departments	814	
Family allowances for wards*	7,844	
Total from public sources		62,340
Donations, subscriptions and bequests	4,198	
Revenue from investments	—	
Contributions from parents for maintenance of wards*	4,476	
Total from private sources		8,674
TOTAL INCOME		$71,014
Deficit		$10,238

* Items directly related to number of wards in the Society's care.

Possibly as a last resort, the Director suggested to one or two members of the staff that the number of wards (and hence the Society's income) might be increased if they visited certain families whose children had been in their care in the past. Increasingly disturbed by this and other developments, the two new men then called on the President to tell her it was becoming more and more difficult for them to play a constructive part in the Society: in effect they offered their resignations. But they were persuaded to stay on. The President was already convinced that a new Director must be found, but she knew her Board was sharply divided on this issue. Shortly afterwards the Director himself offered to resign, saying he no longer felt he had the confidence of his Board. This offer was also refused.

Meanwhile it became clear that influential people in the municipal councils and elsewhere were not willing to rescue the Society unless changes were made in its leadership, and the Director became the focus of a good deal of unpleasant gossip. Eventually, at the end of July 1953, he again offered his resignation and this time it was accepted unanimously. The part-time trained worker (who had become a temporary full-timer and managed to remain on reasonably good terms with all concerned) was asked if he would assume the Directorship, but he refused. The Society's troubles were known in the profession, and no one would apply for the post. Eventually one of the new men was made Director, at first in an acting capacity. The Society's first trained worker (appointed eighteen years earlier) and another social worker resigned.

Meanwhile the costs of maintaining the Society's wards were rising and an application was made to the Magistrates' Court for an increase in the *per diem* rate from $1·15 to $1·41. The application was commenced on October 13, 1953, and opposed by counsel representing some of the municipal authorities which would have to pay the increased charges. After a long hearing, ending on November 3, the Magistrate issued a detailed and carefully reasoned judgement, finding 'with some hesitation' that $1·23 per day was 'a reasonable sum to be paid by a municipality for the maintenance of a child by the Society'. His hesitations arose largely from the fact that the Society had not made (and many thought could not make) a clear distinction between the portion of its expenses incurred for 'protection' work with children in their own homes, and the portion incurred for the maintenance of its wards. He noted the 'apparent animosity between the Society and the municipal councils', and drew attention to the fact that the Society was sole judge of the way in which its work was distributed and its expenses allocated, while the councils had no control whatever over its affairs. True, the councils nominated six of the Society's Board members but 'their qualifications are questionable unless they individually subscribe and so become members'. (He probably knew that the municipal representatives did not play an active part in the Board's work.) Since the municipal liability for maintenance of wards could not be escaped, the Court held it to be the Society's responsibility to draw up accounts distinguishing clearly between the two main parts of its work and to 'limit itself in the protective and preventive aspect of its work to that which can be done with available voluntary contributions no matter how desirable an extension of that phase of its work may seem to the Society'. Meanwhile, the Magistrate pointed out, it was open to the municipal authorities to employ people to investigate wardship applications and to oppose these applications in court, to show when parents of wards were able to contribute to their maintenance, and to ensure that their contributions were fully paid. They might also reduce the numbers of children coming into the Society's care by carrying on their own preventive work or by contributing to such work done by the Society. (Taken together, these suggestions would have virtually amounted to a statutory take-over of the service.)

The Society was sinking fast, for this application had been the last shot in its locker. Questions were being asked about the uses to which family allowances had been put, for this item of income was paid into a separate trust fund which helped to reduce the interest payments on the mounting overdraft. The Honorary President (a Senator and a wealthy and respected member of the community who had given generous support in the past) complained that a large donation made for specified purposes had already been spent in other ways. He resigned, writing that he could no longer be associated with the Society. Finally the Board itself resigned in a body.

At this point the Provincial government's Director of Child Welfare had to intervene. After a preliminary and fruitless meeting with those who had been on the Board, he invited them, the staff, municipal councillors, members and supporters of the Society, to a meeting. At this meeting he urged all present to sink their differences for the good of the cause; he reminded them that he was responsible for the 250 children in their care, and suggested that he could only carry out his responsibilities at the expense of the municipal councils, with the help of a staff of social workers—probably the very people whom the Society had employed, paid salaries quite as generous as those the Society had paid. Thus he made it clear that his Branch was responsible for ensuring that most of the Society's work continued, and had power to fulfil these responsibilities at the expense of the local municipalities. (In fact, so drastic a step would only have been taken as a last resort. It would have been politically unpopular, and the preventive social work—which lay at the root of the crisis—would have had to be abandoned since the Provincial government had no legal powers to carry it out.)

The deadlock then broke. The Board resumed office. A new application was made for revision of the *per diem* rate, supported this time with all the statistics that could be devised and—more important —not opposed by the municipal councils. This application was successful. Some of the councils gave additional grants to the Society. The agency's premises were sold (a large house with rooms originally used for the temporary accommodation of children) and the staff moved to cramped, but businesslike, offices rented in the commercial centre of the town. Subsequent flag days and appeals were more successful, and before long the Society's finances and the morale of its Board and staff were greatly improved. Two years later the new Director joined the supervisory staff of the Provincial Child Welfare Branch and the other 'new man' succeeded him.

Reappraisal

What changes had taken place? What had this crisis been about? The growing emphasis on preventive social work was the development stressed by those leading the Society in 1954. But in fact there had not been a striking change during this period in the distribution of the Society's activities. The 305 children in the Society's care in 1949 had fallen to 248 by 1954. The 51 unmarried parent cases being dealt with had risen to 73—numbers no larger than those found on the Society's books ten years earlier. The 84 'protection' cases had risen to 103, yet the most striking increase in this element of the case-load had taken place not during this period but between 1944 and 1949, when the number of protection cases had more than doubled.

These changes were visible in the Society's accounts—but barely visible. The proportion of total expenditure devoted to 'child care' fell from 83 per cent to 76 per cent between 1949 and 1954, 'investigation and preventive field work' rose from 4 to 7 per cent, and 'administrative and other' expenses rose from 13 to 17 per cent. By 1954 the Society calculated that 30 per cent of its field workers' time, equivalent to 34 per cent of field workers' salaries, was devoted to work with children living in their own homes, and the rest to children in the Society's care. It is even less plausible to suggest that preventive case-work was at this time first accepted as one of the Society's major functions: statements have been quoted which show that this was always thought to be an important function of this and every other Children's Aid Society.

There were cynics who said that nothing more than a palace revolution had occurred. The staff, and particularly the leading people among them, had changed. Yet this was no trivial change. New methods and a new approach appeared in the Society's work: something that can be illustrated more easily than measured.

The Society began as an offshoot of church and school, teaching parents and children to accept the standards for which these institutions stood. This approach, characteristic of a benevolent police force, was still reflected in the Annual Report for 1925, written by the first Director when he had been a member of the Board.
'During childhood character is in the making; good and bad tendencies are struggling for mastery; the soul is in a state of flux. Parents are

entrusted with the most delicate, the most susceptible, the most precious of all raw materials. If they do not mould it, the World, the Flesh and the Devil will ... This problem must be borne by the home, the church and the school. The Children's Aid Society exists to see that these *three agencies* have a chance to function upon every child ... we are endeavouring by persuasion, encouragement and threats to have delinquent parents remedy the existing evils.'

By 1953 a changed emphasis was apparent. A leaflet circulated during the first campaign for voluntary contributions after the appointment of the new Director read as follows:

'Some broken homes can be rebuilt—through making the parents aware of their parental responsibilities—through assisting the parents to strengthen the emotional bonds of family living—through helping the parents to find ways and means of securing the minimum physical standards consistent with their children's health and welfare—through planning with the parents all the details, emotional and physical, necessary for the re-establishment of the home and the return of their children.'

The practical implications of this change sometimes appeared in the Society's case records. In 1944 a social worker visited some foster parents who were having trouble with one of the Society's wards. She reported that 'the foster parents have endeavoured in every conceivable way [to correct his behaviour] by not giving him spending money, sending him to bed, even giving corporal punishment—which was not approved—but with little results. [He] still comes home with pencils, erasers, etc. which belong to other children.' Ten years later the same boy was again giving trouble in another foster home. Another social worker visited him and reported: 'I tried to get [his foster father] to express what [the boy] did or did not do that "griped" him ... he needs a man to whom he can relate and identify ... and resents [his foster father's] rejecting attitude towards him.' The Society's aim in both cases was the same—to help the boy live happily in his foster home—but its approach to the problem was different. In 1954 the Society no longer looked merely at the foster parents' methods of discipline; it studied the unspoken feelings of the boy and his foster parents in an attempt to help them live happily with each other. The report made in 1944 might have come from an experienced layman; the report made in 1954 is that of a professional doing a job for which specific training is required, and for which—rightly or wrongly—a new language had been developed.

A similar contrast may be seen in two letters sent at different periods in the Society's history to unmarried mothers. This was the form used early in 1953:

'The registration of the birth of the above-named child to you has been reported to us as is required by law. The purpose, of course, is that there may be assurance of the welfare of the child and that our report thereon, may be placed with the Department of Public Welfare, Toronto.

'It would appear to be best in the interest of all concerned, that you would first come to see us and give us certain required information and assurance.

'It is, of course, a part of our responsibility to give you assurance of such assistance as is available under the Children of Unmarried Parents Act which we can explain when we see you.

'Please co-operate as suggested and help us to avoid the necessity of other less desirable or convenient approaches.'

This was the form adopted in the following year:

'The registration of the birth of your child has been reported to us as is required by law.

'The law provides help for you, whether or not you are keeping your baby, both in planning for your child's future and in getting financial assistance from the father of the child.

'We are required to send a report to the Provincial Director of Child Welfare. We would like, therefore, to discuss your plans for your child with you as soon as is convenient. Please be assured that all information is confidential.'

The first letter emphasizes the Society's need for 'information' and 'assurance' about the welfare of the child, and threatens 'less desirable or convenient approaches' if co-operation is not forthcoming. The second offers the mother help in making plans for herself and her baby, and promises confidential treatment of the case.

The change in the Society's role in the community is best illustrated by the help its workers sought from other people. In earlier days they frequently consulted others about the families with which they were concerned. In dealing with complaints about a family living on relief a social worker noted in her report that she had asked for the help of the Relieving Officer and 'He called on Mrs Y and warned her very strongly against this drinking party in her home'. The Society sought guidance from ministers, doctors, business people and others, particularly when selecting adopting or foster parents. Later the Society still asked for the help of these people, but it was help of other kinds. It asked them to attend meetings and discuss its work, to sit on its

Board, to organize its fund-raising campaigns and contribute to its funds, to adopt its children and serve as foster parents. It seldom asked for their guidance in its dealings with individual cases.

These conclusions would not be accepted by all who took part in the events described. To some, the central feature of these two years was a struggle for power that ended in victory for the President, retirement for the Director and promotion for two young men. Others saw little in the story but a financial crisis, brought upon themselves by a well-intentioned but unbusinesslike group of people. According to another version, the crisis took the Society one more step away from its origins as a local voluntary organization, controlled and supported by a small group of local citizens, and one more step towards becoming a district office of a Provincial government service. All were agreed that a famous victory had been won, but contenders and observers gave differing accounts of who had won and what they had been fighting about. In our opinion all were at least partly right.

We made no attempt to discover whether the Society's clients were aware that any change had taken place.

DISCUSSION

When those who provide a social service become convinced that their service is bad, perhaps even inhuman, should they press on with reform and turn a blind eye to signals of approaching disruption and bankruptcy, determined that their agency should if necessary die in a good cause? When a man has done more than anyone else to raise a service to its present level and then seems to stand in the way oi further progress in the last years before his retirement, should one maintain the standards of tolerance and kindness that ought to apply in relations between neighbours and fellow citizens, or should further improvement of the service come first? These are important questions, familiar to every experienced administrator. Research can only pose and clarify such problems; it cannot resolve them.

We endeavour here to identify the principal phases of the development described, and the factors that played a part in each. Developments examined in previous studies were initiated partly by changes in the resources available for the provision of a service (as in Bethnal Green's switch to slum clearance) partly by changes in the scale and character of demand for a service (as in the development of the Home

Help service) and partly by changes in the number and character of the people providing the service (as in the cases of the Children's Department and, again, in the Home Help service)—though in none of these cases was the total development due to these factors alone. In the service discussed here—as in others whose character depends primarily on the people providing the service, rather than on financial resources and the terms on which they are made available—it was the growth and character of the staff that played the 'leading' part in the development of policies. But while changes in the staff initiated new developments, many other factors became important once these developments began.

Opportunity for change came with the great increase in staff and resources during the decade after the war. The training and character of the staff recruited did a lot to determine the nature of the developments that followed, but the Society did not recruit its first trained workers at this time—nor even the first from the Toronto School of Social Work. (A trained person with inadequate resources and a vast case-load is often forced to work in ways that differ little from those of the untrained.) More money, more staff, new blood and a light rein on all concerned permitted new elements to develop within the service. But these innovations were expensive, and a growing volume of resources was needed to sustain them. This phase could not continue once the Society was confronted with a growing deficit in its accounts. Differing approaches became conflicting approaches as threatened bankruptcy forced the Society to reappraise its work and its priorities.

Increased resources provide opportunities for experiment and development, but it is the scarcities that often follow from more ambitious work which compel people to choose between abandoning an experiment or accepting it as a recognized part of the service. The limitations which confront those developing new features of an agency's work may appear in the form of a lack of legal powers (as in the Children's Department case, to some extent) in the form of a shortage of staff (as in the Children's Department and Home Help cases) or in the form of other shortages—of office space or equipment, for example. In a voluntary agency, the development of whose work depends on financial resources rather than legal powers, the scope for innovation will often be determined largely by the money available— as in this case. The discretion given to the Society's social workers could not continue unrestricted and the underlying vagueness about the Society's principal functions had to be clarified when further development brought the threat of bankruptcy. Those responsible for the agency were then drawn into increasingly direct and detailed interventions in its daily work. This occurred more or less accidentally, but a tightening of central controls is a common feature in services experiencing a growth of staff and a development of functions until new conventions are established and greater discretion can again be given to field workers. (The same process occurred in the National Assistance Board case.) Clarification of the Society's aims and methods eventually emerged in the course of a struggle for power in which the Board and its staff, the municipal councils, the Provincial Child Welfare Branch, the magistrate's court and private citizens were all involved.

Economic and social changes taking place in the surrounding district exercised a considerable influence on the outcome. The 'professionalization' of the Society's staff and its growing dependence on the Provincial government were only one small example of a similar professionalization and centralization of industry, commerce and government to be seen throughout the district. The 'new young men' among the Society's staff found allies among the new class of migrant middle class people who played an increasingly active and dominant part, both in the affairs of local voluntary bodies and in commercial, industrial and government institutions which were to a growing extent controlled from major centres outside the district and managed by people brought in from outside. As the wife of a migrant factory manager, the President of the Board herself illustrated and represented these economic and social changes.

But no real progress could be made towards the resolution of the Society's problems until every available gun had been brought to bear in the battle and the balance of contending forces became clear. The Provincial Director of Child Welfare provided the final impetus to a solution by threatening to take over the statutory parts of the Society's work and charge their cost to the municipalities, but it is doubtful whether this step would have proved so decisive had it been attempted before every other available solution had been tried and every other source of influence had been brought to bear. The 'timing' of his intervention was well judged. Had he acted earlier his intervention would have been regarded by many as an unjustifiable Provincial government interference in local affairs, but at the point when he called a meeting with all concerned his action merely confronted them with the ultimate consequences of continued intransigeance.

In the case of the London Children's Department it was shown that people approaching a problem with different frames of reference describe the issues at stake in different ways, but are nevertheless capable—without abandoning their different approaches—of collaborating in solutions that accord with the aspirations of each participant. Indeed, each may claim authorship of the solutions devised. In this case, too, the people involved approached a problem with different frames of reference, interpreting the issues in very different ways. But for a while no mutually satisfactory solutions could be found. Their objectives were not merely different; they were irreconcilable.

The deadlock was hardened by other features of the situation. Agencies controlling resources that were vital to the development of the Society—the municipalities in particular—had no effective channel of communication (or failed to use the channels available) for expressing their views or for learning at first hand about the Society's needs. Such a situation inevitably tended to provoke a refusal to participate —'strike action'—when the Society pressed on with developments that were not properly understood or accepted by those who had to play a part in them. In a north American community large sums of money are raised for charity, largely through the organizing capacity and social pressures exerted by local leaders—frequently managers in commercial and industrial firms, who organize fund raising 'campaigns'. But these leaders show a marked reluctance to commit themselves to campaigns that are unlikely to succeed. The social and professional rewards of the heavy work involved depend on the success of the campaign. Thus a change, real or assumed, in public attitudes to a voluntary agency can very quickly have an impact on the agency's financial resources. Meanwhile several members of the staff who were most heavily involved had readily marketable professional qualifications, and three of them had private sources of income. They were thus able to accept the consequences of determined pursuit of their objectives, should resignation become necessary. A solution could only be found when some people withdrew altogether from the Society and the municipal authorities were compelled to accept that the bulk of their financial obligations were inescapable—though they might perhaps be reduced by the growth of the preventive work which the Society was endeavouring to develop.

It is tempting to suggest that the problems revealed in this case were a product of some of the distinctive and forceful personalities in the story. Personalities clearly played a major part in determining the character and intensity of the crisis, but difficulties of the kind that arose in this Society are inherent in its constitution, and the Provincial authorities have had to intervene in similar crises in a number of other Children's Aid Societies. The Society was endeavouring to combine functions which in England are performed by the Children's Departments, the National Society for the Prevention of Cruelty to Children, adoption and moral welfare agencies, and the Probation Service. Many would applaud this attempt to integrate services designed to meet closely related needs, and to cope explicitly with problems that the subdivided English system conceals. Though the stresses on those administering the services may be severe, the children probably benefit. The Society's work, however, was divided up in an odd and arbitrary fashion: a child in trouble at home constituted a 'protection' case, but when he entered the Society's wardship he turned into a 'child care' case, reverting to 'protection' when he went home again; if his sister became inadvertently pregnant she was an 'unmarried mother', and her baby might figure in the 'adoption' case-load. Each of these elements in the Society's case-load tended to become the concern of a different body. The municipal councils were responsible only for the maintenance of wards. The Provincial government's slender resources (considerably enlarged since this study was made) had to be devoted first to its limited statutory responsibilities in the fields of child care, illegitimacy and adoption. Meanwhile the Board tended to make the development of preventive work its special concern. Policies tended to be developed by the Society with guidance from Provincial authorities, while the municipalities which provided most of the Society's income had no control over either. This divorce between policy-making and financing bodies is no new thing—British universities have made a principle of it. But there are dangers in any situation where people hold power in the affairs of an organization (in this case the power of the purse) yet have no effective communication with those holding formal authority. During a period of stability this system can work very well but when the objectives of a Society are being extended and its priorities are changing it takes exceptional leadership to maintain effective communications and to reconcile the diverse interests of all concerned.

These problems cannot be completely solved while Ontario demands social services on a scale that the taxpayer alone can finance, and maintains the structure of voluntary organization and small-scale local government which grew up to meet the needs of another age. In less acute form, the same problems afflicted the schools, health services and public housing ventures, but these were all services which were of immediate interest to large numbers of people—for most of the population has children, and all are anxious to be healthy and well-housed. The Children's Aid movement lacked these firm roots, and had no supporting pressure groups—no equivalent to the parent-teacher associations or the numerous voluntary health associations—to provide the secure political and administrative backing it required.

The surprising thing is not that the Children's Aid Society ran into trouble, but that any organization whose services are unrealistically sub-divided, inspected and controlled by one body, financed by half a dozen, subject to arbitration from several, directed by a self-selected Board and forced to rely for the money to support an important part of its work on fluctuating voluntary contributions, should normally have functioned so smoothly and effectively.

CHAPTER 11

CONSULTATION AMONG SOCIAL WORKERS IN THE FAMILY WELFARE ASSOCIATION

This study deals with another voluntary agency. It traces the evolution of procedures for the improvement of professional skills and working methods in one of the agency's local offices. These procedures were initiated by the agency's staff, in response both to the changing demands being made on their service and to broader developments within the social work profession. The resources required for this innovation were secured from outside bodies which exercised considerable influence on the agency's work, and also through a reduction in case-loads which enabled staff to devote more time to each case. The divergent expectations of those involved and the scarcity of the resources available to them provoked conflicts somewhat similar to those seen in the previous study. The agency's administrative structure was ill-adapted for resolving these conflicts, and the loss of senior staff and committee members posed further difficulties.

THE starting point for this study was one of the seven Area Offices of the Family Welfare Association: Area 4, which included the City of London and much of the north-eastern part of London County—the Boroughs of Holborn, Finsbury, Stepney, Poplar, Shoreditch, Bethnal Green, Hackney and St Pancras. The Area Secretary in charge of this Office mentioned several recent developments in her field, but it was difficult to isolate a topic for study amongst them. However, she referred frequently to the growth of 'supervision' and of procedures for the systematic discussion of cases her staff were dealing with, and she stressed the important part these developments played in the other trends mentioned. With the agreement of the Secretary and her staff this development was selected as the theme of our study which was carried out in 1958.

We shall use the general term 'consultation' to refer to these processes, meaning by this any procedure designed to enable social workers to discuss their current cases with others at regular intervals.

It includes a number of different but comparable activities, all of which were intended to help social workers to improve the standards of their work: 'conferences' at which groups of caseworkers met to discuss individual cases and current problems, with or without the help of an 'expert' of some kind, 'supervision' provided by a senior person (inside or outside the normal administrative structure of the Association) who discussed cases with individual workers and took considerable responsibility for selecting the topics to be explored and posing problems for the worker to consider, and 'consultations' in which workers themselves selected cases and problems on which to seek the guidance of an expert who was normally brought in for this purpose from outside the agency. These different forms of consultation cannot be clearly distinguished since they tended to merge and alternate with each other in practice. Some of them may be termed 'supervision' but the principal purpose of all of them is not to inspect the work done or to control those who do it, but to advance knowledge and skills and to evolve common policies and codes of practice.

The policies of the Family Welfare Association had been debated for several years prior to this study, and the debate still continues. We therefore begin with a brief account of the work and structure of the Association and the changes both were undergoing at this time. We then turn to Area 4 and the development of various forms of 'case consultation' in that Office between 1954 and 1958, explaining the part played by the Association's Central Office in these developments, and concluding with an appraisal of the progress made.

This report is based on interviews with most of the staff and committee members of the Association who took part in the developments described, and on reports, memoranda and records of various kinds. One of the authors served for a period on the Association's Administrative Council and this experience also contributed to the findings presented here. The story was by no means ended when our study took place. A major review of the FWA's policies and organization was beginning as our study closed and important changes, which we do not trace, followed from it.

The Family Welfare Association

The Charity Organization Society was founded in 1869 and re-named 'The Family Welfare Association' in 1946.[1] As late as 1944 its stated aims were still 'to organize charitable effort and to improve the

---

[1] For a history of the Society see Charles Loch Mowat, *The Charity Organisation Society, 1869–1913*. London, Methuen, 1961.

condition of the poor', but wartime pressures and post-war social legislation prompted the Society to provide a full-scale social casework service later described as being designed 'to alleviate the distress which people feel when for any reason they come into conflict with their social environment . . . the phases of this method are (1) to make as thorough a study of their client as is relevant to his social situation, (2) to determine from the knowledge . . . available how best he and his family may be helped, and (3) finally to involve the client and his family in working towards a solution of their difficulties'. In this work the various forms of material help the Society might provide 'are a means to an end, rather than the end itself, which end is the best adjustment which can be effected between the client and his social environment'.[1]

These aims were a reinterpretation of the original objectives of the cos, but they had to be combined with many other tasks which the agency had taken on during its long history. The FWA had an Old People's Homes Committee, established to find appropriate forms of residential care for old people; it was responsible for fourteen Citizen's Advice Bureaux in various parts of London and formed the administrative channel for the distribution of funds provided for them by Metropolitan Boroughs; it undertook a similar service for two Legal Aid Centres assisted by the London County Council; it administered some almshouses, various trusts and eleven pensions funds, and acted as agent for other charities; it provided an Information Service originally designed to expose fraudulent appeals but now mainly used by solicitors and others wishing to trace small charities; and it published a journal—'Social Work'—the 'Annual Charities Register and Digest' and the 'Guide to the Social Services'. More directly related to its family casework service were the Association's long-standing contribution to the training of university students and others interested in social work, and various temporary experimental projects such as those dealing with the treatment of marital disharmony, the welfare of coloured people, and the development of methods of work among 'problem families'.

The development and co-ordination of these activities were the responsibility of the FWA's Administrative Council. Under a constitution drawn up in 1950 (revised again since this study took place) this Council consisted of 30 members. Two were elected to represent each of the seven Area Committees, 2 practising social

---

[1] Unpublished *Review of the Family Welfare Association*, Muriel A. Cunliffe. FWA, 1960.

workers were elected by the Area Secretaries, 1 represented the Citizen's Advice Bureaux, and there were 3 ex officio members (the Chairman, Honorary Treasurer and Assistant Honorary Treasurer). The remaining 10 members were co-opted—some of them from statutory social services and London University. Members of the Council were appointed, and normally re-appointed, every three years. The Council met once a month. It debated and approved policy, and followed up directions from the Annual General Meeting (to which all members of the Association who subscribed at least ten shillings a year might come) and from the special 'Domestic Meetings' of Council and staff which were supposed to be held twice yearly. It was ultimately responsible for the appointment and dismissal of the Central Office staff and all 'casework' staff.

The Council appointed committees and delegated powers to them. The principal committees at this time were the General Purposes Committee (which dealt with most staffing and establishment matters, acted as a supervisory and informative link between the Council and the Area Committees, and dealt with urgent business arising between Council meetings), the Selection and Training Committee (dealing with training, and negotiating with universities and other bodies), the Aims and Policy Committee, and the Finance Committee. Other committees dealt with appeals, press and publicity, grants, and special services and projects such as the Information Service, the Citizen's Advice Bureaux, and placements in old people's homes. All these Committees were entitled to co-opt members in addition to the Council members serving on them. The Association's Central Office at Denison House was directed by the General Secretary, and its senior staff included the Organizing Secretary (responsible for casework staff and training matters, and deputy to the General Secretary) the National Casework Secretary (responsible for dealing with enquiries about individual cases from all over the country) and the Accountant.

It can be seen that the central body in this structure—the Administrative Council—met frequently enough to play an active part in the Association's management but had a large membership representing diverse interests and including paid staff, volunteers and outside experts of various kinds. It was responsible to two different general assemblies—the Annual General Meeting and the Domestic Meeting —and carried out its work through a very large number of committees, each of which could co-opt further members.

Since 1954 the Association's casework service had been provided from seven Area Offices. Each had its own Area Committee of at least twelve members elected annually. Committee members included representatives of voluntary and statutory services and various other local interests. Under the 1950 Constitution they were required to meet between four and twelve times a year for the purpose of raising and administering funds, teaching and training workers in the principles, methods and administration of family casework (using whatever methods they thought fit), and establishing centres offering advice and guidance on matters of family welfare. They managed FWA affairs in their Areas, elected members to the central committees, and appointed representatives to the committees of other agencies. The organization of fund-raising appeals and the supervision of Area finances was normally delegated to sub-committees. The Area Committee might also elect a 'Cases Sub-committee', not more than one-third of whose members might be co-opted from outside the Association. This sub-committee would 'consider and make decisions on all cases submitted to them but delegating authority to the Area Secretary in dealing with cases coming within the defined policy of the Association'. It, or the Area Committee, had to authorize expenditure exceeding £35 on any one case. It had also to make recommendations to the Area Committee on all questions of policy affecting individual cases, and report any cases in which a change of policy was required or implied. Each Area office was run by an Area Secretary who was a senior social worker responsible for directing the other caseworkers in the office, the small clerical staff, and a number of voluntary workers. She was responsible to her committee for the social work service, the training of students and general administration. Her casework staff would normally consist of one or two Assistant Secretaries, and possibly another in training. In earlier years the Association's local Areas (then called 'Districts') were smaller and more numerous—there had been twenty-one of them in 1948, and a maximum of thirty-nine during the nineteenth century. In the past their Secretaries frequently had no fully trained staff, but they could call on the assistance of a larger number of unpaid voluntary workers. Thus at the Area level, too, the Association had made a partial but incomplete adaptation to change. The Area Committees' control of casework, training methods and the distribution of material help—originally complete—was loosened and left for each to clarify for itself. The Committees included a growing proportion of 'expert' members, employed in neighbouring social services, alongside the 'lay' volunteers who represented the traditional source of the Association's membership. The COS had always been a fairly loose federation of local units. At the time of this study the Central Office's growing control over the Areas hinged largely on its power to appoint and pay casework staff, but the Areas' capacity to raise funds of their own—and hence their real autonomy—varied considerably, though none were financially self-supporting.

At this stage in its history the FWA was responding to a number of external developments which may be briefly summarized. Full employment, rising incomes, and the establishment of the National Assistance Board and other statutory services—several of which have been described in earlier studies in this series—had deprived the Association of many of its earlier relief-giving functions. The scarcity of leisured local gentry, and the Association's growing reliance on trained social work staff shifted the balance of expenditure and power within the agency, conferring greater influence on trained workers and the Central Office which paid their salaries. Meanwhile the gathering national drive for more trained social workers (to be most forcefully represented by the report of the Younghusband Committee[1] which was being written at the time of this study) posed serious problems for the FWA; although it had always played an active part in this campaign, the Association did not have the financial resources to compete with the salaries offered by the big statutory services, and to recruit good staff it had to offer other inducements such as the opportunity of doing interesting work in a professionally stimulating environment. In the past, COS workers had concentrated on helping the most 'helpable'—those whom an earlier generation described as 'the deserving poor'—but the FWA had come increasingly, though never unanimously, to concentrate on the most intractable cases for which the statutory services often proved least effective. The distribution of material help, though never an end in itself, had been the COS's best known and most extensive task; but the 'harder' cases the Association was now dealing with, coupled with the new outlook and training of many of its staff, made the skilled use of human relationships the principal instrument of its work. The COS had been suspicious of the growth of government and unwilling to render itself or its clients dependent on public money; but the FWA was gradually compelled to seek financial help from the Home Office, the Boroughs and the London County Council.

The Association's 'ordinary income' rose from £18,751 in 1946–7 to £54,504 in 1957–8, but the largest part of this increase came from central and local government grants for specific projects, while income from subscriptions and donations available to meet general expenditure only increased from £10,391 to £18,829 during this period. As a

[1] *Report of the Working Party on Social Workers,* Ministry of Health, HMSO, 1959.

result the annual deficit fluctuated between £750 and £27,562, and had been increasing for four consecutive years at the time of this study. It was covered, thanks to a large but unpredictable flow of legacies, and net assets actually rose slightly. But to maintain this position the Treasurer was compelled to demand repeated economies.

During the decade after the war the FWA carried out successive reviews of its functions and administrative structure, and reduced the number of its Area offices—and hence its caseload—from twenty-one to seven. In 1947–8 it received 17,433 new applications for help; by 1955–6 this number had fallen to 4,059 and then continued at approximately this level.

Although the attempt to organize procedures for 'case consultation' among the staff of Area 4 was only a minor aspect of the general course of development outlined here, it nevertheless constituted a central thread in the story. The COS had provided for consultation through 'case committees' in each Area which controlled the distribution of material help and supervised the work of the staff. Since committee members were often attracted to devote their time to this task by the opportunity it provided for first-hand contact with practical social work, and since Area Committees were supposed to be ultimately responsible for their Areas' debts, the Case Committees had compelling reasons for supervising the work of their staff closely. But the assumptions and outlook underlying this system had become unacceptable to many in the FWA—particularly among the new generation of trained social workers. Thus the search for new methods of consultation was prompted by a determination to work out new policies and conventions, to improve social work practice, to provide the stimulating and progressive professional environment that would encourage the new training courses to send their students to the FWA, and to attract graduates from such courses to join the staff. But the structure and traditions of the FWA could not easily accommodate consultants or supervisors, and the financial resources to employ such people were hard to come by. This case therefore throws a good deal of light on the general progress of the Association at this time and cannot be understood unless that broader context is kept in mind.

'Case Consultation' in Area 4

The FWA Area that forms the basis of this study was the product of a series of amalgamations. In 1949, after the first of these, its territory had a population of 65,000 and its staff of one senior caseworker and two juniors dealt with 1,017 new applications for help during the following year. At the end of 1950 its territory was extended again to cover two more Boroughs, providing a total population of 238,000, and the same number of staff dealt with a little over 800 new applications during the following year. In 1954 parts of two neighbouring Areas were incorporated to give Area 4 a population of 650,000 from which 689 new applications were dealt with in the following year by six trained workers, one of whom left halfway through the year. These figures showing the increasing territory to be covered, and the falling case-load (falling for the office and, even more strikingly, for its workers) indicate the changing character of the Area's work which was becoming more selective and intensive.

The amalgamation of 1954 was more than just another in the series; it was part of a bigger reorganization that followed a comprehensive reappraisal of the FWA's aims and methods. The new Area, with an office in Myddleton Square, was one of two centres set up at this time to experiment with new ideas about social work and the organization of a family casework service. Its paid staff of six trained caseworkers was larger than the FWA had ever envisaged before, though the size of the Area's population was equally unprecedented. These staff had been chosen to form a 'progressive' team of experienced workers, sympathetic to the aims of the new centre. All had volunteered to take part in the experiment.

In a paper presented to her committee some years later, the Area Secretary described features of the old COS from which she and her colleagues wished to break away. 'The responsibility for ensuring that clients were deserving seemed to override the normal regard for the rights of the client as an individual.' '. . . there was a general assumption that the Committee knew what was best for a client . . . (and there were) definite standards in the minds of Committee and workers as to right and wrong.'[1] Clients were usually interviewed in rooms occupied by other workers and clients; they were asked to name two referees who would substantiate their statements, and some checking up was done without seeking the clients' consent—with the Public Assistance Committee and the Mutual Register of Assistance, for example. (Consent seems generally to have been sought, however, for inquiries among employers, landlords and others outside the social services.) Emphasis was placed upon material circumstances and honest, upright behaviour, rather than upon feelings, and relationships. Cases were often dealt with by more than one worker in order to maintain

[1] Mary Keenleyside: 'Development in Casework Method', *Social Work*. (October 1958, Vol. 15, No. 4, p. 516.)

'impartiality'. She felt that plans had been made *for* people, not *with* people.

At that time some workers formed the opinion that more attention should be paid to the feelings and motives of clients and social workers alike. They wanted to learn more about human behaviour, and make more deliberate and effective use of the relationships that developed between clients and workers. This change in outlook was linked with the spread of knowledge about psychology and psychiatric methods. In a second paper presented to the committee,[1] another member of staff outlined three principal ideas used in the new approach to family case-work: the influence of unconscious forces upon human behaviour, the importance of childhood experience in determining adult personality, and the sexual origins of much human feeling. These ideas, together with an appreciation of psychological mechanisms such as 'projection', 'reaction-formation' and 'identification', were used to seek a deeper understanding of the client's needs and to attempt a solution of his problems through a controlled, professional relationship with the social worker.

The development and application of these ideas called for careful thought and expert guidance—guidance of a different kind from that provided by the weekly meetings of Case Committees still operating in several Areas. This had been recognized in 1953 in the report of a Reorganization Sub-Committee which led to the establishment of the new experimental offices. The sub-committee quoted Dr Young-husband ('Modern casework involves practising casework under super-vision and good supervision necessarily implies good casework is being done in the agency') and described consultation and supervision as 'the two essentials for good casework practice'; 'neither of these is adequately provided for in the present structure of the Association'.

These recommendations, which dealt with many other matters besides, were accepted after a good deal of argument and modification. In February 1954, just after the new Area 4 was established, a Super-visor/Consultant was appointed to work from the Central Office. (Some Area Secretaries were still uneasy about the implications of the term 'supervisor'.) This step was facilitated by two other developments. The Association hoped for support from the Home Office which eventually agreed to contribute to the Supervisor's salary on the grounds that her work would provide tuition in marriage counselling. Meanwhile plans were being made for the establishment of a new

[1] S. I. Briskin: 'Casework and Present Day Trends', *Social Work*. (October 1958, Vol. 15, No. 4, p. 521.)

training course for social workers at the London School of Economics and Political Science; the Association and the School were hoping to establish training centres in Area Offices for students on this course, and a Supervisor could help to achieve these aspirations.

The Supervisor/Consultant, a psychiatric social worker who continued at the Central Office until February 1957, was asked to devote most of her attention to the five 'ordinary' Area Offices and the two larger experimental offices saw little of her. Her appointment meant that some decision had to be taken on the future role of the Case Committees, with whom responsibility for case decisions had hitherto rested. Areas were left free to work out their own plans: to retain, modify or abolish their Cases Committees, or to supplement their work with case conferences held with the Supervisor/Consultant or other experts. At a Domestic Meeting called in April 1954 (at the request of Area 4) to discuss the Committees, the Chairman reaffirmed the Administrative Council's opinion that adaptations to new conditions were essential, but that Areas wishing to maintain their Case Committees should be free to do so. During the next two years the Aims and Policy Committee watched the variations in practice that developed in the Areas, but although experiments with case conferences were judged to have been very successful, no pressure was brought to bear on those Areas which still preferred to submit their cases to the decision of a lay committee.

The staff and committee for the new Area Office at Myddleton Square was drawn from three different Areas. One of these had followed the traditional aims and methods of the Association, in another there had been greater willingness to consider new departures, and the third provided many of the staff and committee members who had been most active in working out new ideas. The two post-war Secretaries in this third office had been unusually able and energetic, and had done much to win the co-operation of their committee. Nevertheless the committee had retained its decisive power and exercised it when necessary. In 1951, for instance, it refused to allow the staff to attempt intensive casework and provide help with household management among 'problem families' since their numbers and training were not considered adequate for this work. Their Chairman (who later chaired the new Area Committee) had had considerable war-time experience in another voluntary agency—the Personal Service League —and she had been drawn to the FWA by her interest in casework. She had herself worked in the Area for a time as a trainee, and she was an active member of the Administrative Council and several of its committees, including the Reorganization Sub-Committee of 1953.

Staff from all three Areas had attended discussion groups on case-work arranged at various times since 1948 with a psychiatrist, a psychiatric social worker on the staff of the London School of Economics, and staff of the Tavistock Clinic. The Area Secretary had been encouraged by this introduction to the application of psychiatric principals in social work to take a year's course in advanced social casework at the Tavistock Clinic, returning in time to take over the new Area.

Three months before the new Area opened, the staff appointed to it began regular consultative meetings with a specially appointed worker. In August 1953 the General Secretary of the FWA had attended a United Nations Seminar in Italy, and had there met a member of its staff—a Hungarian-born American caseworker and university teacher then working in Europe on a Fulbright scholarship. He was impressed by her teaching ability, and on his return proposed that the Council should appoint her as a temporary consultant to the staffs of the two experimental areas. She began work in October 1953, three months before the amalgamation took place, and continued until the following May. She held weekly group sessions, lasting about two and a half hours, for the staff who were to be transferred to Myddleton Square. Her final report shows that she found it necessary to give consultation that was both broader in scope and more precise than she considered usual by American standards, since the staff needed to be taught something of the psychology of normal human behaviour, pathological behaviour and psychosomatic illness, in addition to casework tech-niques. She also found much uncertainty among the staff about future goals and prospects.

The group based their discussion on cases prepared by the workers and circulated in advance of the meetings. The consultant also read the case papers. Afterwards the workers responsible for the cases discussed made a summary of the discussion which was checked by the con-sultant and attached to the case papers. The topics considered included material relief-giving, the nature and use of relationships, and the psychological mechanisms underlying human behaviour. There were in all twenty-seven meetings, two on intake procedure, two and a half on statistical techniques, one on material assistance, one on unmarried mothers and one and a half on a self-evaluation of the group; the remaining nineteen dealt with case material and points arising from it.

The consultant felt she ought to have continuous contact with the workers in order to create the mutual trust without which it was virtually impossible to teach or to learn; she also tried to gain a thorough knowledge of the organization and the workers in it. She concluded that the experiment had proved stimulating—workers had acquired a good deal of knowledge and had consolidated their considerable previous experience. In this sense they were more confident of themselves and of the aims and value of their profession. But the process of acquiring knowledge and developing new techniques in place of rejected ones, involving critical self-examination, produced considerable anxiety, and for this reason the consultant considered it necessary for the staff to have continuous and close supervision and more teaching. While she considered group sessions better for some things, a more satisfactory integration of theory and practice would be achieved by individual supervision. She was firm in asserting that supervision 'properly conceived and executed does not undermine self development and self reliance, but enhances it by giving it guidance and encouragement...'

When the new Office was set up the staff persuaded a majority of the Committee to do without a Case Committee. Instead members were invited to serve on a 'Cases Advisory Panel' whose advice the staff could seek when necessary. In fact the Panel was infrequently used during the first year and thereafter fell into abeyance. In general, decisions about cases were left to the staff, after discussion with their consultant or in their own weekly staff meetings. This decision was referred to the Central Office and the General Secretary advised the Area that under the Constitution cases on which £35 or more were to be spent must be referred to the Area Committee, but that its approval could if necessary be regarded as automatic. Some Committee members still felt strongly that the change was unwise, both from the casework point of view and because it would lose local support. At least one member refused to serve on any committee whose role was advisory rather than executive. The Area staff were worried by this division of opinion, and hence asked for the Domestic Meeting mentioned previously. The Area's decision to keep decisions on cases in the hands of the staff was not seriously challenged after that, but the difficulty of maintaining the interest and full co-operation of a lay committee which had no direct contact with casework remained a source of concern.

When the temporary consultant left, the staff of Area 4 felt strongly the need for further support and teaching and asked for more group sessions with additional individual supervision—though they were aware of greater confidence in themselves and in their ability to help clients. They still felt embarrassed by the giving of material help, realizing that such help was sometimes necessary and that it could be given constructively within a casework plan, but still feeling hampered by attitudes towards the provision of material help which stemmed from the days when 'relief-giving' had been a symbol of traditional cos policies. They also felt a need for help in developing satisfactory methods for their initial 'intake interviews' and for recording the work done on each case. The freedom gained by abolishing the Case Committee brought new and heavy responsibilities, for social workers alone now had to decide whom to help and whom to turn away, what help to give and what to withhold. Many of the anxieties and uncertainties they expressed at this time centred on these questions.

These views were reported to the Administrative Council and its Training and Selection Committee, together with an outline of two experiments the Area proposed to make—an analysis of intake interviews over the next three months, and the introduction of an appointments system fixing the time and duration of all but emergency interviews. Lack of funds and suitable personnel made it impossible to replace the Consultant when her contract ended in May 1954. The Supervisor/Consultant at Central could provide no help and for a while Area 4 was left to fend for itself. The staff derived a certain amount of support from their own weekly meetings where all matters concerning the Area were discussed: office administration, statistical and recording techniques, casework skills, cases, and policy involving relations within the Association and with outside agencies. The focus of these discussions varied with changing needs: when consultation was not available, discussion of cases predominated, although a good deal of thought was devoted to the analysis of new cases and recording processes. A recurrent topic for staff discussion throughout the period was the function of the Area Committee.

In September 1954, the Administrative Council was informed of negotiations between the FWA and the Institute of Almoners (one of whose representatives had been a member both of the Council and the Aims and Policy Committee) to obtain a grant from the Sir Halley Stewart Trust to finance a joint experiment in supervision, for which the name of an American casework consultant was put forward. She accepted the appointment for only eight months but at that time there were hopes of another American—a Fulbright scholar—being found to take her place. This project, while designed to meet the needs of the experimental Areas, was equally a reflection of the FWA's determination to maintain and develop its role as a major training body for caseworkers, both for its own staff and for students sent by the universities. The necessity for the FWA to offer two centres capable of providing training and supervision of the calibre required by the new course begun at the London School of Economics in October 1954 had been a strong argument in favour of the creation of the two experimental offices. But the Secretaries were not clear whether the new supervisor was to supervise them or train them to supervise others. Like other measures promoted by the Central Office, it was intended to do both, for the Association wanted to build up a group of supervisors among its casework staff.

Area 4 had hoped to receive both individual supervision and group sessions. After preliminary talks with the staff the new Consultant decided on the latter for the ten FWA caseworkers and the four almoners involved. She did this because the FWA staff already had experience of working in groups, and quicker results would thus be achieved in integrating theory and practice (speed was important because of the LSE students who were about to arrive), and because tuition in supervision was particularly important for the almoners.

This programme, she reported, provided 'consultation'—rather than 'supervision' in the American sense of the word. In America, 'the supervisor is a fellow member of the staff who has considerable administrative responsibility for supervisees and their work as well as that of teaching students and beginning workers and/or helping more experienced workers in their continuing professional development'. That is to say she is an administrator and policy-maker as well as a teacher. The second consultant was at least as skilled in administration as in casework, and she was able to help the staff clarify a number of administrative problems. The topics covered included the classification of cases and an experiment carried out in analysing new applications for help. The consultant pointed out that caseworkers were tending to overestimate the psychological factors in family tensions and to play down social factors. The caseworkers were ready to acknowledge this, but found it difficult to share the supervisor's horror at the poor standards of living considered acceptable by the FWA. American standards of material well-being prompted her to be more generous with material help than seemed realistic to them. They agreed, however, that research was needed to help them in assessing family budgets. The supervisor also argued that many of the Association's difficulties arose from the fact that it had incomplete control over the funds available for its work and an inappropriate administrative structure.

She approved the new aims of the FWA and, 'since organization and administration are so closely related to creating the proper "climate" in which casework can grow and develop', suggested a thorough reorganization aimed at 'strengthening and clarifying lines of responsibility'. 'In the present structure it may be inevitable that there will be feelings of separateness and rivalry which are not conducive to growth and progress.'

In June 1955 the consultant returned to the USA and Area 4 was once again left without supervision, although still feeling greatly in need of it. Cases came to the fore again in the discussions at staff meetings and the Area Secretary began to devote one hour a week to each of her social workers in order to discuss their work. This was an approach to supervision in the American sense, but it increased the heavy responsibilities she already carried in her own casework, in supervising students and administering the Area Office. The burden borne by Area Secretaries had been an increasing problem for a number of years; as early as July 1948 the suggestion had been made in the Council that each Area should have an administrative as well as a casework Secretary. By taking on a bigger Area Office and supervising students for the LSE the Secretary was compelled to abandon half her own casework. One social worker had left the new office six months after its creation and had never been replaced, so the Area did not have the full complement of staff planned for it. Various attempts were made to relieve the Area Secretary, by appointing an administrative worker (who left after a month, partly owing to the small salary she was paid), and by distributing some of her more routine duties among the senior staff. The latter arrangement was only partly successful, for senior workers also had little time to spare, and additional difficulties arose from the strain of experimental work on a small group in unsettled circumstances which made it hard to develop a smoothly operating team.

In July 1955 the Central Office suggested that Area 4 might receive supervision from the caseworker who had run the Association's Problem Family Project and was now on the regular staff of another Area. Area 4 considered that their supervisor should ideally be a part of their own casework team, but since this worker was known to be highly skilled and in any case there seemed to be no alternative, they welcomed the suggestion although she would not be available until the following January. Later in the year, however, it was found that her commitments were too heavy to permit this extra work, and the Area was again left without any prospect of help.

Early in June 1956 the Area Secretary talked to the General Secretary about the possibility of getting supervisory help from the Family Discussion Bureau, a marriage counselling agency originally established by the FWA in 1948 in collaboration with the Tavistock Clinic to whom it was about to be transferred owing to lack of the financial resources required for it. With the Bureau would go the Home Office grant for marriage counselling services which helped to maintain this work, and the FWA was anxious to qualify independently for such a grant by virtue of the Areas' work on marital cases. The Secretaries' Meeting sympathized with this aim, and was generally eager to increase skill in marriage counselling. In July they discussed the matter with a worker from the Bureau who suggested something on the lines of the group they ran for a number of psychiatric social workers in Middlesex.

The Home Office was prepared to regard such supervision as a qualification for a grant, and the Family Discussion Bureau was willing to undertake the work, and was interested to compare this type of training with the practical course given in their own office. The Area staff were not entirely happy with the proposal—it seemed to them an expensive and inadequate substitute for what was really needed. Preliminary talks with FDB workers did not altogether remove their doubts, but the Area Secretary persuaded her colleagues to make a three months' trial from November 1956. Two members of the Bureau staff were to take a group weekly for one and a half hours' discussion of problems arising from difficult marital cases. One of these workers had spent ten years with the FWA as an Assistant Secretary and had transferred to the FDB when it was first started.

The staff of Area 4 then reorganized their own weekly meetings, and decided on a 'work plan' which they hoped would lead to better formulation of goals and more disciplined thinking. In this move they had been influenced by a Canadian casework tutor who had been running short courses at the London School of Economics that year. When the FDB group had been running for three months an attempt was made to assess its value. The caseworkers were still unsure—they felt there was too strict a limitation to marital cases and too few general implications were studied, and they were still worried about problems of relief-giving. They tentatively suggested a further trial period of three months. The FDB workers, on the other hand, felt the group was going well, and was useful from their own standpoint in throwing light on the treatment of marital problems in a general casework setting. Indeed, they were now inclined to think that the best preparation for marriage guidance work lay in specialized training of experienced caseworkers drawn from a general social work agency. The Area Office staff, strongly encouraged by their Secretary, 'rather lamely' agreed to continue group discussions of all kinds of personal relationship problems until the end of the University year. During the following months the group became much more effective, and by the end of the session the staff decided unanimously and with enthusiasm that it should be continued indefinitely after the summer break. (The FDB worked to university terms.)

During the year the Council's Selection and Training Committee had examined the whole question of supervision and concluded that group supervision best served the needs of the FWA. The Central Supervisor/Consultant's contract expired in February 1957, and at her own request it was not renewed. It was agreed that the duties and responsibilities attaching to the post at that time were too great to be borne by one person. The post had been advertised with revised duties and a suitable applicant found—a worker from the FDB—but by then a thorough-going review of the work of the Association had been authorized by the Council, and the appointment was therefore left in abeyance until the review should be completed. However, the applicant from FDB agreed to take over for a while a weekly case conference group in one of the Areas: and Area 7 (the second experimental Area) after a period of 'consolidation' without supervision, had arranged individual supervision at the Tavistock Clinic for its four senior case-workers, but now wanted to set up a group similar to that in Area 4.

The Selection and Training Committee discussed plans for setting up four groups—three covering all Areas, and one for workers supervising junior staff. The latter had to be dropped for financial reasons, but the other three came into operation in the autumn of 1958 when Area 4 was joined by Area 3's staff for its group meetings with FDB workers, who also started another group with Areas 6 and 7. The other three Areas combined in a group led by a psychiatric social worker from the Tavistock Clinic.

Meanwhile Area 4 had been discussing the problem of its Area Secretary's overwork. She raised the matter with her Committee in October and November 1957, dividing her duties into the delegable and non-delegable, and proposing that the former be taken over by an Administrative Secretary. The Committee sympathized strongly with her, but were worried about the status such an officer would have, and the general feeling was that administration should remain under the control of a caseworker. A working party from the staff was set up to consider the problem, and their findings referred back to the Committee, who then submitted a plan to Council for the appointment of an administrative officer who should not only take over routine office matters from the Area Secretary and be the office manager, but should be able to speak with authority on casework, and act as a public relations officer. A long argument about the financing of this plan ensued—the Area claiming that it could find the money from a legacy recently made to it, and the Administrative Council and its Finance Committee pointing out that all the Association's resources would be needed to weather yet another financial storm that was blowing up at this time. Eventually an outside source of funds was found to back the experiment, and the Administrative Officer—a social worker trained in the new course at the London School of Economics—was appointed in the autumn of 1958, at the time this study was being completed. At the same time a review of the Association's aims and organization —the third major review since the war—was beginning.

Conclusion

This account of the development of case consultation is a confusing and inconclusive story. Had any other aspect of the FWA's work been examined the result would probably have been the same, for the Association itself was in a transitional stage.

Several things had been happening at once. The Association's case-load had shrunk and the needs to be met were changing, owing to rising living standards and the development of other social services. The staff found that more of their work had to be devoted to dealing with intractable personal problems calling for more skilled treatment based on a deeper understanding of human behaviour. Wider developments in the social work profession encouraged some of the staff to seek opportunities of improving their knowledge and practice, particularly with the aid of psychoanalytic insights. It may be, too, that their clients expected more considerate and sensitive treatment than they did in the past; such a development would be in line with a trend to be seen in many other spheres—in the growing interest in 'labour relations', 'public relations', 'mass communications' and the elaboration of 'service industries' of all kinds, as well as in the development of the social services. Advances in knowledge about human behaviour and motivation, mostly made before the war, have spread to a wider audience and gained wider application since the war, in social work as in other fields. As the Association's staff assumed more of the responsibilities originally borne by voluntary committee members, many of them became increasingly concerned about the inadequacy of their knowledge. Their search for expert guidance and training followed from all these developments. And when such help was provided it reinforced the trend, extending both their knowledge and their awareness of ignorance, and whetting their appetite for further study and more critical evaluation of their own work.

Throughout this period the FWA was engaged in a continuous struggle to redefine its functions and reorganize its structure—a struggle conducted under the shadow of bankruptcy and amidst repeated attempts to economize. Each of the groups set up to reappraise the FWA's aims and methods reached broadly similar conclusions: family casework ought to be the FWA's main function; there should be fewer Area offices, and each should have a larger and more highly trained staff who should bear full responsibility for decisions about casework; and skilled supervision should play an important part in these developments. But although a number of steps had been taken in these directions, the most striking thing about the FWA's attempts to reorganize itself was the cycle—repeated every two or three years—of crisis, reappraisal, discussion, minor modification and crisis. Why was progress so slow and uncertain—in the development of supervision as in other spheres?

There seem to be several reasons for this. It was repeatedly pointed out that the development of new and more effective forms of casework among people whose needs were not adequately met by the large statutory services was a natural evolution of COS traditions. This was true. But several aspects of this development were peculiarly difficult to reconcile with these traditions. It concentrated the agency's resources on helping the kind of people whom the COS would often have rejected as 'unhelpable' or 'undeserving'; it called for increasing reliance on paid staff and a restriction of the powers of the voluntary, 'lay' committees which had formed the backbone of the COS; it conferred increasing power on the Central Office; it cost money, and compelled the Association to collaborate increasingly closely with government, and with bodies such as the London County Council and the London School of Economics—institutions which had in the distant past been the spiritual homes of some of the COS's most formidable opponents.

In considering the FWA's response to these dilemmas it must be remembered that the Association was a federation of Area Offices, financially dependant upon a Central Office, but never completely subject to central direction. The jurisdiction of Area and Central organizations had never been precisely defined; each Area had financial resources of its own and was encouraged to raise money for itself, but in the last resort the resources of all Areas could be called on to pay the Association's debts. Thus disputes about the Areas' freedom to spend their 'own' money and disputes about the Central Office's powers to appoint and move caseworkers continued throughout the period covered by this study—and indeed throughout the lifetime of the cos. Generally speaking, the Central Office tended to exercise most power at times of financial stringency and the Areas gained greater freedom once each crisis was past. The Areas with the largest resources and those individuals noted for their capacity to raise money held a stronger hand that others.

Differences in outlook and training meant that different people— among staff and committee members alike—reacted in different and sometimes conflicting ways to proposals for reform. 'Lay' committee members had little opportunity to test the new methods or convince themselves of their effectiveness; and the traditions of the Society with which they were familiar—the network of small local offices, the discriminate giving of material relief, the judgement of 'character' (with honesty, respectability and independence their recurring theme) —were all called in question by these new methods. The Chairman of Area 4, who was noted for her support of the 'progressives' within the Association, said that she herself would probably not have joined the FWA had it not been for the opportunity of serving on a Case Committee. Others who lacked her faith in the new methods were much less willing to abandon the old. The FWA was passing through a phase to be seen at one time or another in many services. It was about the beginning of the last century that the distinctive roles of 'professional' and 'lay' workers were recognized and established in civil engineering services building roads and bridges; the schools and public health departments followed suit later, and many branches of social work— beginning with the psychiatric and medical social workers—are now passing through a similar phase. It is significant that many of the committee members who took leading parts in working out new policies within the FWA were themselves professional workers (predominantly psychiatric social workers and almoners). Their role was criticized by some of the 'lay' committee members who at Administrative Council meetings in 1958 argued (unsuccessfully) that members who held staff positions in other social services should not be permitted to serve on certain committees. This criticism was not accepted at the time, but it was undoubtedly true that the FWA's attempt to incorporate new trends of thought in its management by appointing members of its own professional staff and staff from neighbouring statutory services to its Central and Area Committees sometimes led to a confusion of roles and an unhelpful identification of certain viewpoints with particular personalities or interests.

As in other federations of diverse local units (the Labour Party for example) the fact that a decision had been reached at one level of the administrative structure did not deter exponents of the defeated point of view from raising the issue again at other levels and in other committees: the primary loyalties of the members of the Association's numerous committees were often attached to the particular Area or the particular branch of the FWA's services they had been chosen to 'represent'. Such a system calls for exceptionally consistent and compelling leadership; those responsible for managing the Association could not rely on formal authority or a unitary hierarchy to impose decisions. Thus the fact that the FWA lost several of its key senior officers in the mid-1950's may help to explain why progress was somewhat uncertain at this time. The Chairman of the Administrative Council, the President, the General Secretary and the Organizing Secretary all changed within two years.

Meanwhile no way of assuring financial stability could be found, and this made it difficult to pursue consistent policies. Voluntary sources of funds were inadequate to keep pace with rising costs. Modest grants were made by the Home Office, and some Area offices had occasionally received contributions of up to £250 from Metropolitan Boroughs, but it was not till the closing weeks of this study that the Association first made a more general appeal to the London County Council. The LCC had already given generous grants to other voluntary family casework services—notably the Family Service Units—but the FWA seems to have felt that a whole-hearted appeal to the local authorities should only be made as a last resort.

All these uncertainties affected the development of consultation. It was never accepted that regular and uniform procedures for consultation should be adopted throughout the Areas, and this form of help was regarded by many as an 'extra' to be provided when resources could be spared for it. Even the enlarged Area 4 may have been too small to justify an appointment for this purpose, but when a Supervisor was added to the Central staff she was unable to provide the help this Area needed. It was therefore impossible to work out and apply the 'best' methods of consultation; help had to be got from whoever happened to be available at the time, paid for with whatever funds could be found, and linked with other (and possibly irrelevant) developments in order to qualify for grants. Moreover, though caseworkers in Area 4 were agreed that the old Case Committee could not help them, they were uncertain what should take its place. When the Area Secretary herself began to provide supervision for her staff and students the resulting pressure of work became intolerable for her. Some new distribution of duties had to be worked out, and the appointment of an Administrative Officer was but the latest in a series of attempts to reorganize the structure of an Area Office in accordance with the needs of a modern social work service.

Consultation therefore developed in a groping and hesitant fashion, depending upon the help of consultants from other agencies, other countries, other professions or other branches of social work. Experiments in consultation received a mixed welcome from those they were designed to help, and when they came to an end altogether new procedures had to be set up which might owe little to the lessons of previous experience. Yet, by one means or another, the Staff of Area 4 repeatedly returned to the task of learning more about their work and seeking guidance and support in their dealings with their clients, whether through staff discussions, supervision or other methods.

DISCUSSION

The principal features of this development and many of the problems it posed have already been considered. Here we discuss some of its more general administrative implications and draw comparisons with other studies in this series. Although the evolution of consultation in this Area Office was only a minor aspect of the FWA's history, it was so closely related to the development of the whole agency at this time that it must be considered in this context.

Post-war modifications in the work of the FWA were first brought about by external economic and social changes, but their implications were rapidly taken up and developed by some of the agency's staff and committee members. As in the Children's Aid Society and the London Children's Department, changes in aims and working methods depended on the application of increased time, manpower and skill to each case. In previous cases this was achieved by an increase in staff, but the resources of the FWA permitted no general increase in manpower. The same effect was achieved in Area 4 by an amalgamation of Areas and a considerable reduction in each worker's case-load. In other Areas, where earlier patterns of social work continued unchanged, case-loads were not reduced in this way. The broad and unspecific character of a social service's aims, noted in previous studies, again appears in this case: even the new definition of the agency's principal functions, quoted at the start of this report, was open to many different interpretations. As in other developments we have traced, the interpretations were hammered out in the course of day-to-day adaptations and improvisations, punctuated by occasional more general reappraisal and debate. The three main groups of factors playing a part in this process are again familiar: the influence of outside authorities controlling resources required by the agency—the Home Office, the Family Discussion Bureau and the University, for example —the aspirations and outlook of staff and committee members actually providing the agency's services, and changes in the demands made on these services. (We have paid least attention to the demands made on the service because they played a smaller part in the particular development chosen for this study; they were a product of many factors, including social conditions in the surrounding area, the reputation of local FWA offices, the links between the FWA and the large number of agencies referring cases to it—nearly 150 different agencies referred the 2,000 cases that were 'active' at the time of this study[1]—and the priorities applied by workers responsible for selecting the cases to be served.)

Features of its situation which rendered it particularly difficult for the FWA to combine these influences and make them a basis for a consistent and continuing evolution of its policies have already been identified. The objectives to be achieved were ill-defined and controversial. The Children's Department and the Children's Aid Society, considered in previous cases, were able to develop family casework as an *adjunct* to their principal, highly practical and widely recognized job of caring for children, with less anxiety about the need for consultation and supervision—though similar demands were expressed by staff working in those agencies, too. But the FWA's staff, lacking the security provided by a central, practical task of this kind, felt greater need for discussion, guidance and education. In the Area Offices that still confined themselves mainly to the discriminating distribution of material help—also a practical and clearly understood task—there was less demand for consultation. Meanwhile the objectives of the various interests playing a part in the evolution of the FWA's work, inside and outside the agency, could not readily be reconciled. As in other cases we have considered, there were discrepancies between the formal or 'manifest' explanations of the agency's work and objectives, the prac-

[1] *Review of the Family Welfare Association.*

tical or 'assumed' interpretation of these objectives, and the future aspirations of those concerned. But these discrepancies did not lead in a cumulative, reconcilable and smoothly evolving direction; they were often contradictory.

It is at this point in the analysis that we have learnt to look for the groups and individuals whose roles compel them to contend with such conflicting pressures and produce a fruitful synthesis or compromise. But the FWA's patterns of communication and decision-making proved particularly weak at this point. Some confrontation had to be achieved between the diverse approaches to family casework, and the many other interests within the Association—the Citizen's Advice Bureaux, the Old People's Homes Committee, the Information Service, experimental projects of various kinds and other services, all competing for a share of the same funds. Only at the level of the Administrative Council was this confrontation possible. The status and authority of such 'representative' bodies always tends to be uncertain in a voluntary association: a similar problem of sovereignty appeared in the Children's Aid Society. In the FWA a large Council was recruited in a manner designed to encourage people to represent rather than reconcile their interests, and further appeals from its decisions could then be made to the Domestic Meeting and, potentially, to the Annual General Meeting. The agency's 'federal' structure helps to explain why decisions were less authoritative, more cautious—and less disruptive—than those traced in the previous case.

Meanwhile the social workers in Area 4, like their colleagues in other studies, were passing through a phase of professional development in which they needed to identify the crucial and distinctive features of their work and concentrate upon strictly professional concerns. The structure of the Association might have been designed to encourage the less desirable features of this phase by shifting the consideration of more general questions, such as the priorities to be accorded to the agency's different activities and Areas, to a distant and indecisive forum. The consultations, staff meetings and supervisory sessions in Area 4 were not only a means of professional development but also an attempt to sort out these priorities at the local level, dealing frequently with intake procedures and the selection of cases, the role of the Area Committee, the principles to be adopted in providing material help, and so on. But if appropriate procedures for determining priorities in an agency's work are not available, decisions have nevertheless to be made—often in inappropriate places. The outcome of this continuing attempt to fashion new aims and methods, going on at the same time in many branches of the Association, emerged in the form of irreconcileable demands on the financial resources available—as it did in the case of the Children's Aid Society. This process inevitably transferred many of the ultimate decisions on the allocation of resources to those responsible for the Association's finances. The professional staff sometimes complained that decisions about the development of social work services were taken on the basis of irrelevant financial criteria, but the Honorary Treasurer retorted— justifiably enough—that he had at least to ensure that deficits on current account were restricted to a level which would in the last resort leave him two years' grace in which to wind up the Association and meet all its debts and obligations. If others could not restrict the Association's expenditure to this level, he had no alternative but to pose the problem himself, for decision by any authority capable of acting. Consultative and educational procedures for the staff in Area 4 were amongst the occasional casualties of this procedure.

Thus the development examined in this study was a central feature of the attempts made by the staff in one Area office to cope with changed demands on their service in the light of new ideas then developing throughout their profession. By gaining greater discretion in determining the selection and numbers of cases to be served, the methods to be employed and the aims to be adopted, these workers were able to make considerable changes in the character of their service. But the increased responsibilities they assumed in this way and the fundamental questions these developments posed about the ill-defined objectives of the service led them to seek new forms of guidance and new procedures for learning about their work. These new forms of supervision called for additional expenditure which could not be assured on a planned and continuing basis because the assumptions on which they were based were not generally understood and accepted throughout the agency. Effective procedures were not available at this time for reconciling the conflicting objectives of different branches and interests within the agency and for determining the priorities to be accorded to each. Procedures for consultation and supervision were nevertheless improvised in an intermittent fashion, largely as an adjunct to other activities and requirements of the agency. These and many other problems of the FWA were examined in the course of a major review conducted just after this study was made, and a major reorganization has since been carried through in an attempt to resolve them.

CHAPTER 12

FORMULATING A POLICY FOR
SECONDARY EDUCATION IN CROYDON

This study deals with an attempt to adapt a social service to changes in the demands being made upon it. But the major development proposed by the director of the service in response to initial expressions of public concern could not begin without the participation of the principal people providing the service and the consent of others capable of influencing its growth. Thus conflicts which emerged at a later phase in other cases we have studied had here to be resolved at the outset. This study traces the course of these negotiations and the parts played in them by the various groups involved. A growing circle of outside interests was brought into the debate and a determined drive for decisions rendered it difficult for the governing body of the service to maintain an independent standpoint or to formulate a fruitful synthesis from the diverse views presented to it.

THIS study deals with two attempts to recast the system of secondary education in a County Borough. The first took place between 1954 and 1956; the second began in 1961 and was still under discussion in 1964 when the study ends. The study was carried out by a Borough Councillor[1] and has the advantage—and possibly some of the disadvantages—of being based largely on a diary and on current records assembled by an active participant in some of the events to be described. Unlike most of the previous studies, this case deals with the preparation of plans for a new development, not with their implementation. These plans called for a wholesale reorganization of complex and firmly rooted institutions, a reorganization which could not be worked out gradually and pragmatically; major decisions had to be taken about the future structure of the system before any reform could begin. The case deals with negotiations, still in progress, which may eventually lead to new developments. The social services considered in most of the previous cases had something like a monopoly of the

[1] Kenneth Urwin.

particular type of service examined; in this case the Education Department was collaborating closely (and some of its schools were competing directly) with a parallel system of private schools, and these relationships with outside bodies played a considerable part in the story. Yet, despite these distinctive features, many elements of the story will already be familiar from the analysis of previous cases: the initial recognition of stresses calling for reappraisal of the system, the formulation of different—and sometimes conflicting—interpretations of this situation among groups with divergent frames of reference, the involvement of a widening circle of interests capable of exercising influence on the decisions to be made, and the concentration of pressures focussed upon the body responsible for those decisions—all these phases of the policy making process will be familiar. The way in which they were handled by the Education Authority provides distinctive variations on this theme, and may account for the Authority's failure—thus far—to bring about any major reform.

Croydon and its Secondary Education

Croydon has a population, according to the 1961 census, of 252,500: by the middle of 1963 this figure was estimated to have risen to 254,100 —an addition due to a birth rate that is well above the average for England and Wales. Croydon is an integral part of the London conurbation. Its centre lies ten miles south of Charing Cross. But, like West Ham and East Ham in the same conurbation, it constituted a separate County Borough for local government purposes at the time of this study. Thus its immediate neighbours—Beckenham and Bromley in Kent, Mitcham and Sutton in Surrey—had limited powers and were subject to the Kent and Surrey County Councils for many purposes. But Croydon's Council was responsible for all local government functions within its territory. Under the reorganization of Greater London government, due in 1965, the boundaries of the local authority are to be substantially enlarged.

The town is not merely a dormitory suburb of London. Despite its large commuting population, it has a strong commercial position in its own right. Its manufacturing industries include electrical components, computers and electronic gear, small cars, and so on—a variety of fairly specialized engineering enterprises. But commercial undertakings now hold pride of place. With the steep rise in rents in central London, more and more companies have sought out the office space which Croydon's own schemes of development have recently offered. In 1956 (when its existing office accommodation was almost negligible) the town promoted in Parliament a private Bill which triggered off major re-development in the central area. Early projects—the fruit of collaboration between the Council and private developers—coincided with the Government's growing determination to discourage further office development in Central London; and Croydon's stake has since grown to such an extent that the Location of Offices Bureau expects the town to rank as the fifth largest commercial office centre in the country by 1970—its office population, then numbering between 25,000 and 30,000, would be exceeded only by those of London, Birmingham, Manchester and Liverpool. As the developers include considerable shopping areas in their office blocks, Croydon also has a growing reputation as a shopping and service centre.

The town returns three members to Parliament and has since 1950 been represented by Conservatives, with majorities ranging in the 1959 Election from 6,000 to 10,000. The balance on the Borough Council swung to give the Labour group a slight edge in 1963, with twenty-five elected representatives to the Conservative-Independents' twenty-three. But the allocation of aldermanic seats prevented the Labour group from taking control.

The Council of Croydon is the accredited Local Education Authority—one of 146 in England and Wales. For most practical purposes the responsibilities of the Council are vested in its Education Committee, made up of eighteen Councillors and Aldermen. The terms of membership of the Education Committee differ from those for other Committees of the Council, in that its members serve for three years at a time, six being elected each year. The Committee normally meets every four weeks, and it has a number of sub-committees whose meetings also follow a regular cycle. These deal with Schools, Further Education, the Youth Service, Youth Employment, Reconstruction, and Finance and General Purposes. The agenda on each occasion is drawn up by the senior officers of the Education Department, normally after consulting the elected Chairman—though any member may request in advance that a specific item come up for discussion. The meetings of the Education Committee—but not of its sub-committees—are open to the public and the press. Exceptionally, as in the matter under review here, a special ad hoc sub-committee may be created, reporting direct to the full Committee. All policy recommendations must receive the final ratification of a majority vote in Council.

The Education Committee's professional advisers consist of administrators with substantial teaching experience, and a number of expert

technical officers. There is also a local Inspectorate. The Chief Education Officer's principal colleagues are the Deputy Education Officer
and the Chief Inspector. The Principal School Medical Officer, who
is also the Borough's Medical Officer of Health, is responsible for
medical matters. The Chief Inspector has a staff of five Inspectors, and
other senior officials include the Principal School Architect, two
Assistant Education Officers responsible respectively for Schools and
Further Education, the Supplies Officer, the Youth Officer, and the
Youth Employment Officer.

Education is compulsory from the age of five years. This means
that the Education Authority is responsible, under the 1944 Education
Act, for providing schools of different kinds for children from five to
the statutory school leaving age of fifteen. A considerable number
of children will choose to stay at school beyond this age, and the
Authority must provide schooling for those who want it until the
end of their eighteenth year. Croydon's experience in this respect is
important, for the proportion of the town's children staying into their
fifth, sixth and seventh year of secondary schooling is well above the
national average. Comparable figures for London, and for Boroughs
about the same size as Croydon are shown in the accompanying table.

PERCENTAGE OF CHILDREN REMAINING AT SCHOOL BEYOND
MINIMUM SCHOOL LEAVING AGE, 1963

*Numbers in age-groups shown, as percentages of
same groups at the age of thirteen*

	15-year-olds Boys	Girls	16-year-olds Boys	Girls	17-year-olds Boys	Girls
Croydon	64	54	35	26	27	10
London County	51	49	27	25	13	11
Leicester	38	28	20	14	12	6
Stoke-on-Trent	22	19	16	11	10	7
Newcastle-on-Tyne	34	31	17	14	9	6
Counties	44	42	24	22	12	10
County Boroughs	38	33	20	17	11	8
England	42	39	23	20	12	10

Source: Ministry of Education, *Secondary Education in Each Local Education Authority
Area.* List 69. HMSO, 1964.

In this table the figures refer to pupils for whom the Authorities had direct financial responsibility. The majority of these pupils were in the Authorities' own schools—the 'maintained schools'. A few of them had places, by the deliberate choice of the Authority concerned, in independent and direct grant schools[1] of the neighbourhood and their fees were paid by the Authority. In Croydon the population of children so placed in any year is over 5 per cent of the total number for whom the Authority is financially responsible: this relatively high figure indicates a marked wealth of opportunity in Croydon's own situation, for in and around the Borough are 9 independent and direct-grant schools, 5 for boys and 4 for girls, all of them with a long educational tradition, where the Authority contracts to take free places for some of its pupils. These places are allotted to children gaining a high position in competitive transfer tests set by the Authority in the last year or so of the primary school: every parent of a primary child can express preferences for particular schools in the secondary range, but the child's ranking in the transfer tests is the principal means of selection.

A number of parents choose to pay fees for education at secondary schools not provided by the Authority, either for religious reasons, or because they feel that private schooling has special advantages. These children may at any time transfer to a maintained school, but their placing will be at the discretion of the authority.

In this study we are concerned with the pattern of secondary education which developed in Croydon after the 1944 Act, and with Croydon's own evaluation of the selective processes which largely determined the placing of children within that system. Broadly speaking, this system is divided into three parts: Grammar, Technical, and Modern. Two 'maintained' grammar schools, one for boys and one for girls, were already in existence in 1944, and these were continued. As the school population grew, and as it became obvious that many more children could cope with work at least up to 'Ordinary' level, so other secondary schools were converted into grammar schools, further 'selective' schools (including technical schools) were created,

---

[1] An 'independent school' is one financed solely from endowments and fees for pupils. Normally no Authority would buy places at an independent school unless the school is a good one—at least being 'recognized as efficient' by the Ministry. The independent schools in which Croydon takes free places are 2 prominent boys' public schools (1 within, the other just outside the Borough boundaries) and 4 denominational schools, 1 Anglican (girls) and 3 Roman Catholic (2 for boys, 1 for girls). Normally 'direct grant schools' are one-time independent schools now receiving a grant from the Ministry of Education in return for an arrangement to receive free-place pupils (either 25 per cent or 50 per cent of entry) from Local Authorities. Croydon takes a substantial number of places at 2 such schools, 1 for boys and 1 for girls.

and finally 'academic' courses with 'O' level objectives were begun in a limited number of 'non-selective' secondary modern schools. This enlargement of selective education continued throughout the post-war period, and by 1963 there had been added to the two 'maintained' and one 'aided' grammar schools existing in 1944: five new grammar schools (ex-'central' schools), a selective school without a sixth form (ex-secondary modern), two technical schools with sixth forms, and academic courses leading to 'O' level examinations in ten secondary modern schools. By 1963 the thirteen-year-olds for whose education Croydon was responsible were distributed in the manner shown in the table opposite. In comparison with other authorities, Croydon had an exceptionally large number of children in independent and direct grant schools, and an average proportion in grammar schools; but the smaller numbers in intervening types of school left a proportion in the secondary modern schools that was also larger than average.

Each school has a considerable measure of independence, and the Authority is at pains to interfere as little as possible in their internal administration. Their development therefore reflects a delicate balance between head teacher and staff, parents and pupils, and the Borough Inspectorate. A Governing Body, normally composed of eight members headed by an Alderman or Councillor, is established for each school, and its members appointed every three years by the Council. Membership of these bodies tends to follow the lines of political grouping in the town, though non-political organizations may offer nominees to the Council. In the case of schools with a denominational background which are now aided or controlled by the Authority, members are appointed to represent the denominational interest. The duties of Governors are restricted mainly to the school, and they have no part in shaping the overall policy of the Authority, though they may legitimately comment on the application of that policy to their own school.

Behind these local groups intimately connected with each school—Council and Education Committee, Governing Body, administrators, teaching staff and parents—stands the Ministry of Education (since renamed the Department of Education and Science). The Minister has considerable powers to maintain standards in individual schools. The 1944 Act required him to 'secure the effective execution by local authorities, under his control and direction, of the national policy for providing a varied and comprehensive educational service in every area'. Thus every Authority had to produce a Development Plan, indicating in detail the siting, area and general character of its schools,

	Primary (all-age)		Secondary Modern		Technical		Comprehensive		Other Secondary		Grammar		Direct Grant		Independent	
	Boys	Girls	Boys	Girls	Boys	Girls	Boys	Girls	Boys	Girls	Boys	Girls	Boys	Girls	Boys	Girls
Croydon	0	0	67	69	8	*	1	1	3	4	16	20	2	6	4	1
London County	1	*	15	15	2	*	48	46	19	21	15	17	1	1	1	*
Leicester	0	0	73	71	6	0	0	0	6	7	15	22	0	0	*	*
Stoke-on-Trent	2	1	49	54	7	3	0	0	29	30	11	10	2	2	0	0
Newcastle-on-Tyne	4	6	55	51	17	18	7	7	0	0	13	14	4	3	0	2
Counties	2	2	65	64	2	2	6	6	5	5	19	20	1	1	1	1
County Boroughs	3	3	63	64	6	4	5	4	4	6	16	17	2	2	*	1
England	2	2	65	64	3	2	6	5	5	5	18	19	2	2	1	1

* Less than 0.5 per cent.

Source: Ministry of Education, *Secondary Education in each Local Education Authority Area*. List 69. HMSO, 1964.

actual and potential. But despite the intentions of the Act, a Development Plan has no force in law. Section 12 of the Act, which empowered the Minister to make 'local education orders', has not been applied. Under Section 13 an Authority must consult the Ministry about any proposal to establish a new school or to close an existing school, and the Minister is empowered to veto or modify proposals of either type; and under Section 67 (4) he has on occasion prevented expansions of existing schools which appeared to him to amount to the establishment of a new school. Croydon was never certain whether its plan for reorganizing secondary education required the Minister's approval or not.

HM Inspectors of Schools—who are appointed by Order in Council and technically independent of the Ministry—provide advice and a means of informal consultation linking the Ministry and the Education Authorities. The Ministry used also to distribute the funds provided for the Authorities by the Treasury, but since the Local Government Act of 1958 this function has been exercised by the Ministry of Housing and Local Government whose general grants cover about 60 per cent of the Authorities' current expenditure on education.

A school has real, if limited, independence. But it operates within a framework determined by the Council and its committees, who depend on the advice of the administrative officers and inspectors in the town hall; it is influenced by the Ministry and the central government's inspectors, the professional associations to which its staff belong, the parents of its children, and sometimes an association of old pupils. All these bodies play some part in the study that follows.

The main features of Croydon's situation may be summarized before proceeding to the developments to be traced in this study. The Borough had a rapidly increasing and reasonably prosperous population, depending mainly on work in central London or in local commercial, service and engineering industries. A large proportion of these people were determined to secure the best available education for their children. (The demand for selective secondary education was much greater here than in the other two County Boroughs in the London area.) The selective procedures which determined educational opportunities—mainly in the children's eleventh year—had thus assumed major economic and social significance, and were followed with the keenest interest. The existence of an exceptionally large number of independent and direct grant schools in and around Croydon and the opportunity for securing free places in them, sharpened the comparisons made—by parents and teachers alike—between the relative merits of different secondary schools. The independent and direct grant schools provided a small but enormously important part of Croydon's secondary system, yet they were in no way under the Borough's control, and could only be aligned with any general reform by their own agreement. The Council might decide to reduce the numbers of children it sent to these schools, but their places could readily be filled from other sources. A considerable number of influential people in the town had themselves attended the better known schools in the district and could not regard debates about their future as an abstract or remote question of educational policy. The Borough Council and its officers worked in close proximity to the Ministry, and also to the London County Council—which at this time was pressing on with the creation of an entirely different pattern of secondary education relying mainly on comprehensive schools. Croydon's Council was jealous of its independence, but aware of national and regional developments which constituted a potential challenge to its own policies. These policies assumed the basic soundness of the structure bequeathed from the pre-war period, and were designed to provide an increasingly generous variety of secondary education within the framework of a conventional tripartite division between grammar, technical and modern schools—helped out at the 'top' end with places in the independent schools. This system was described by the Borough's new Chief Education Officer as 'the first thoughts of most Authorities on their obligations under the 1944 Act to make secondary education for all a reality'. What were to be Croydon's second thoughts?

First Attempt at a Reform

In July 1954 the Council accepted a motion put forward by two members of the minority (Labour) group. It read: 'As the number of grammar school places in Croydon is already below the national average both for boys and girls, the Education Committee is requested to inform the Council what steps it proposes to take—within, say, the next three years—to provide the extra grammar school places which Croydon obviously needs if it is to take its proper share in making provision for the education and well-being of the nation.' This proposition raised questions both about the quality of non-selective secondary schools and about the scarcity of selective places.

To this motion the Education Committee reacted in September with a preliminary report, prepared by its officers, indicating some limited steps which could help make good the deficiency in selective places; and in October it set up a special Sub-committee to review the grammar school situation on a broad front. Late in November a memorandum signed by the Chief Education Officer (who had held his appointment only a few months) and by the Chief Inspector was made public. The timing of its appearance was probably an accident, due to a leak of information to the local press, but the fact of its publication at a premature point—before even the Sub-committee had considered it—produced immediate difficulties. The document in fact put forward an imaginative scheme for amalgamating the sixth forms of grammar schools in Croydon to form a two-year 'Junior College'; this College would provide places for pupils from all the sixteen maintained schools in which 'O' level examinations offered access to more advanced work. The creation of such a College, it was argued, would result in the kind of economies of staffing and equipment which the situation in Croydon called for, and would afford students of sixteen to eighteen years a wider variety of courses than could be provided by any one secondary school.

The memorandum had not been discussed with any representative group of teachers. They were unaware that these ideas were being considered and it thus became a focus of contention in educational circles. The Chief Education Officer recognized that 'a revolutionary change from the present pattern of the English Grammar School' was being proposed. *The Times Educational Supplement* described the plan as 'a proposal to interfere with the best of our English schools to meet a particular difficulty'. The grammar school heads in Croydon wrote defensively: 'The sixth form is the backbone of every grammar school. Its standard reflects the standard of the school as a whole.'

Representative deputations of teachers—not all of them unsympathetic to the proposal—then met the Sub-committee. The following spring the Director of the Oxford University Institute of Education was invited (at the personal suggestion of the Chief Education Officer) to advise the sub-committee as a consultant. By November the subcommittee, having met seven times, had reached a considered (though not unanimous) opposition to the project, and this view ultimately prevailed in the Council debate. The Education Committee's report to the Council stressed that their Consultant had advised solely from the educational and not from the economic angle. It quoted him as favouring the idea of a pooling of teaching resources at sixth-form level, but as opposed to the plan as it stood. In a letter to *The Times Educational Supplement* the Consultant outlined his objections thus:

(a) A sixth form depends on continuity with what has gone before.

(b) Sixth form teaching is best given by those who are concurrently teaching at different levels.

(c) A sixth form should include opportunities for those who would never qualify for the intellectual hotbed of a Junior College.

(d) A feeling of responsibility and the exercise of authority is important in the intellectual development of a young person.

The Chief Education Officer had, of course, touched on some of these points in making his case. Thus he had argued that sixteen-nineteen year olds (with 'A' or 'S' level objectives) would be able to work most satisfactorily in a new kind of teaching institution. 'He or she (the sixteen-year-old) has emerged from the age of adolescence and can be said to have reached a stage of early manhood or woman-hood. It is usually in these years, when the young person is conscious of becoming an integrated adult personality, that the foundations are laid for real intellectual or cultural achievement in later life. For those who might aspire to first-class intellectual attainment it is quite essential that their education during these early adult years should be in com-petent hands, under the guidance of men and women of high intel-lectual qualifications.' The Chief Education Officer was prepared for sixth form pupils to get away from the often unacceptable idea of 'staying on at school'. 'They would,' he wrote, 'be going on to a college which might in a very short time be able to establish for itself a considerable cultural and intellectual reputation . . . The young adult of seventeen wishes to be treated as an adult and to have a different relation with his leaders from that of the adolescent . . . Five years in one school is long enough, and the growing personality is stimulated by changes of environment, so long as they are not too frequent.'

His memorandum had criticized the prevailing organization of sixth form work as wasteful of staff, space and equipment. Because of these defects, he thought, pupils were being refused their first choice of 'A' level subjects because facilities in their school were not available; and he suspected that some who left at sixteen might have given up because of the known difficulty of providing certain courses. While minority subjects demanded special attention, no school, he wrote, could afford to divert staff to take charge of them to the extent of arranging whole periods of individual tuition.

He entered an interesting caveat against any assumption by the grammar schools that they could emulate public schools in their sixth form work. (His own teaching experience had been gained in a well-known public school.) The fact was that the public school would always carry a sixth form proportionately larger. 'For reasons which are in large part historical, the grammar school, in competition with the large public school in gaining University places, is at a permanent disadvantage . . . One might use the touchstone of Oxford and Cambridge awards . . . In competition for these the pupil from an independent school has a better chance . . . This is not due to any prejudice on the part of the Universities in favour of certain schools . . . Nor, surely, could it be contested that the native ability of the boys at independent schools is higher than the others.' The advantage of large numbers, he suggested, accounted for the better quality of sixth form work within the public schools.

This proved to be a far from convincing argument, and the comparison with public schools served further to alienate grammar school opinion within the town. In fact, at local level the grammar schools might with some justice regard themselves as impoverished to the exact proportion that neighbouring independent and direct grant schools were enriched. For these latter received the considerable asset of able free-place pupils—almost certainly potential sixth form material of good calibre. The grammar schools, competing for good pupils and striving to offer opportunities for all-round development to all of them, could not avoid emulating the public schools in their approach to advanced work. The threat of 'decapitation'—as the loss of sixth forms came to be called—appeared devastating. As the grammar school heads wrote in a second brief: 'The sixth form develops in gifted boys and girls an astonishing maturity. A break at sixteen would cut across the intentions of the GCE course—which envisage "O" and "A" level work as part of the same continuous undertaking; would hamper the transition from an imposed discipline to self-discipline; and would mean a loss of roots without time in six terms to put down new ones.'

One corollary of the Junior College project in Croydon was that the heads of the non-selective schools might reasonably expect the Authority—if it accepted the proposal—to carry through a reappraisal of their part in the secondary pattern. On the one hand they might pillory—as some did—the anxieties which the grammar school heads expressed about the social effects of co-education (in the Junior College): one-third of the non-selective schools were co-educational. A majority of the non-selective heads welcomed the Chief Education Officer's plan. They argued that the more capable children in the non-selective range would merit still larger opportunities of achieving 'O' level standards and so of finding a place in the Junior College. They recognized that with this end in view the Authority would seek to strengthen their staffing and improve their equipment. However, their expectations could not be too sanguine. It had to be accepted that even with a radical change of policy in Croydon it would take a generation to bring all the older schools up to a reasonable standard in buildings and equipment. Moreover teachers do not live for ever. In default of tangible evidence that the Authority was able to plan extensive re-building schemes—and no such opportunity was open to any LEA—the grammar schools would maintain many of their preponderating advantages. There were those too who remarked that the Consultant had shown no enthusiasm for the demise of the grammar school: they regretfully summed up his intervention as that of a distinguished but remote Oxonian who, like the Devil invoking Einstein against Newton on another occasion, had shouted 'Ho'— and restored the status quo.

Thus the Council, at the end of this first series of discussions, acquiesced in very restricted change. The imminent closure of two Polytechnics provided room for a physical expansion of grammar school work, and Croydon's selective intake grew in 1956 and subsequent years to about 30 per cent of the age-group concerned. At the same time 'academic' courses were planned in certain of the non-selective schools.

Progress thus far may be briefly summarized. A new Chief Education Officer and his immediate colleagues took the opportunity provided by the Council's first serious expression of dissatisfaction with the secondary system to propose far-reaching reforms which would have created a new type of sixth form college at the cost of 'decapitating' the Borough's grammar schools. These proposals were supported by a considerable wealth of statistical—and emotive— argument. They provoked immediate opposition in the schools most obviously due to suffer from such a change, and after considerable discussion and a generally unfavourable report from an outside consultant they were abandoned. The arguments advanced so far were mainly derived from two fundamentally different points of view. Those concerned with the development of education throughout the Borough dwelt on the wider educational opportunities, the more efficient deployment of teaching resources, and the more acceptable educational environment which the reform would offer in the long run. Those concerned with the development of existing grammar schools dwelt on the serious damage such a reform would bring about in those schools in the immediate future. Many more arguments were to be advanced in subsequent years, but these basic differences in outlook still constituted the principal obstacle to agreement. Though the Council and its committees had been given a great deal of evidence to consider, no serious attempt had yet been made to achieve a reasoned reconciliation of views and interests among the schools themselves. Prolonged and detailed discussion of these questions would be required before any progress could be made.

A Second Attempt

Croydon's second investigation of its secondary education began at Committee level in 1961. This time the initial problems provoking discussion were different: they were the unreliable selection procedure, and the apparent waste of grammar school places. By now the principle and practice of competitive selection at eleven plus had been called in question in many parts of the country. Croydon's contribution to the national debate was to correlate transfer test results with the subsequent scores of pupils at 'O' level. This investigation showed how uncertain a predictor the eleven plus procedure was: there were disturbingly poor 'O' level achievements among grammar school pupils, and signs of good 'O' level potentialities among a limited number of children in non-selective schools. At the same time the Chief Education Officer's passionate interest in the Junior College scheme reasserted itself, and he tried to build a new and stronger case for the Junior College upon opposition to the eleven plus.

The papers prepared by the administration from 1956 onwards all showed concern at the quality of response to grammar school opportunity as evinced by those with a poor record in examinations for the General Certificate of Education. These enquiries deserve special mention. What the administration did was to establish its own yardstick of reasonable achievement within the grammar school. This was to be two or more passes at 'O' level in English Language, Mathematics, a Science, or a Foreign Language—so-called 'basic' subjects. Such a criterion can be challenged, but no other systematic method of evaluating the performance of grammar school children was seriously proposed. Those who felt that the yardstick of GCE success was a poor one would assert that to restrict the analysis to 'basic' subjects was even less revealing.

These points emerged from the analyses made by the Education Department:[1]

(a) In 1956 and 1957, only 10 per cent of maintained school entrants passed in the four 'basic' subjects.

[1] 'Secondary Education in Croydon. A Consolidated Report.' July 1962.

(b) In 1958, the figure was higher at 14 per cent, but there were 41 per cent who passed in one subject only or in none.

(c) The children taking free places in independent and direct grant schools did considerably better, on average, than those in maintained schools.

(d) When the assessment of IQS quoted at the time of the transfer tests was correlated with GCE 'O' level results five years later, the following pattern emerged for the maintained schools:

IQS AND 'O' LEVEL RESULTS

IQ level at transfer	Average passes in 'basic' subjects		Average passes in all academic subjects	
	Boys	Girls	Boys	Girls
127+	2·3	3·2	4·7	5·2
123-6	2·35	2·6	4·0	4·4
119-22	2·3	2·1	4·5	3·7
115-18	2·0	1·7	3·2	3·0
111-14	1·6	1·5	2·7	2·5
107-10	1·65	1·4	2·6	2·6
103-6	1·7	0·9	2·4	1·0
99-102	1·4	1·1	2·2	2·2

There is no reliable basis for a comparison between the results obtained in selective and non-selective schools. Until recently, for example, there had been no provision for foreign language work to 'O' level in non-selective schools. However, in one year, 1958, ninety-four pupils in non-selective schools took 'O' level subjects. The results achieved by these children are shown below. The ranking of the 'catchment' pupils in the original transfer tests had not justified any expectations of a useful result in 'O' level work five years later, yet they, and fifty-six other pupils, had achieved encouraging results.

	No. of children	Average passes in academic subjects	Average IQ
'Selected' for academic course	19	3·4	108
Recommended by Junior School Heads	37	3·2	107
'Catchment' pupils	38	3·2	100

Now a grammar school place at eleven plus was a prized social asset, and 84 per cent of Croydon parents opted for grammar school at the time of their child's transfer. But in the light of these findings the Chief Education Officer wrote in 1961: 'A considerable proportion of pupils in grammar and selective schools have failed to some degree in a curriculum which they might have been expected to tackle ... It might be held that unless after five years in the secondary school a pupil can obtain a pass in two or more of these basic subjects, he has not in the event justified his place in the grammar school or selective school course ... What emerges therefore is the need to retain flexibility within the secondary school course, since to make too rigid a division at eleven plus means subsequent wastage in both directions (i.e. children selected and failing to justify their selection, other children making a presentable showing in GCE work despite having been unselected).'

These reports, and the administration's recommendations based on them, went to a new Sub-Committee of the Education Committee which began seriously to consider the problem in June 1961. In April the Education Committee had asked for a general report on 'the state of the schools'. The sub-committee was made up of four members of the majority group and two of the minority. Their objective was to consider the whole character of secondary schools in Croydon and to propose some change in pattern. The trend of the administration's proposals was towards common secondary schools, capped as before by a Junior College; but there were sidelong glances at other possibilities of reform which came to assume greater importance as the discussions went on.

The Chief Education Officer submitted his reports to the Director of the National Foundation for Educational Research, and to the Director of the London University Institute of Education. In his comments, the former stressed the advantages of the large school—with eight form entry as a desirable size—and urged flexibility of curriculum, especially during the first three years of secondary education. The latter made written observations and visited Croydon—at the suggestion of the Chairman—to speak to the Education Committee. He was concerned that the present structure of secondary education fixed things too soon and too finally; he appreciated the merits of 'academic' streams in non-selective schools, but recognized the difficulties of making proper provision at the top end of secondary schools without a very large entry at their base. So (while disclaiming any intimate knowledge of Croydon's secondary pattern) he felt that: (a) four form entry common schools might be educationally satisfactory until choice of subjects had to be made at about fourteen plus; (b) some selection would have to follow 'O' level, and this fact might lead a pioneering authority towards a Junior College. To this extent, at least, he presented views at variance with those of the consultant who had advised the Council seven years before.

The Chief Education Officer was at this time endeavouring to drive matters rapidly to a conclusive point, urging the Sub-committee to make a recommendation about the general lines on which change in Croydon could be based, and leaving to future consultation with head teachers the detailed work of implementation. This was considerably further than the Sub-committee was prepared to go. The staffs of schools had at no point been officially advised of the administration's reports and had therefore been offered no opportunity to comment upon them. It was unthinkable that far-reaching decisions by the Education Committee could be envisaged while teachers remained entirely outside the discussions.

However, the draft of the report of the sub-committee in July 1962—incorporating most of the administration's findings and the views of the two consultants—was positive in its tone and detailed in its manner of presentation. It prompted conjecture that decisions had already been taken since it stated: 'They (the Sub-committee) consider that it should be the Council's policy to move progressively towards the pattern of a common school at the secondary school stage between eleven and sixteen, so that competitive selection at eleven plus may be suspended . . . They consider establishing a new pattern of work for GCE 'A' level and for University admission, and have returned to the proposal discussed seven years ago . . . for the pooling of this work for all maintained secondary schools in the borough.' The report included a sketch time-table by which the early stages of the plan could be made effective. Its publication gave rise to the widespread impression—shared by such journals as *The Times Educational Supplement* and the *Observer*—that the 'Croydon Plan' was being put into effect.

But the scheme outlined was prefaced by the words—'The Sub-committee have in mind . . .'—and when the report was presented to Council the Chairman of the Education Committee emphasized that no final decision was being sought. The Committee recommended discussion of the proposals with the Ministry of Education, and meetings with head teachers to consider both the principles involved in the proposals and the methods by which they might be implemented. The Chief Education Officer proceeded to make personal contact with heads of schools to acquaint them with the background to the whole enquiry.

At the beginning of the new term in September deputations representing staff in the schools moved in upon the Sub-committee. Initial reactions followed the same kind of alignments as in 1954–5. But public, as distinct from professional, comment was more favourable to change than it had been during the earlier debate. Thus the *Croydon Advertiser* declared: 'When seven years ago, we opposed the idea of a sixth form college in Croydon, absorbing and replacing the sixth forms of the existing grammar schools, we were wrong. It was a judgement based too much upon a sentimental attachment to the established order, too little upon an appreciation of desirable developments to meet new needs ... The arguments now put forward to support it are convincing, even, virtually, unanswerable.'

In all, four deputations met the sub-committee. They came from the Head Teachers' Association, from the National Union of Teachers, from the Joint Four Association—staffs of maintained grammar, independent and direct grant schools—and from the National Association of Schoolmasters. The Head Teachers' group, divided as it was along expected lines, could give no impression of unity: their representatives put forward divergent views, with the primary heads eager for the ending of competitive selection, the secondary non-selective heads supporting the tentative plan, and the grammar heads arguing the merits of a seven-year course and preferring—if change there had to be—fully multilateral or comprehensive secondary schools. The deputations from the Joint Four Association and from the NUT could claim near unanimity among their members—the former opposing the plan, and the second supporting it. But while the Joint Four ignored their dissentients, the NUT actually included in their deputation a grammar school spokesman to represent their minority viewpoint. The NAS speakers put individual rather than corporate points.

Written memoranda were also sent to the sub-committee. Some of these reflected the concern of the governing bodies of selective schools that their voice be heard. Others had a political orientation, and local ratepayer, Labour, Liberal, and Communist groups ventilated their judgements. A newly formed Croydon branch of the Association for the Advancement of State Education set up a working party which prepared an analysis of the Report, but considered it inappropriate to express an opinion on the merits of the scheme.

The most incisive statement opposing the plan for reorganization was prepared by the headmasters of two long established and widely respected boys' schools of Croydon, sharing the same well-endowed Foundation. The first Whitgift School was founded in 1600 by John Whitgift, Archbishop of Canterbury. In 1837, when national ferment about educational provision was beginning to grow, the Charity Commissioners began an enquiry into the school's work, and as a result a decision was made in 1853 to divide the school into a 'Middle' school and a 'Poor' school. The significance of these titles has long since faded. One (Whitgift School) is now independent, the other (Trinity School of John Whitgift) has direct grant status: both depend substantially upon fee-payers, the first to the extent of 90 per cent and the second to the extent of 45 per cent of its boys.

The Whitgift Foundation, by the very strength of its tradition, has come to claim a dominant place in the educational life of Croydon. Its Governors tend, in the main, to be closely identified with the civic life of the town, and the Chairman of the Foundation was for many years —in a different capacity—leader of the majority group on Croydon Council. The Council for its part nominates three Governors to the Foundation. Nevertheless, the two schools stand quite outside the sector of maintained schools and are in no way subject to the Council's control. It was to be expected that their headmasters would play a forceful part in the controversy.

One of the basic administrative problems facing a local education authority, they wrote, is to decide on the age at which to 'select' its pupils. They noted the diversity of practice in developed countries: if Western European countries still hold to selection about eleven, the USA and USSR select very much later—the USA, in effect, as late as the second year at University. The heads accepted the need for early selection if it met the ever-growing need for highly educated men and women, and they went on to argue that an alliance of independent, direct-grant and grammar schools was essential to this end.

They stressed that the Report contained two major propositions which did not cohere. The first dealt with the problem of 'overlap'— the discrepancy between eleven plus performance and 'O' level results among children selected and not selected. The authors of the Report clearly saw this overlap as cause for grave concern; but the heads replied that four-fifths of selective school entrants appeared to justify their places. The second proposition in the Report was its call for a major reorganization, and this, said the heads, could not be founded merely upon the problem of the overlap. Hence they argued that the Report was lame in its more important leg: for reorganization—especially in the drastic form proposed—could not be justified if Croydon's own analysis of its situation was all that could be found to justify it.

The Whitgift Heads saw the 'common school' as a direct threat to the proper education of Croydon's more able children. 'The Report,' they wrote, 'shows a lamentable lack of concern about the likely effect on the able children whose needs are so well met by the grammar school pattern. Social justice for them demands that they shall be put in as favourable a position academically as their counterparts in the independent and direct grant schools. There *is*, pace the Report, a type of child who can fairly be described as academic in the sense that his abilities and inclinations are, on the whole, mainly intellectual. How is their lot going to be improved by attendance at an unselective school? It is absurdly unrealistic to suppose that such a school, shorn of its sixth form, will attract the service of able graduates. The admirable general-degree man ... is not the answer for the abler child, who must if possible be taught by teachers whose academic horizons are as distant as his own will eventually become. The independent and direct grant schools work on this assumption, and, equally, nothing less than the best available is good enough for the grammar school child. In short, they need as lively a milieu as can be found for them ... Academic quality, which is more hardly won in the maintained grammar school than in the independent school, takes years to build up. To disperse it is folly.' They concluded that the age of eleven was by no means too early a point to find and encourage the abler child, and called for an extension of the practice of arranging later transfers at thirteen for those missing the first opportunity. (But Croydon's experience with late transfers, whether at thirteen or at 'O' level, has shown how difficult to operate this procedure can be. The brighter children in secondary modern schools are handicapped because they have not followed a full grammar school curriculum. Meanwhile the attempt to develop more academic teaching in these schools may be frustrated by the loss of their best pupils.)

This line of reasoning pursued by the Whitgift Heads served to reiterate in Croydon's situation a recent judgement of Sir Edward Boyle, Minister of Education, whose actual words they quoted with approval. 'The grammar schools are still the strongest and most valued elements in our system of state education ... We should not destroy them, but they in their turn must show themselves responsive to the times and must learn to deal with the less bright boys and girls, who can, none the less, gain by working in an intellectual atmosphere.'

The publication of this paper was an important stage in the discussion of proposals for a change. Yet it was significant as much for the areas of the Report on which it did not comment as for those on which it did. The Chief Education Officer, in a memorandum replying to the two heads' observations which he prepared for the Sub-committee, noted that a concern for 4,300 children in Croydon's grammar schools could apparently be advanced as a reason for ignoring the 31,000 other children for whom the Education Committee was responsible. He came more and more to base his own case upon the inequities of eleven plus selection. 'The concept behind the proposals is the absolute necessity in the state educational system of retaining flexibility in secondary education between the age of eleven and the normal school leaving age (about sixteen in Croydon) . . . The present pattern results in an alarming waste of latent ability and an inefficient use of teaching power.' He chided the Whitgift heads for their attachment to educational patterns designed to meet bygone social and economic needs. 'We are going through a period when the accepted social and economic pattern is disintegrating . . . The countries whose methods are disparaged in the Whitgift report, the USA and USSR, are the very ones who in their different ways seem to have grasped the significance of the present changes better than the older countries of Europe, and are forging ahead. For ourselves it is clear that overall educational standards have got to be raised higher than we have ever before imagined: and we cannot afford a system which does not leave the doors of educational opportunity open as long as possible.'

This written debate between the Whitgift heads and the Chief Education Officer went to the heart of the whole controversy. An analysis of the other memoranda received by the sub-committee reveals nothing quite as provocative. Save for a representative group of primary school heads, no one troubled to comment on the quality of the junior school in Croydon or tried to relate the secondary school to its junior school foundations. This may not be surprising as the whole exercise bore upon the future of the secondary schools, but the absence of any reference to the ethos of junior schools suggests that the task of preparing the child for transfer to secondary school—as distinct from helping him to follow a curriculum to an agreed level—was not seen to present any special difficulty. Several papers deprecated the effect upon individual children of competitive transfer testing. Thus, the Advancement of State Education group wrote: 'The use of a test for transfer at eleven plus imposes psychological strains on some children, mostly as a result of parental anxiety.' The non-selective school heads wrote of the tests as 'bringing a sense of failure and denial of opportunity to those who do not pass'.

The prospect of common schools in the Borough worried the grammar heads, particularly in view of the proximity of their competitors, the independent and direct grant schools. 'We shall have independent and direct grant schools providing one kind of education and one kind of staff, and common schools providing a quite different kind of education, with a different quality of staff.' Moreover, the loss of sixth forms would be irreparable: the connection between the sixth form and the rest of the school was held to benefit the sixth former, the pupil on his way to the sixth, and the pupil who was never going to reach the sixth. The non-selective heads, by contrast, had no fears of the common school concept. The schools, they argued, would be integrated social groups; there would be more effective deployment of staff; girls (in mixed schools) would have real opportunities of technical education for the first time; the ladder of attainment would be there for all who could to climb.

In October 1962 three members of the Sub-committee and the Chief Education Officer discussed their tentative plan with representatives of the Ministry of Education, among them the Under-Secretary of the Schools Branch and the Chief Inspector for secondary schools. The Ministry spokesmen indicated that Croydon's experience of difficulties in the grammar schools was by no means unique and did not in itself make a compelling case for the total abrogation of seven-year courses. They said there was not, in Croydon's presentation of its arguments, any integral relationship between its concern about the inequities of competitive transfer at eleven plus and its interest in the 'device' (the Ministry's word) of a Junior College. Further, as Croydon representatives already knew, the approach of reorganization in Greater London meant that a new London Borough of Croydon—including Coulsdon and Purley, then still part of Surrey—would be responsible for implementing any plans that might be agreed. Thus the final formulation of a scheme would have to wait upon the creation of the new Borough, whose members would be elected in 1964, and representatives of the existing Coulsdon and Purley area would at that point have a voice in determining both the principle and the detail of organization in the new Croydon's schools.

This point had not been lost on Croydon. It tended now to slow down the tempo of discussion. And a further development imposed new delay. The Chief Education Officer's health broke down, and he was intermittently absent over a period of several months. Eventually, in the summer of 1963, he had to retire from office on grounds of ill health. A new judgement—that of the Deputy Education Officer—was brought to bear on the situation: without prior commitment to any plan, but with increasing command of the issues to be resolved. He was appointed Chief Education Officer in November. He and a new Chief Inspector wrote an additional report in which four separate schemes of reorganization were set out.

These were: (a) the original proposal, i.e. common schools from 11 to 16 with a Junior College after 16; (b) a plan to model Croydon's pattern of schools on the Leicestershire experiment, with a break at 14; (c) a mixed scheme founded both on 11-14 year schools and on 11-16 year schools, to be followed jointly by grammar schools and a junior college; and (d) a proposition that existing schools could be grouped to form large multilateral units, with 9-12 form entry and sixth forms. By the end of the year the Sub-committee had asked the Chief Education Officer to concentrate his study on the second and third of these proposals, and to consider the additional possibility of one multilateral school with a seven-year course.

Under the Leicestershire scheme, existing non-selective schools in Croydon would become junior secondary schools for pupils from 11 to 14, and existing selective schools would become senior secondary (or grammar) schools for those from 14 to 18 plus. Though the character of schools and the age of their pupils would change, each school could remain in its existing building, with few exceptions and a minimum of modifications. It was calculated that sixth forms in the senior schools would be of the order of 120 pupils, which was less than the administration would ideally recommend.

The other 'composite' plan envisaged the establishment of relatively large secondary schools for pupils of 11 to 16 through amalgamations of schools whose buildings were close enough to each other. Smaller and more widely separated schools would become, as in the Leicestershire project, junior secondary schools for pupils from 11 to 14, with a natural sequence to similar sized schools catering for those between 14 and 18. A junior college would be founded to provide post 'O' level facilities for pupils from the first group of schools. In effect, therefore, the Borough would have two parallel kinds of sixth form at work, and it was argued that there could be flexibility of entry arrangements to suit pupils' objectives.

Early in 1964 the framework of these two schemes (together with the possibility of a multilateral school for children between 11 and 18) was outlined to the teachers' organizations of the Borough, and a series of consultations was held between the administration and teachers' representatives. On this occasion the Governing Bodies of the denominational schools within the Borough were approached for their views. But neither scheme found real favour with any section of teacher opinion. Since the first round of meetings with teachers' representatives in the autumn of 1962 three new points of resistance had clarified themselves. First, the teachers who opposed most actively the continuance of competitive selection were dismayed at the prospect of a surviving 5 per cent selection for independent and direct grant places: they argued that this destroyed the main virtues of the reform since pressures within the junior school would be even further intensified by competition for the few remaining selective places. Second, the Borough's non-selective schools were becoming increasingly concerned about the loss of their 'academic' work—to 'O' level standard. Although some non-selective schools still provided no 'O' level opportunities, the great majority hoped they might, and thus even within a year had found new reasons for cherishing some aspects of the status quo. Third, the notion of a distinction between common schools (implicit in the composite scheme which provided for some schools dealing with the ages from 11 to 14 and others dealing with the ages from 11 to 16) was repugnant, for it suggested yet another hierarchy within the authority's pattern of schools—a hierarchy for which there was no sort of justification.

The teachers were not in a position to obstruct all change in the Borough. Firm positions had not been taken up, and the arts of persuasion may still bring about some modification of these views. But in face of the collective opposition of the teachers' associations— with whom unanimity is a rare phenomenon—the Sub-committee and administration had again to go back over their tracks. The Sub-committee continued to search for a formula which it could commend to the new Croydon without in any way committing its successors. In the end, however, it had to be content with a statement of principle. This was accepted by the Education Committee, whose report to the last meeting of Croydon Council before the elections for the new Borough stated: 'Because the Committee recognize that it will be for the Council of the London Borough of Croydon to decide on the form of Secondary organization, they are not recommending a particular scheme, as they are of the opinion that the Council of the new Borough should have the opportunity of examining possible schemes. They do, however, consider that they should express themselves on certain matters of principle and conclude:

(1) That selection at eleven plus for maintained schools should be abolished;

(2) That the Authority must continue to take places at Direct Grant and Independent Schools;

(3) That any scheme of reorganization adopted must be shown to be superior to the present tripartite system in that:

    (a) it allows to every pupil that opportunity in terms of his his age, ability and aptitude which the 1944 Act laid down as a principle;

    (b) it recognizes that this opportunity must be made real for pupils of all degrees of ability; and

    (c) it must be flexible enough to permit a pupil that rate of progress through a Secondary course which his ability demands.

(4) That as planning for additional secondary schools must begin within the next year, it is essential to establish principles according to which new secondary school places must be built.'

The Council, by 55 votes to 1, accepted this Report, with its implications for an eventual reorganization of secondary education to produce secondary schools providing for a full range of ability. Its four conclusions were commended to the new Borough of Croydon.

This second attempt at reform originated from a more general concern with the inadequacies of the educational system, and developed against the background of nationwide discussion of the same issues. By 1961 it was becoming clear that further expansion of existing forms of selective education—the only positive outcome of the first attempt at reform—would not resolve the problems. Indeed the record of 'O' level performances in the enlarged grammar schools suggested this form of development might even render matters worse. A system of common primary schools, succeeded at the age of eleven by a tripartite pattern which owed more to the accidents of past history than to the Borough's current needs and potentialities, called for more radical reforms. The negotiations that followed during the next three years produced no such reform. But they were not altogether fruitless. Before its amalgamation with neighbouring local authorities, the County Borough had resolved that means must be devised to abolish competitive selection tests at the age of eleven. This procedure would be maintained for places in direct grant and independent schools only. This decision, limited and negative though it might be, was a long step forward in the process of formulating a policy for secondary education. It remains to be seen how it will be received by the representatives of the new Greater London Borough of Croydon.

H

DISCUSSION

Although the negotiations traced in this study failed to produce any conclusive result during the period covered, they nevertheless provide a revealing glimpse of the policy making process and an opportunity for applying some of the concepts derived from previous studies in this series. The form and character of an educational system changes slowly and is always liable to be rendered obsolete by continuing economic and social development. Croydon lies in one of the more prosperous segments of the London suburbs and is thus affected by all the social changes occurring in this most rapidly developing region of the country. There are several long established schools of high reputation in the district, and the Borough's system of secondary education owes a great deal to the traditions they have helped to create. The task of adapting this system to the social changes proceeding around it is thus likely to be peculiarly difficult.

The inadequacy of the system and the need for reappraisal and reform was forced upon public and professional attention in a number of ways. The scarcity of opportunities for academic education, the increasing competition for places in selective schools, and the waste of talent among potentially able pupils excluded from these schools; the difficulty of providing more advanced and specialized teaching in schools too small to support an adequate sixth form, and the wasteful use of the sixth form teaching resources available; the inefficiency and unpopularity of selection procedures at the age of eleven, the distortions of primary education they produced, and the difficulty of arranging any effective opportunity for selection at later stages of schooling; the need to provide for the education of growing numbers of 'young adults', many of whom preferred to escape from the restrictions imposed by traditional forms of schooling and seek the freedom offered by the labour market: these were among the problems to be contended with.

When his Council expressed concern about some of these issues, the new Chief Education Officer seized the opportunity to propose a radical reform of the whole system. Such a reform called for a wholesale reorganization of many well established institutions and could not be brought about without the support of at least a large proportion of the people directing these institutions. Some of the most influential schools playing a part in the system were not maintained by the Borough, and the constitution of the others could not be radically altered without the consent of the Ministry. It was clear that the interests of those who would have to participate in this reform were liable to conflict; these interests, moreover, were represented in a number of well entrenched professional associations. An attempt would therefore have to be made to find some common ground between them, and to work out a reconciliation of divergent aspirations through the formulation of plans that would offer advantages of some kind to most of those concerned. This might have been the point at which representatives of those providing the service—administrative and technical officers, inspectors and head teachers—could have been brought together in working parties to formulate viable solutions. But that step was not taken, and the anxieties of many of these people were sharpened by premature publication of proposals to be considered by elected members. Thus key people among the providers of the service were compelled to present their views in the form of an attack on these proposals, and to commit themselves to an increasingly public opposition both to each other and to the administration. An outside consultant was then brought in to advise the Council in a situation which forced him to assume the role of an arbitrator. He was not prepared to support the reform proposed, and the Education Committee was unwilling to press on with it. In any case this proposal for reorganization, whatever its long-term value, did not promise any immediate solution to the particular problems the Council had originally posed for discussion.

The second attempt at a reappraisal of Croydon's secondary education followed a remarkably similar course until the point at which the Chief Education Officer resigned owing to ill-health. Once again an expression of concern about specific problems arising from the general structure of Croydon's system of secondary education was taken as an opportunity for proposing the same reforms. Once again the Education Committee and its sub-committee were called upon to discuss these proposals before the staff actually providing the service had a chance to consider them; and again a plan for reform was published in a manner that provoked opposition to the administration and dissension between those who would have to collaborate in implementing it. Two new consultants were called in to give their verdict—a rather more favourable one this time. The arguments presented on all sides were elaborated at greater length, and public attitudes to the problem had changed since the earlier debate. A new group of citizens, concerned with the advancement of state education, appraised the administration's scheme in a balanced fashion; but the Council—which had so far reached no decision of policy—made no attempt to enlist such public support. The Whitgift Schools, though entirely independent of the Borough's education service, threw their formidable weight against the plan. Meanwhile the fundamental differences between the outlook of the principal groups involved remained much the same as in the previous negotiations. Head teachers were concerned with the development of their own type of school and the opportunities of the children they were immediately responsible for. Their differing responsibilities led them to favour or oppose different features of the administration's proposals; but none of them were able to consider the evolution of the *whole* system and the educational opportunities of *all* Croydon children—those in school and those at work—in quite the comprehensive manner in which these questions presented themselves to the Committee and its senior officers. All these points of view were reasonably clear by the time the Authority consulted the Ministry, and the Ministry's officials refused to support the proposed reform, commenting that the Borough had not demonstrated that this was the only solution for the recognized difficulties it faced.

With a change in its leadership the Education Department reconsidered its plans for the future, and a more flexible and varied choice of solutions was formulated. But by now the interests involved were publicly committed to a number of conflicting aspirations and it proved as difficult as ever to secure agreement. This was the point at which the forthcoming reform of local government interposed a pause in the drive for decisions which may yet provide opportunities for a reconsideration of these issues and the modification of intransigent standpoints.

The course of these events suggests that despite the wealth of telling statistics prepared by the Education Department, those providing the service—both in the schools and in the town hall—were never enabled to formulate a common approach to the problems confronting them. Complete agreement might have proved impossible, but the course adopted compelled them to approach the problem, not as teachers sharing a common concern for education throughout the Borough, but as exponents of different types of schooling. The Council had shown itself to be concerned about particular problems, but had not expressed any general preference for solutions. Its role might therefore have been to define broad objectives and to consider alternative means proposed for attaining them; but it became involved in the detailed formulation of one solution and allowed itself to be aligned with certain interests within the service before rival interests had been heard. It is proper for the officials who are responsible for the development of a social service to 'educate' their governing body and urge particular courses of action upon it, but they should do their utmost to secure agreement among their colleagues before involving their masters in controversy. Consultation with the Ministry, which bore the final responsibility for arbitrating in cases of dispute, was postponed until late in the proceedings—perhaps too late to be of much value. A variety of alternative solutions were then examined and time will tell whether these may offer an escape from the deadlock. Nevertheless, despite their inconclusive outcome, these negotiations had at least brought about a widespread recognition—publicly endorsed by the Council—that the existing pattern of secondary education was no longer adequate. This consensus may yet form the basis for a major new departure.

Previous studies have shown that the staff providing a social service, those controlling the resources required for it, and those determining the demands made upon it must all play a part in any major development of the service. The general objectives of the social services are often ill defined and capable of being interpreted in diverse ways. This diversity need provoke no conflict provided the aspirations of participants are satisfied to a sufficient extent. But when important groups among those providing the service suffer, or expect to suffer, a serious loss of resources, powers or status, conflicts arise among them which will spread, if pressed sufficiently far, to a widening circle of outside interests capable of influencing the development of the service. The timing of decisions about this development then calls for sensitive judgment. For premature attempts to resolve such conflicts may commit those responsible for these decisions to standpoints which provoke unnecessarily intransigent opposition among those who must eventually play a part in the evolution of the service. Major participants in this evolution may then be compelled to resign, or evolution itself may be brought to a halt.

PART III

CHAPTER 13

CONCLUSIONS

Introduction

The previous chapters will be read for various purposes and various conclusions will be drawn from them—not always those which their authors had in mind. We must therefore begin by explaining what it is we propose to draw conclusions about. This book is designed to throw light on the evolution of social policies by showing how changes come about in the work done by local units of the social services and by clarifying the roles of those who play a part in this process. Other studies of administration have dealt with the growth and character of bureaucracies, the communications and relationships that make up the 'social systems' of working groups, the logical processes of decision making, and the methods of administration and management to be prescribed for successful practice in these fields. In many of these studies the service provided—the 'task' of the organization—is disregarded, or treated as the outcome of an economic, social or logical system that forms the principal object of analysis. Our own work has a different purpose. It takes the evolution of the services provided by an organization as its focal point; other elements in the administrative system have not been examined for their own sake, but are treated as factors contributing to that evolution. We have not attempted to prescribe rules for good administration, because that would call for a definition of administrative 'success' and hence a specification of the task to be performed, the evolution of which is the subject of our studies. Although recent research on administrative organization has been of considerable help to us, our own approach is more like that of a historian who seeks to discover how the work and objectives of particular organizations evolved and why they take the patterns he finds.

We have not attempted to deal with administration in general but only with particular processes in particular types of agency: the processes which bring about changes in the volume, character or distribution of the services provided by local units of the social services. These agencies may be voluntary or statutory, national or local. They operate within a framework of legislation that must for the time being be accepted as 'given'; they have no appreciable reserve of unused resources, but they have considerable opportunities for securing additional resources—given time and the creation of certain conditions which they can help to bring about. The changes we have studied are reasonably typical of a middle range of local administrative developments, lying somewhere between the 'internal' reorganization of existing resources and working methods (such as the establishment of a typing pool or of new record-keeping procedures) and the creation of altogether new institutions (such as the establishment of new public services arising from a change in the law). Such developments are taking place all the time, they constitute the most important parts of a social administrator's work; and although they lack the radical and dramatic character of a change in national social policies they frequently provide the experimental groundwork that is later consolidated and codified by legislation, and they determine the manner in which Parliament's intentions are eventually interpreted and applied.

We begin our conclusions by identifying and clarifying some of the principal elements in the structure of administrative organization, indicating the relationships linking these elements. This provides little more than a clarification and reappraisal of the concepts already employed in discussions of each case. Next we identify the principal phases through which the developments we have studied appear to proceed, and examine the parts that different people play in each phase. Although no conclusive generalizations can be derived from so small a sample of cases, we present our hypotheses in an assertive, pragmatic fashion. They should at least be capable of being refuted in subsequent studies. Finally we consider some more general implications of this work which may be of interest to others researching, teaching or practicing in the fields we are concerned with.

The Elements of Administrative Organization

For our purposes 'administration' has been described, not as a distinctive activity or technique, but as consisting of all the processes that play a part in determining the volume, character and distribution of the service being studied. The 'service' is the outcome of these processes—the product provided for the public—not the agency providing it. The people who contribute to these processes may be approximately divided into three groups. The first we shall call the 'providers' of the service, and they depend for the performance of their tasks on the other two groups: those controlling the resources they require—resources which the 'providers' convert into a service—and those determining the demands met by the service. This tripartite division of the participants into 'providers', 'controllers of resources', and 'determiners of demand' must immediately be qualified in various ways. These groups may not consist of physically different people: the members of a 'self help' housing association who pool their savings to build houses for themselves with their own labour play all three parts in the process—though they may also depend on money lenders, land owners, local planning authorities and suppliers of building materials who control some of the resources they require. It will be remembered that half the members of the Finsbury Housing Committee (Chapter 9) were tenants of Council flats; they too were providers and recipients of their own service. Democratically elected governing bodies are one of the focal points of communication between the three types of participant we have identified, and, depending on the service in question and the manner in which they actually operate, they act as providers, controllers of resources, determiners of demand, or a combination of all three. We discuss their role in greater detail later in this chapter. Thus it is more useful to regard these elements of an administrative organization as three 'spheres of activity', rather than as separate groups of people, for there is often no precisely definable boundary line between the people involved. The providers are those committed to the provision, development and general success of the service in virtue of their contracts of employment, the work they actually do, their personal involvement and motivation. They are 'responsible' for it in the sense that they are liable to gain credit for its success and blame for its failure. Since the 'services' we have studied are activities or tasks, not agencies or administrative groups, they may be difficult to define, and the activities which constitute a service may change in the course of time or for the purposes of different discussions. Hence the boundary line between the providers and the controllers of resources may shift. In our study of the Family Welfare Association, for example (Chapter 11), we dealt with social casework in an Area office (whose staff constituted the 'providers') and also with the broader range of services provided by the whole Association (whose providers were a much larger group, including people who would be regarded as controllers of resources from the Area office's point of view). Those determining the demands made on a social service are also an ill-defined group. In the Home Helps study (Chapter 7) they included the clients of the service and the doctors, hospitals and other social agencies which helped to select clients, to refer them to the service and stress or assess the urgency of their needs. The Home Help Organizers who selected the households to be served also play a part in determining the demands met by the service. Thus these three elements of an organization can only be distinguished with reference to the particular tasks under discussion. The provision of a service rests with an 'internal' group who secure relatively undifferentiated resources or 'inputs'—of labour, money, equipment, land and so on—from 'external' groups who may not actually own these things or have any official title to them, but exercise some control over their supply and allocation. The providers then convert these resources into specific services that are received by another 'external' group of clients. When a new innovation is being considered which is introduced by an internal subgroup that has to rely on support, or overcome opposition, from others regarded as providers of a more general range of services, the boundary line that distinguishes providers of the service from controllers of resources must be tightened to include only those responsible for the particular development under discussion.

All this may seem a complicated and imprecise way of describing familiar and simple things. But, despite their approximate nature, these distinctions draw attention to important features of the administrative process. A three-part model helps to dispose of a common and frequently misleading tendency to think in terms of two-part models. 'Supply and demand', 'bureaucrats and the public', 'the state and the citizen'—such phrases establish pervasive assumptions about the nature of the administrative process. Assumptions about the roles of the partners in such transactions are then further elaborated by common parlance derived from ill-defined beliefs about the origins of social institutions. It is said, for example, that 'social services are designed to serve their clients' (or that 'firms are designed to maximize profits'). Such statements are not derived from systematic observation; they express a particular ideology. They are useful in certain contexts, but on occasion it may be equally appropriate and at least as revealing to say—for instance—that a probation service is 'designed to protect the social order whose leaders control the resources it requires', or that a teaching hospital is 'designed to advance the knowledge of those who provide its services' (or that a firm is 'designed to provide a living for its employees, or services for its customers').

A three-part model also helps to establish the central and crucial role of the providers of the service. They are not simply the instruments of their governing body—an impersonal link between the committee and its clients. They create, and continually modify, the service. And for this purpose they conduct transactions in two 'markets': the market for the resources they require and the market for the services they provide. The currency for these transactions may be rules, regulations and personal influence, rather than money; but the survival and character of the service depends none the less upon their outcome. All three types of participant must play some part in determining the volume, type and distribution of the services provided, and each is capable of frustrating or distorting any change in the service which the others may intend. Those providing the service are concerned with the improvement and development of their work, within the limits determined by available powers and resources, and according to aspirations derived from their colleagues, their training, their professional loyalties and personal needs. Those controlling the resources they require and those determining the demands made on the service are 'external' groups who must be concerned with many other factors, some of which would be regarded by the providers as irrelevant to the service itself. The hospital seeking home help services for the aged as a means of freeing beds for the use of other patients, the factory exercising its right to delay a building project as a means of securing parking space, the headmaster of an influential independent school opposing a plan for the reform of local authority schools as a means of promoting the forms of education he favours, the central government department withholding loan sanctions as a means of restraining inflation throughout the economy—such influences on the development of social services may be regarded as desirable or undesirable, but all are an entirely normal feature of social administration, and all play a part in determining the character and outcome of social policies.

This formulation also helps to focus attention on the points in the structure and the phases in the process at which the interests and aspirations of these three groups have to be confronted and reconciled. It is not the demands made on a service which ultimately shape its character but the demands that are met, or 'made effective'. The number and the selection of clients served depends on the decisions of the providers responsible for accepting applications, the impression of their aims and capacities they convey to the public, the relations they establish with others who refer potential clients to them, and other activities on the boundary lines between the providers and their clientele. Likewise the resources actually made available to the service ultimately depend not on the interests of those controlling them but on the transactions which take place on the boundary lines between them and the providers—on the claims the providers make for their service, the commitments they are prepared to enter into or to leave unspecified, the length of the delays they are able to tolerate, and the general understanding of the aims and importance of the service conveyed by the providers to those who control the resources they need. The points on the boundary lines at which these transactions take place can seldom be predicted in advance by researchers or precisely controlled by constitution makers. The governing body responsible for a social service and advisory committees that may be attached to the service are natural channels of communication, both with the controllers of resources, and with those determining demand. Particular members of the providing group may carry most of the responsibility for such communications—as the architect did in the Finsbury High Flats case, for example (Chapter 9). The members of a municipal Council are expected to communicate information about potential demands for a service to the staff who provide it (the architect commented: 'it's the housewife's opinion that counts—and she may be on the Council') and they also conduct some of the negotiations with those controlling resources (sending a delegation to the Ministry, for example, to discuss building plans and subsidies). But staff at all levels of the hierarchy may communicate with staff in 'neighbouring' services, with professional associations, with clients and other external groups. Since the providers of social services are full members of the community within which they operate, any of them may be found to play a part in these boundary line transactions.

External influences of this kind played some part—and usually a very important part—in shaping the character of all the services we have examined. The Children's Department (Chapter 8) had to secure the assent of the chairmen and chief officers responsible for other Council services before embarking on its intensive casework experiment. The evolution of the Home Help Service was largely determined by the demands made upon it by its clients and those referring people to it for help. The two Housing Authorities studied (Chapters 5 and 9) had to steer a course that would be sufficiently acceptable to the

Ministry, the County Council, local property owners and others. The evolution of Croydon's secondary education (Chapter 12) depended to a considerable extent upon the views and interests of those running independent schools in the district. The National Assistance Board's part in the Legal Aid Scheme (Chapter 6) is a classic example of the 'boundary line' processes (the Board's assessment procedures) which determined the demands actually met by a service. When those responsible for a service are asked to name 'the most important developments or changes which have occurred in your department in the last few years' they will almost inevitably select developments of the kind which call for some participation from both the types of external grouping we have considered.

In most of these cases the influence of those controlling resources appeared to play a more important part in shaping the outcome than the influence of those determining demand. This, we suspect, is a genuine reflection of reality in the social services, for they usually face a potential demand which far outstrips the services they can provide: resources are scarce, clients are plentiful. But it would be rash to press that conclusion too far since the influences of resource controllers tend to be more 'visible', being expressed in specific steps or phases of the administrative process—in budgetary procedures, applications for planning permissions or compulsory purchase orders, appointments of new staff, and so on. The influence of clients and of others determining the demands met by these services was by no means negligible: it was expressed in a continuing though unobtrusive fashion through elected councils and committees; it played a major part in the Home Helps case, and the developments studied in Croydon arose initially from growing public demand for selective education.

The Evolution of Social Policies

Since these were exploratory studies that were deliberately designed to give administrators the main responsibility for identifying significant developments in their work, the procedure for selecting our cases was very simple, and produced a wide variety of developments, ranging from major reforms of a service to relatively minor modifications of working methods. Moreover these developments were examined at various stages in their progress. The Croydon case dealt with the initial and inconclusive discussion of proposals for a major reform; the Family Welfare Association case dealt with an intermittent series of similar short term developments that were still continuing at the time of our study; the Home Helps case dealt with the general evolution of a newly established service; the Bethnal Green and Children's Department cases and the Canadian case (Chapter 10) each dealt with all stages of a major development within a service; the High Flats case dealt with a piece of capital investment; and the Legal Aid case dealt with the improvement of working procedures during the aftermath of an expansion of the National Assistance Board's responsibilities. But provided it is remembered that the conclusions to be derived from these studies amount to no more than a set of hypotheses calling for further analysis and testing, this variety of cases may not be an insuperable handicap. It may help us to identify crucial features of administration which recur in entirely different settings; and the various phases of administrative development included in the series may afford a more comprehensive picture of the sequence of such phases than could be derived from a similar number of more strictly standardized cases.

In this section we attempt to provide a fairly comprehensive outline of certain features and phases of the policy making process in local units of the social services. This outline is derived from the cases we have presented, but is not restricted to that source alone. If the particular development examined in one case threw light on earlier or later phases of a bigger, longer-term process of development we have not hesitated to draw on that more extensive information. Likewise we have incorporated ideas derived from other studies, both empirical and theoretical, in so far as these seemed to throw light on our own findings. And at some points we have drawn fairly heavily on our unpublished study of a University. (This case proved exceptionally valuable, being based on extensive interviews and on a diary kept by one of the participants in the development examined.) Thus we do not assert that each of the developments examined in the previous chapters accords precisely with the model to be outlined here, but only that they accord with the main features of those phases of the model's operations which they represent.

It is often difficult to identify the origins of new developments of this kind. The first initiative may come from those controlling the resources an agency requires, or from its clients or those referring and representing them. But our studies suggest that the providers of the service usually take this initiative—sometimes under the compulsion of a foreseen change in resources (as in the Bethnal Green case) but usually in an attempt to meet in a more appropriate or satisfying way the actual or potential demands they perceive. Thus their perceptions of the needs to be met and the standards of service they regard as fitting are crucial. These perceptions depend largely on the education and previous experience of the staff, and the climate of opinion they establish amongst themselves. The initiative for change is particularly likely to come from those providing the service when they are trained and skilled, when they are given considerable discretion in the practice of their own work, and when the services they provide depend largely on their own direct contacts with those served. Services which call for costly capital investment or the provision of cash payments for clients must depend more heavily on the financial resources available and on those who control them. But 'ideas' are not enough: the 'external' participants in the service must respond before the providers can bring about appreciable changes.

Initially the providers tend to be fully employed in coping with their existing responsibilities. But these responsibilities are imprecisely defined and leave them considerable discretion to shape the character of their own service. Changes in the service—or, indeed, the opportunity for thinking about and preparing such changes—usually call for extra staff. Plans for change may be generated after extra staff are appointed, as in the Canadian and Children's Department cases; or they may emerge, in effect, from 'overtime' work among existing staff which leads later to an increase in resources for the extra work already planned or begun. Frequently both processes occur. To be more precise, what is required at this stage is a change in the ratio between the providers' resources and the demands met by their service. This usually comes about through an increase in resources, but it may arise, as in the Family Welfare Association, from a restriction of the case-load carried by the service. A change in the ratio could also arise from increasing mastery of skills—or rising productivity—among the providers, a portion of whose energies are then set free to expand and develop their service. But although something of this kind undoubtedly happened in some of our cases, the scope for increasing productivity in professional services tends to be small.

To secure the additional resources they need, influential members of the providing group must gain the assent or support of others, *outside* their own agency and not directly responsible for their service, who exercise some control over these resources. These controls operate in many different ways. They may be derived from formal authority (of the kind held by a central government department, or by the Treasurer and Establishments Officer of a municipal council) or from well established procedures of varying degrees of formality (such as regular meetings of chief officers, designed to ensure that each proceeds with the agreement of his senior colleagues) or from personal, political or professional influence (based on the personal status and connections of local councillors, professional leaders and others) or from the choices made by able people who must be persuaded to join the providing group before the desired development can be brought about (for authority to appoint additional staff will be of little value unless good recruits can be found). To gain the support of all these people the providers must commit themselves to achieving certain objectives regarded as valuable or acceptable by those controlling the resources they need. To this extent they must sacrifice some of the freedom to run the service in their own way which they would retain if they chose the quieter life available to a group that seeks no major changes or developments in its work. The providers may be compelled at this stage to commit themselves to general or specific objectives: to 're-ducing the numbers of children coming into public care', to 'abolishing the eleven plus' or to providing particular facilities sought by a lease-holder who is capable of delaying or blocking a development, for example. The commitments and claims, offered as an inducement to secure the resources required at this stage, tend either to be specific but unimportant, or important but ill-defined. This is because the pro-viders seek to retain as much control of their service as possible, and because the interests whose support they require are often so diverse that objectives which were important and precisely specified would be likely to alienate some of them. The proposals made by the Chief Education officer in Croydon were in fact so radical and specific that they provoked insuperable opposition. Likewise, in the High Flats case, the attempt to satisfy both a leaseholder and a tenants' association led to serious trouble, and further delays arose before the conflicting interests of the Ministry and the County Planning Department could be reconciled. But more general commitments—to 'preserve the family', for example, or to 'advance knowledge about marital prob-lems' (seen in the Children's Department, Children's Aid Society and FWA cases)—are less likely to prove disruptive or too precisely binding.

Having secured the additional resources they require, the providing group has to convert these into services—or, more often, into a modifi-cation, expansion or redeployment of existing services. The eventual outcome—the change in policy actually realized—often takes years to emerge and is difficult to predict with any precision. That is because the conversion of money, labour, materials and equipment into a service is a complex and gradual process. It depends on the people who do the work and the relationships established between them, and on the people who seek the service or help to shape the demands for it. Exchanges on the margins between the providers and receivers continually mould the character of the service, extending it in some directions and eroding it elsewhere—rather as wind and tide shape a coastline over the years. Even when the objectives of a service are defined with fair precision, as in a slum clearance programme, it has been shown that the selection of the areas to be served (in Bethnal Green) and of the individual households to be served (in Finsbury) may present considerable problems and leave considerable scope for discretion and bargaining among those participating in the process. In a professional service where heavy capital expenditure is not involved, the evolution of the service generally proceeds without precisely defined objectives or constraints and this characteristic calls for further explanation.

The aims of the social services are usually of the most general kind, as can be seen in the legislation establishing them, in the constitutions of voluntary agencies, or in the basic memoranda on new developments prepared for the approval of appropriate committees and governing bodies. Though these objectives have to be clarified to some extent when additional resources are required for new developments, the final determination of the character, volume and distribution of the services actually provided for clients is seldom governed by precisely specified aims—and for at least three reasons. (a) Many social services call for a concentration of some of the most highly skilled staff in the 'front line' from which the provision of the service takes place; doctors, teachers and others must be permitted considerable discretion in developing their work, in adapting it to the needs of particular cases and in selecting those to be served. While the social work services may not be 'professionalized' to this extent, they nevertheless show many of these characteristics. Thus the providers need *discretion* to operate freely within a broadly defined professional and administrative framework. (b) Frequently, too, they cannot clearly foresee the character of the demands that will be made on them, or of the resources—of new knowledge as well as more tangible things—that will be available to them. The demands made on the Home Help and Children's Department services were largely unforeseen at the time when they were established, and the impact of wartime and postwar developments had an equally important and unpredictable effect on older agencies such as the Family Welfare Association and the Children's Aid Society. To some extent, therefore, the social services must recognize the uncertainty they have to live with; they must be capable of responding to changes in their environment, and their objectives are genuinely and necessarily *vague*. (c) Many of those actively involved in various capacities as providers of the service will have different frames of reference from which they derive interpretations of the existing situation and aspirations for the future which diverge or conflict. They depend for the development of their service on an even more varied range of potentially conflicting outside interests. The long term plans for their services envisaged by senior officers may call eventually for new legislation, a rise in the rates, a resignation or two within their own departments, and take-over bids for services at present performed by other agencies. Meanwhile junior staff may find their discretion is extended if their superiors are not too well informed about developments and aspirations at junior levels of the hierarchy. Thus each of those engaged in the process of social administration have three 'pictures' of their service in mind: a picture, first, of the service as officially prescribed in the relevant literature; second an interpretation of the service as it actually is; and third a prospect of the service as it ought eventually to become. These three perceptions of the service resemble the successive frames of a moving picture. But while the film starts for each person with approximately the same officially prescribed image, it moves thereafter in different ways and at different speeds. If we are right in concluding that the providers of a service will usually initiate change and must always carry it through, then it is essential that many of them should have such 'moving pictures' in mind. But if the objectives and aspirations of all of them were made entirely explicit, collaboration amongst colleagues and the orderly development of public services would be disrupted. Thus many of the people concerned have respectable (i.e. rationally justifiable) reasons for being *unexplicit* about their objectives. These three types of indeterminacy—'discretion', 'vagueness' and 'unexplicitness'—necessarily characterize the objectives of the social services and pervade their development.

This is *not* an argument for tolerating unnecessary or damaging uncertainty, or for abandoning attempts to plan or evaluate the development of a social service. Discretion, vagueness and unexplicitness are only tolerable and useful if their limits are reasonably clear and their implications restricted in scope. Objectives which are too precisely defined tend to be restrictive, if cautious, or disruptive, if radical. (Our studies of the National Assistance Board and of Croydon's secondary schools may provide examples of these two extremes.) But objectives which are too vague tend to destroy a sense of purpose, and provide no foundation upon which to establish proper standards of performance. (The social workers in the FWA Area office were endeavouring to clarify objectives which had been left exceedingly vague by more senior authorities in the Association.)

Once a new development has begun it often produces further off-shoots and calls for yet more resources. Indeed there are signs that continuous modification and development of a social service are most likely to occur when those providing it secure a continuous increase in resources—not simply because the extra resources enable them to do more work, but because the process of growth ensures there is always a margin of unused human resources available for planning, promoting and developing new things. If the increase in resources comes to an end, or if new recruits are so inexperienced and untrained that they demand a great deal of supervision from more experienced staff (which amounts to the same thing), then there is no longer any margin of time and energy available for innovating activities. Thus the process of *growth* (meaning an increase in resources) and the process of *development* (meaning changes in the character of the service) tend to be linked—growth promoting development—especially in the types of service in which innovating activities cannot be centralized and specialized but depend heavily on active contributions from a considerable number of professionally trained staff.

But growth does not operate to a uniform scale throughout the organization. It brings about an uneven development of the service and the working groups providing it, with potentially serious implications for the status, influence, discretion and satisfactions of those concerned. The film moves on: the actual state of the service is seen to be departing further from its original, formally approved, description, and structures and procedures designed for an earlier pattern shown signs of strain. Sooner or later a reappraisal of policies and priorities will be required to bring about a closer reconciliation between the formal (or 'manifest') and the actual (or 'extant') versions of the organization. This phase is often postponed for as long as possible, because it may prove painful and because the indeterminacies already mentioned conceal the need for it. But those providing the service will eventually be compelled to attempt some such reappraisal; without it further development is liable to produce a tendency to overspend the budget, a scarcity of staff at points in the structure which were not expanded sufficiently to cope with the extra work being generated at other points, or a tendency to outstrip the legal or constitutional powers of the agency. The Children's Aid Society clearly ran into a situation of this kind and similar features appeared in other studies. Often it is only when confronted with the limitations on their resources that the providers explicitly accept—or reject—a change in policy. This phase may prove disruptive, or it may pass off smoothly. How soon it appears and how sharp its effects prove to be will depend partly on the providers themselves—and particularly on their more senior members—and partly on the rate at which they can acquire additional resources to sustain continued development of their activities without the necessity for discriminating explicitly against any of them.

Conflict

This is one of the points in the evolutionary process at which conflicts are liable to arise. Priorities have to be determined which threaten to alter the existing patterns of service, and the resulting distributions of discretion, satisfaction, influence and status. In the Croydon case, owing to the nature of the service, such a conflict had to be faced at the start, before any change could be attempted. In the Canadian case, conflict became acute in the final phase of reappraisal. Somewhat similar conflicts can be glimpsed in the High Flats, Children's Department, and Family Welfare Association cases, though the picture in the last two of these is less clear. Such conflicts show recurring features and phases justifying separate analysis.

It is often those amongst the providing group who are most directly affected by changes, proceeding or threatened, who first perceive a need for a 'decision' on policies, priorities, responsibilities or the distribution of resources—as case-loads or overtime increase, as rumours circulate, personal relations deteriorate or other signs of stress appear. They begin to form groups and cliques that define the nature of the problem and the 'issues at stake', and canvass solutions. Different interpretations of the situation, different aspirations and different personalities do *not* produce conflict, provided all concerned can satisfy their aspirations within the same general pattern of development—as was indicated in the Children's Department case. We repeatedly found that if their objectives can be reconciled in this way, people with divergent views have a remarkable capacity for supporting—and indeed for claiming to have originated—developments whose purpose and significance they describe in very different terms. Conflict begins seriously when different interests and aspirations cannot be reconciled in this way; when someone *has* to suffer—or be excluded from the group providing the service concerned (though not necessarily from the agency in which he is employed). Contending groups then seek the support of those responsible for taking the 'decisions' they ask for. This may be the first that senior staff of an agency hear of the conflict. There tends at this stage to be a polarization of opinions. The contenders search for satisfactory definitions of the issues at stake among like-minded associates, rather than among their opponents; and having established a circle with a common outlook on these issues they appraise and evaluate any solutions proposed by the response accorded to it in this circle.

If no decision is made, or if the decision proves unsatisfactory to some, those most anxious or dissatisfied tend to seek the support of any outside groups capable of exerting influence on the decision, if they are able to gain access to such groups. Typically these outsiders will be found amongst those controlling resources required by the providers. 'Outward' appeals of this kind encourage others amongst the providers to make counter-appeals to other outsiders likely to support alternative points of view. A widening circle of outside interests may then be brought into play, and their influence is concentrated on those responsible for a decision, and subsequently on those at more senior levels of the hierarchy who are capable of reversing that decision. If the conflict is likely to be pursued to extremes, those with authority to take the necessary decisions have to wait until all available guns have been brought to bear in the battle. To make a decision sooner only invites attempts to modify or reverse it which may disrupt the agency and discredit authority. Some reconciliation of conflicting interests and aspirations may be achieved at any stage of this conflict; it may, for example, prove possible to find additional resources which satisfy the aspirations of all concerned. But if no reconciliation is possible a solution may have to be achieved through a bargaining process which establishes the balance of power between contending forces. How far these 'bargaining strengths' depend on the distribution of formal authority, the value of individual participants' contributions to the service, the ease with which substitutes for their contributions can be found, the strength and character of their loyalties to the agency, or on other factors, will depend on the nature of the case—and particularly on the participants and the conventional patterns of authority previously established among them. Provided they are kept within bounds, uncertainty about the future and the anxieties it provokes encourage innovation and enable people to adapt to change. But when heightened in the course of conflict they tend to have the opposite effects. Meanwhile, people who have for long treated each other as colleagues, or even as friends, may find that the situation compels them to adopt the altogether different relationships of formal authority or competitive bargaining. Such relationships, which are normal and acceptable in the army or the market place, often prove peculiarly harrowing and destructive within a working team of this kind. But this situation cannot continue indefinitely. A decision must eventually be reached if the service is to continue. Though the formal approval of such decisions by an appropriate authority may simply set a seal on a much lengthier process of development, negotiation and conflict, the announcement of it is often the first that the public at large will hear of the decision in question.

The eventual outcome, however, may not accord closely with this decision. It will depend heavily on the people who are left in positions which give them effective responsibility for implementing the decision. (Many a point sacrificed by compromises made in the course of a conflict has been recovered when the opposition resigns.)

The Structure of Administration

The foregoing hypotheses about the processes of administration have a number of implications for its structure, and it is time to return to the participants whose roles and relationships make up this structure.

It is clear that the selection of the social services' clients merits far more detailed study than we have been able to attempt. All the services we have examined faced a bigger demand than they could meet, and we know little in detail of the processes that determine which clients are selected and which services these people actually receive. Moreover a social service frequently benefits several people simultaneously, even if only one of them would be recognized as its client in a particular 'case'; thus the distribution of help amongst those involved in one case also calls for careful study. The social worker in a Children's Department may be called upon to help children, their parents and foster parents. The Children's Aid Society's services for unmarried mothers involved responsibilities to the mother, her baby and the Provincial Child Welfare authorities. The National Assistance Board officer dealing with Legal Aid Assessments is serving the Law Society for whom these assessments are made, but in practice we found he could not simply disregard the needs of the people whose resources he was assessing. The Home Help Organizer knows that her service may be of vital importance, not only to old people and their families, but also to hospitals, general practitioners, old people's homes and other social services. Similar situations appear elsewhere: a probation officer, for example, may be responsible to the magistrates for a young probationer whose welfare depends largely on his parents, and the officer must be concerned with all of these people. Thus the character and development of a social service depends heavily on the willingness of clients to use such agencies and the selection the clients make of the services available, on the procedures bringing clients to the attention of those providing the service (procedures often reflecting the needs of other services), on the selection of applicants made by those providing the service and the manner in which they interpret their responsibilities to the various people who may be concerned in one 'case'.

What has been said about the client indicates the importance and complexity of the roles of those directly providing services for him—particularly when the services call for considerable skill and give wide discretion to the staff concerned. The aims of such services cannot be considered in isolation from the methods employed in providing them. Quotations from the files of the Children's Aid Society show how much the character of a service may alter when there are changes in the outlook, methods and skills of the workers providing it. Field staff in the London Children's Department and the Family Welfare Association also brought about major changes in the aims and methods of their services. Moreover the capacity of field staff to handle and develop their relationships with staff in other agencies may play as large a part in this process as their capacity to deal directly with clients. Formally approved 'changes in policy' announced by the governing body may simply recognize and codify a process worked out over several years by people at humbler levels of the providing group.

The next group of participants to be considered appear at the middle and more senior levels of the social services' management. They are not empowered to make major decisions but they have considerable discretion to allocate the resources required for the service and to control and supervise the uses to which they are put. Their responsibilities frequently place them at 'junctions' in the communication system linking specialists and sub-groups who have divergent interests and aspirations. They act as 'filters', selecting and interpreting information that passes up and down the hierarchy and between one agency and another. They must be capable of speaking and understanding the different professional and administrative 'languages' of those with whom they communicate and reconciling minor divergencies among them. They often prepare the plans and the memoranda relied on by more senior staff—who may subsequently be given the credit (or the blame) for them. They are sufficiently close to the field staff and to those at the top of the hierarchy to be familiar with the weaknesses of both, yet they must be prepared to shore up such weaknesses in unobtrusive ways if the service is to develop effectively. They require a sensitive appreciation of the trends of development likely to prove acceptable to various participants, the distinctions between 'discretion', 'vagueness' and 'unexplicitness', and the restrictions to be imposed on each. They may have begun their careers as general administrators or as professionally qualified specialists, but to be fully effective they must have developed loyalties to the various organizations in which they work—loyalties which transcend the horizons of a particular agency or profession. The Deputy Town Clerk in Bethnal Green, the Senior Child Care Officer in the Children's Department, and the architect in Finsbury all bore such responsibilities in different ways and for different reasons, and the success of the developments in which they were engaged owed a great deal to them. It may not be a coincidence that no one appeared to fill this role effectively in the cases in which more serious conflicts and difficulties arose. It should be noted in passing that many of the people who now hold such positions entered the public services as general administrators just before the war and gained valuable experience in other fields during the war. Had they been born a decade later many of them would have gone to Universities and entered the public services—if at all—in professional capacities (as engineers, medical officers, accountants and so on) or as civil servants in the central government's administrative class. Studies of administration tend to deal with the top or bottom levels of the structure: democratically elected bodies and their chief officers at one end; clients and those who serve them at the other. We neglect middle management at our peril.

It should now be clear that the role of the directors of social services, though important, is a restricted one. The influence exerted on the development of a social service by those already considered, and the fact that staff in these services cannot normally be removed from their posts except in cases of the gravest error or scandal, gives chief officers limited room for manoeuvre. They generally bear the principal responsibilities for dealing with outside interests controlling the resources required for the service. They are called upon to convey, inside and outside the providing group, a sense of purpose and direction, and of the value and importance of what is being done, and to shape the general level of aspiration amongst those providing a service. If they fail to seek and secure the support of those controlling the resources required for expansion—including potential recruits to the agency—the services they provide are unlikely to develop, though the existing pattern may become or remain efficient. They are called upon to look further ahead than any of the other participants we have considered, fostering fruitful lines of innovation (which will often be initiated by more junior staff). The commitments they enter into with senior colleagues, the procedures they sanction for the evaluation of their services, the recruits selected to join their staff, the resources acquired for their agency—all these must be chosen in a manner that opens rather than closes the doors for future development (development for which their successors will often gain the credit). The timing of crucial decisions made at this level of the hierarchy often calls for exceptional skill, and our studies suggest that the temptation to make prompt and explicit decisions may be as seductive and dangerous as the temptation to procrastinate. Chief Officers are responsible for the agencies they direct, but our studies show that some of the social services' most important tasks are performed by staff in several different agencies. The term 'service' is commonly used to refer both to an agency and to the work it does, and it can be peculiarly difficult for chief officers to appreciate the distinction between these concepts. Fruitful development of the work often calls for the participation of many people outside the agency, and a willingness to subordinate the interests of the agency to those of the people to be served; otherwise the evolution of social policies may be frustrated or wastefully distorted.

The role of an agency's governing body varies widely according to its constitution and traditions, and it is difficult to generalize fruitfully about it. Only in the Croydon and Finsbury cases could an elected Council or Committee be said to have initiated the developments we have studied. But in several of the other cases such bodies played an important part at a later stage. The Board of the Children's Aid Society exercised considerable influence on the character and outcome of the development studied; and the Housing Committee in Bethnal Green established a general climate of determined opinion that provided a firm foundation for the work of their officials.

Because the members of these bodies are elected by the public—or by the fairly small minority that chooses to vote in local elections—they are sometimes expected to conduct a direct 'democratic' management of their services. Commentators then make depressing references to the 'encroachment of bureaucracy' or the 'decay of local democracy' when the reality turns out to be different. A century and more ago the members of Vestries, Boards of Guardians, charitable committees and similar bodies themselves carried out much of the daily work they were responsible for, and faint traces of this tradition are still to be seen in our study of the Family Welfare Association. But the assumptions encouraged by such folk memories are liable to be misleading and needlessly derogatory to those who now perform the difficult and time consuming duties of committee membership. (The parallel myth that boards of directors are supposed to represent the shareholders that elect them produces a similarly confusing mixture of truth and illusion.) In fact, the governing body of a social service is only one of the channels of communication between the public and those providing the service, and 'the public' is itself an abstract and largely mythical entity. The architect in the Finsbury case had to deal with the County Council and the Ministry, representing respectively a regional and a national 'public'; the Borough's Housing Manager had to deal with the tenants originally living on the site and those subsequently selected for the new flats; and other participants had to deal with neighbouring land owners and leaseholders—all 'publics' of different kinds. The Children's Aid Society had to deal with private donors and subscribers, several municipal Councils, departments of the Provincial and Federal governments, foster parents, adopters, and the families it served. *Some* of the Society's communications with *some* of these 'publics' were channelled through its Board. Examples could be multiplied indefinitely, but these may show that the distinctive features of the governing body's role do not arise from any monopoly of relationships with the external community that uses and pays for a social service. It is true that the governing body's tenure of office may depend, formally speaking, on public approval, and it may be responsible for raising much of the money for its services. But the committees of the two voluntary bodies we have dealt with selected themselves, in effect; and among the local authorities dealt with, only the Croydon Council had suffered a turnover of members since the war which was sufficient to threaten the position of its majority party. Meanwhile a large part (and often the majority) of the tax revenues required for these services was levied by other bodies—typically by the central government. No one would deny that elections do sometimes bring about important changes in the policies of local social services: we only wish to establish that such changes usually originate from other sources, that the role of governing bodies does not consist mainly of initiating or directing changes in policy, and that others engaged in providing the service may be at least equally active in communicating with the public, and equally anxious about the quality of their relationships with the public.

Governing bodies have many other responsibilities. They are particularly concerned with establishing and maintaining relationships with those who control the resources required for their services, and they form one (but only one) of the principal channels of communication with such groups. They often devote at least as much effort to keeping the public informed about the service as to keeping its providers informed about public opinion. They constitute a means of arbitrating between contending interests amongst the providers, and the existence of this 'court of appeal' may be very important, even in an agency where most people choose to settle out of court. They also perform certain formal duties which have symbolic importance—inaugurating new institutions, receiving distinguished visitors, bidding farewell to retiring members of staff, and so on.

But when dealing with the type of development we have studied, the governing body's principal role is to approve, modify or reject decisions which commit the providers to significant changes in their objectives, to courses of action which involve risks or impinge on other services, and to significant expenditures or redistributions of resources. Such decisions may call for consideration of technical evidence, but they require more than an appraisal of facts and methods; they require a judgment about priorities, objectives and risks. The staff providing a service are not compelled to consider the other services which may have to be foregone if their own is to expand, nor to determine how much it is worth paying to minimize certain risks inherent in their proposals, nor to weigh the effect on neighbouring services of precedents (in their methods of dealing with clients, the salary scales of staff, or payments to foster parents, for example) which they may seek to establish in their own service. They may indeed consider all these things, but they are not compelled to do so; they are often ill equipped to weigh and appreciate the factors involved, and it might be inappropriate for them to devote too much energy to such tasks. It is the responsibility of social workers, engineers, doctors, teachers and others who work in the social services to concentrate on providing and perfecting the service they are capable of; no one else can do that for them. But someone does have to consider what sacrifices should be made to secure these standards. The governing body, provided it is adequately advised by appropriate senior officials, should be equipped for this purpose. Paid staff require a sensitive appreciation of this role if they are to distinguish the things the governing body should consider from the things it need not be aware of. Thus there was clearly no need for Finsbury's Housing Committee to understand the technology required for digging preliminary bore holes on a building site, but when these holes showed there were dangers of subsidence or a delay that could only be avoided by sinking further holes at a cost of £1,200, problems of cost, time and risk were posed which fell within the Committee's sphere of decision.

It is often difficult to secure and maintain a clear appreciation of these distinctions. The governing body's members may understandably wish to 'keep in touch' with the operations of the services for which they are responsible. For this and other reasons they may be tempted to spend a lot of time on executive or near-executive work which confuses their role and wastes their energies. The Family Welfare Association's local Case Committees, the Finsbury Housing Committee's personal participation in the selection of tenants, the time spent by Children's Committee members on the Managing Committees of residential homes and schools, and the Croydon Education Committee's detailed analysis of proposals for reforms that had not yet been considered by senior staff in their own service—all these appear to be examples of such confusion. The governing body's job is not to provide the service, but to find and appoint the staff who can do this—and, if necessary, to remove those who cannot. Its work is at least as difficult as the task of managing the service, and it should offer a sufficiently exacting and satisfying challenge. Equally damaging confusions arise if the staff providing a service 'counter attack' by assuming some of the responsibilities of the governing body. The participation of paid staff as full members of the Family Welfare Association's Administrative Council illustrates this opposite tendency. More often, the staff are liable to submerge their governing body in a mass of confusing detail because they do not know how to pose clearly the questions which the committee really needs to consider, or simply because they feel that sufficient material must somehow be found to fill every meeting.

These comments on the roles of participants in the administrative process have tended at points to become prescriptive—even hortatory. Our evaluation of administrative structure is based on the assumption that innovation and development are its most important tasks, and that effective means must be found for completing each phase of the processes outlined earlier. But any prescription for action rests on some statement of the objectives to be attained and the conditions involved.

To a governing body and paid staff who cannot trust each other, and to those who assume the burdens of committee membership for the personal satisfactions or political influence to be gained from participation in the distribution of services, some of the morals drawn from the preceding paragraphs will naturally seem unconvincing. The committee may take on executive work because that is what its members got themselves elected for, its staff may wring decisions from it through confusion and exhaustion, and both may be prepared to pay any price involved. We only point out that there may be a price.

Some Implications

Our attempt to construct a model that may help to explain the development of local social services has inevitably produced an abstract and over-simplified account of the process. In a large agency there may in real life be several developments of this kind proceeding simultaneously, some of them spilling over into other agencies, or involving people and institutions outside the social services altogether. Each of these developments is likely to have begun at different times, and to proceed on a different scale and at a different pace. The importance and duration of the different phases in each will vary. Some developments will be abandoned, bogged down or transposed into new forms, and others will be completed more or less according to plan. Thus the model of these processes we offer will seldom correspond precisely to reality. But it may alert those entering the social services to some of the problems they will have to deal with and some of the factors they should be aware of. It may help them to ask the right questions, even if it provides few of the answers. We conclude this discussion with a more speculative essay on some broader implications of our findings.

The developments we have studied appear typically to proceed through a cycle, starting from general commitments—entered into for the sake of securing additional resources controlled by outside interests—and leading eventually to formal 'policy decisions' which codify the outcome of internal experiment, adjustment, and (occasionally) conflict. The spark that ignites this process of innovation may come from various quarters, but the driving force that propels it comes from those deeply involved in providing the service—paid staff, who may be employed in different agencies. The strength of this force depends on the aspirations of these people—the opportunities they perceive, and the dissatisfaction they feel with current standards and patterns of service—and these things depend on their outlook and training, and the climate of opinion they create amongst themselves.

We would do well to remember that in a wealthy, industrial society such as our own the labour force is replaced very slowly; those now entering training courses in our universities and colleges will still be at work in the twenty-first century, and many of them will not reach senior posts in the social services until the eighties and nineties of this century. Since the changes in needs and knowledge likely to occur in these decades will be at least as great as those experienced in the past, the provision of opportunities for further education is not a temporary necessity for under-manned social services but an urgent and permanent requirement. Systematic preparation for work in the social services, provided in universities, colleges of further education and professional institutions, is largely designed for the training of field staff. Little has yet been done to equip these people for the more senior administrative posts many of them will have to fill in ten or twenty years' time.[1]

But innovation and a continued momentum of development in these services call for the acquisition of additional resources. A meagre environment that furnishes no margin of resources beyond those required to meet current commitments does not merely delay innovation; it prevents the generation of new ideas (for ideas call for time and energy, and some prospect of realization), it encourages the ambitious to leave in search of more favourable fields, and lowers the aspirations of those who remain. It should not be forgotten that those who receive the service also help to shape its development. But those providing the service can never meet all the needs they perceive, even among the people concerned in one 'case'. The extent to which a service is attuned to meet the most urgent needs in the most appropriate ways depends heavily on the capacity of those providing it to sense and appraise the wants of others, to foresee changes in these wants brought about by economic and social development, and to alert a wider public to these changes. From the community's point of view this is a potentially weak link in the system: a social service may be 'efficient' without being effectively attuned to the needs of the times.

If this account of the evolution of policies in the social services is sound it explains why too little light has been thrown on the process by social scientists, excellent though their work may be for other purposes. The development of these services does not proceed as a continuous equilibrium-seeking response to marginal changes in external, impersonal forces (as economic analysis of organizations

[1] For a discussion of this problem, see D. V. Donnison, *Education for Social Administration*, C. S. Loch Memorial Lecture. London. Family Welfare Association 1964.

often suggests). It is begun and driven forward by *people, within* the groups providing the service; its progress is partly self-sustaining—growth promoting further growth—and it is not uniform and continuous, but passes, like a drama, through succeeding 'acts' of uncertain duration and differing character. Some have treated administrative agencies as 'social systems' and examined the mechanisms that promote cohesion, maintain order and ensure their stability and survival. Such studies provide revealing side lights on the problems we have examined. Nevertheless their methodology and concepts tend to be peculiarly inappropriate for the analysis of change (not stability), brought about through a process of conflict (rather than cohesion), occurring in services frequently provided by several different agencies (not by one social system). Much research on the character of human relationships within working groups also tends to be tangential to our own concerns for similar reasons; for changes which are derived from dissatisfaction with present standards and patterns of work, and changes which sometimes call for painful redistributions of resources, influence and status, are not most easily analysed with a conceptual framework devised by those concerned with the maximization of satisfaction and the minimization of conflict. Studies of management, administration or the theory of games, designed to reveal the most logical and efficient patterns of decision-making, also tend to be ill-suited to our needs because they usually require that the objectives of organization be defined or simply assumed, whereas the objectives of the social services are changing and necessarily somewhat unclear, and their evolution should itself be the focal point of research. 'Decisions' are often difficult to identify in these services, and those we have discovered often follow and confirm action rather than precede it. Meanwhile classical studies of 'bureaucracy' also tend to omit crucial elements of our subject matter. The behaviour of highly mobile, innovating, professional staff does not conform to that of the stable, disciplined hierarchy often assumed to be typical of this institution; the objectives of the organization are not sufficiently specific or static to permit a stable and strictly 'rational' deployment of resources for their attainment; '*the* bureaucracy' breaks up on serious inspection into a variety of separate, competing and bargaining organizations; and these organizations do not present a monolithic face to '*the* public' but are interpenetrated and allied with a variety of 'publics' which exercise considerable influence on their operations.

These observations are not a criticism of the lines of research referred to. Our debt to many of them is made clear in the appendix that follows. Each is designed for purposes other than our own and is valid within its own terms of reference. 'Firms', 'organizations', 'bureaucracies', and similar concepts employed by social scientists are in fact abstractions designed to throw light on general problems that interest the researchers concerned—the allocation of resources, the mechanisms of social control and communication, human relationships, the logic of decision-making, and so on. Provided their purpose is made clear, we should not be too dismayed if they fail to correspond closely with the behaviour of the organizations we have chosen to study.

The stress we have laid on the uncertain and changing character of the social services' objectives may leave the impression that their aims are the outcome of accident or a socially meaningless struggle for power. This question merits more serious examination.

For each service there will typically be a generally accepted but imprecisely defined formal statement of objectives. In practice, some selective interpretation of objectives, falling within the discretionary limits of this statement, will have been worked out by those providing the service, and each of these people can provide approximate but slightly different explanations of it. (The way the service really works in practice can only be discovered by examining the collective experience of its clients.) More uncertain and more varied still will be the partly explicit accounts people give of the way the service *ought* to work. The disparities between these explanations are evidence of past development and an essential prerequisite for further development. So much has already been explained. Policies are created by people. But how do people form their opinions about policies, and how do they change these opinions?

Observation suggests that previous training and experience provide a general outlook, and a framework of acceptable statements—which may have rather greater influence on verbal explanations of practice than upon practice itself. Current objectives and aspirations for the future evolve in the course of practice. Though people must sometimes sit back and reflect upon what they are doing in order to make plans for the future, the clarification and modification of objectives emerge directly from experience; 'policy' and 'practice' cannot be considered in isolation from each other. Views on particular aspects of a service are sharpened in times of conflict. In such phases the contenders proceed by selecting and defining the issues at stake with the aid of like-minded groups of people. This concept of 'the issues at stake' is a crucial one. When a conflict is over, people may agree that a famous victory has been won, but often they still give different explanations of what the battle was *about*. Thus there is a strong psychological link between a man's perceptions of the world he lives in and the judgments he makes about it—the two are part of the same intellectual and emotional experience.

It may be helpful, as many philosophers have found, to distinguish statements of fact and technique from 'appraisals' or 'value judgments'; the two have different logical characteristics. But the distinction is espoused for rather less reputable reasons by administrators ('The Council decides on policy. We only carry it out') and by professional workers of various kinds ('In my capacity as an Economist I can tell you six ways of preventing inflation; but I cannot tell you what to *do* about it'). Such statements secure a sound reputation for objectivity and avoid distressing conflicts. But they are apt to suggest that opinions and knowledge are derived from different experiences—different processes of thought—and produced by different people. In practice, however, a municipal Council (and doubtless the Cabinet too) wants advice about objectives as well as information about 'the facts'. For these bodies have to form views about the issues at stake—to identify which 'facts' are most important, and why. 'Facts' are not 'bits of experience' lying around waiting to be collected; they are facts *about* something, assembled by particular procedures of investigation and measurement which cannot be set in train until someone decides, on the basis of a judgment about the issues at stake, which 'things' are sufficiently relevant or important to investigate and measure. Thus although statements of fact have different logical characteristics from statements of opinion, knowledge and opinions cannot in real life be divorced from each other: they evolve together. Likewise, there is no cut-off point in the administrative hierarchy, with people below it deliberating the facts, while people above exchange value judgements. There may indeed be levels of the hierarchy above which the decisions to be made become more complex and important, each decision being unique and unrepeatable, and producing non-reversible results that take longer to appear. This is a useful distinction, sometimes employed to identify what are called 'policy decisions'. But the making of such decisions—or of any choice—calls for some understanding of the situation or context involved, *and* some selection of objectives; the two processes are part of the same experience.

People normally change their views and their behaviour, not by abandoning their moral judgements, but by extending their frames of reference to encompass a broader understanding of the issues at stake.

Their definition of the context within which decisions are to be taken expands. In fact, they are capable of *learning*—and educational examples may illustrate the point. A man who favours corporal and capital punishment may change his views as he learns more about delinquency and delinquents, *not* because he finds these are ineffective methods of attaining his unchanged objective of preventing crime, but because he no longer feels disposed to treat people in this fashion, even if such methods *are* effective. Arguments about this aspect of justice have taken on a different meaning for him; he perceives the issues at stake in a different way. Likewise a man whose views on old age pensions are derived from a frame of reference in which the responsibilities of the family hold a central place—'People should (or should not) support their parents' is his principal contribution to the debate —may also change his views, *without* abandoning that imperative, as his frame of reference expands to encompass a broader understanding of the issues at stake. He may perhaps have learnt more about human capacity to adapt to social change, about the workings of the wage system and the class structure, and about the redistribution of incomes between earners and dependants brought about by inflation and by increases in the gross national product. The context for the decision has expanded, and new factors have to be taken into account.

It is this capacity for education which ultimately determines the scope for developments in social policy (and for the human race generally). Changes occur in the social services as all who participate in their evolution—clients and controllers of resources, as well as the paid staff providing the service—extend their frames of reference to accommodate a new understanding of the issues at stake. These services, despite the hopes and fears they have engendered, can produce neither a hell nor a heaven upon earth; they are deeply rooted in the economic and social structure of the country, and can be no better and no worse than the society from which they spring and our capacity to understand that society. Thus there can be no ultimate or perfect pattern of social policies; they will continue to evolve so long as economic and social changes throw up new needs, and so long as people are capable of learning more about the world they live in.

I

APPENDIX 1

AN INTRODUCTION TO THE LITERATURES

SINCE the evolution of social policies is entangled with the whole development of an industrial society, scholars from every branch of the social sciences have had something to say about the questions that interest us. But each major branch of scholarship has been designed—and rightly so—to develop a coherent body of knowledge, ideas and methods, contributing to an understanding of a general range of intellectual problems rather than to the solution of the specific problems of particular institutions and professions. Therefore the student who pursues the questions examined in this book will find no main stream of literature to help him: he must explore selected reaches of many streams and his selection should lead him furthest along those which personal taste, past training and experience render most useful to him. His principal objective should not be to learn a technique but to extend and sharpen his perceptions of particular types of situation and problem. He may achieve this by studying philosophy and the development of political ideas, by reading historical or sociological research, or by applying mathematical or economic analysis, biological analogy, or psychological insights into human behaviour and its unconscious motivations. All are available. We can provide no more than an introduction to sources that seem fruitful to us, giving a few examples chosen for their quality and for the leads they provide to further reading. But first we should outline some of the main streams of scholarship to be considered. This sketch may whet the reader's appetite for exploration and suggest where he should go next, but it cannot do justice to the variety and depth of the literatures it touches upon. To the authors mentioned and the vastly greater number not mentioned we apologize in advance.

There are books describing the social services of England,[1] their powers, structure, growth and mode of operation—but few on other parts of the British Isles. Some deal with the needs of particular types of clients and the services provided for them.[2] Others with the development of particular professions playing a major part in the social services,[3] with the history of particular types of service,[4] with particular phases in the growth of the

---

[1] E.g. Penelope M. Hall, *The Social Services of Modern England*. London, Routledge & Kegan Paul, 1960.
[2] E.g. Peter Townsend, *The Last Refuge*. London, Routledge & Kegan Paul, 1963.
[3] E.g. Asher Tropp, *The School Teachers*. London, Heinemann, 1957.
[4] E.g. Jean S. Heywood, *Children in Care*. London, Routledge & Kegan Paul, 1959.

whole system,[1] or with the lives of those who contributed to the development of these services.[2] Biographies and diaries[3] often provide the most valuable insight into the evolution of social policies, blinkered though they must be by the obligation to focus on one participant. Much of this work describes human needs and the structure and growth of professions and agencies organized to meet them, but often it throws little light on the processes of administration and innovation—on what actually goes on from day to day in the town hall, and the manner in which this changes.

An altogether different stream of scholarship began from an attempt to identify, codify and prescribe the techniques of administration. Administrators, it was argued, could be trained for their jobs, just as engineers, chemists and accountants are trained for theirs. Much of this work dealt with the subdivision and specialization of tasks and the related problem of co-ordinating the parts of an administrative organization. It tended to draw on large, authoritarian organizations for its examples (the army and the Catholic Church, for instance), and produced a profusion of organization charts and general 'principles' which had the merit of being reasonably clear (even if wrong) and thus provoking further thought. The endeavour to establish that administration is a difficult and responsible job for which training is required—rather than appropriate political loyalties or kinship—must be respected; but the mechanistic approach adopted by its early exponents excluded the influence of past history, personal relationships and informal patterns of behaviour, it stressed the roles of managers treating the managed as cogs in the machine—and it was based on the assumption that objectives could always be clearly specified: the administrator's task was to organize effective means for the attainment of agreed ends.

If administration was not a technology then it might all be a matter of human relationships, and much useful research began on relationships in working groups and their implications. This approach had the merit of penetrating beyond the high command of large organizations to the small department and local office—the levels at which most people's administrative experience begins and ends. It brought human beings and change back into the picture; but change was still treated as an occasional intrusion upon normality originating from outside, rather than as a central feature of the life of organizations, originating from within them. Moreover some authors were tempted to present uplifting exhortations stressing the virtues of co-operation, loyalty, leadership and mutual understanding, without any systematic analysis of the evolution of the objectives which people are to be cooperative, loyal, etc. about. The possibility that conflict might be a necessary and productive phenomenon was too often disregarded, and the

---

[1] E.g. Richard M. Titmuss, *Problems of Social Policy*. London, HMSO and Longmans Green, 1950.

[2] E.g. Royston Lambert, *Sir John Simon, 1816-1904, and English Social Administration*. London, MacGibbon & Kee, 1963.

[3] E.g. Beatrice Webb, *Our Partnership*. Barbara Drake and Margaret I. Cole, Eds. London, Longmans, 1948.

few scholars who endeavoured to discover whether happy, friendly organizations are more productive than unhappy, strife-ridden organizations tended to come up with embarrassing answers.

In other quarters the attempt to theorize and generalize was abandoned altogether and efforts were concentrated on the more time-consuming but intellectually less demanding task of making case studies, particularly to serve the needs of schools of business administration. The instinct was sound—it was time to make a detailed and objective exploration of the manner in which administration really works—and cases that deal with major examples of policy-making are particularly useful for our purposes. But case studies which do not begin from a definition of the underlying problems to be examined deprive their authors of conclusions (for what are they to draw conclusions about?) and prevent them from performing the full task of a scientist or a teacher. More interesting were studies prepared by those whose principal concern was to explore the development of particular institutions or services. Government reports unravelling the responsibilities for disaster—for the destruction of the airship R.101[1] or the death of a foster child,[2] for instance—also contribute to our understanding of these processes.

Economists have long had a well developed 'theory of the firm' which was designed to throw light on the manner in which the volume of production may be determined by price relationships under specified conditions, but they had little to offer to people who actually worked in firms or to those who wrote histories of them. More recently—as public attention has turned from the full employment of resources to the mechanisms of economic growth—economists have set about examining real firms, what goes on within them, and how they grow. And this combination of historical and theoretical analysis is proving exceedingly valuable, for our purposes as well as theirs. Innovation and the internally generated processes of growth are at last gaining the attention they deserve.

Sociological studies of bureaucracy also have a long pedigree, derived from a continuing concern with the processes producing differentiations of role, status and opportunity, and the mechanisms ensuring order, cohesion and social control. Attention has recently been focused more closely and systematically on the operation of complex organizations, though still largely for the purpose of deriving conclusions about social controls, the survival of organizations, roles and the relationships between them, and other general features of social behaviour. The character of the work actually done by these organizations and the manner in which it develops seldom takes a central place in these studies; but the 'moving parts' of the organizational model are being identified, and as economists' 'firms' and sociologists' 'organizations' assume a closer resemblance to the real phenomena from

[1] Cmd. 3825, 1931. (Simon Report).
[2] Cmd. 6636, 1945. (Monckton Report).

which these abstract constructs are derived—and a closer resemblance to each other—more fruitful techniques of analysis are being developed for all concerned.

Meanwhile there has been a potent revival of thought and research on 'administrative science', starting from the viewpoint that the central feature of the administrative process is the making of decisions. Hence the analysis of the logic and practical procedures of decision making is the principal task of its students. This approach turned the organization charts of its predecessors upside down, showing that decisions were not simply made at the top and implemented below, but that all concerned—including the clients, customers and others outside the organization—played a part in determining and modifying decisions. It brought 'values' and aspirations back into the picture, not as assumptions derived from outside the sphere of academic analysis, but as major elements among the phenomena to be studied; it showed that conflict was a necessary and healthy element in the decision-making process, requiring systematic study; and it gave new life and cohesion to research on public administration which had too often been restricted to descriptive accounts of an arbitrarily selected set of institutions, or to the analysis of particular administrative and political processes—committees, pressure groups, electoral behaviour and so on. 'Decisions', however, were difficult to identify and isolate in practice, and the 'basic unanalysable units' that had to be employed in studying them were 'premises'[1] (the assumptions, attitudes and aspirations in the minds of participants) which appear equally difficult to run to earth. This approach has now produced an array of precisely defined and interrelated hypotheses about the workings of administration, the validation of which will call for a formidable amount of detailed empirical research.

Equally striking has been the progress recently made in studies of industrial management. Psychological methods and insights have been integrated more effectively with the analysis of administrative structure, and concepts have been defined more rigorously—though the validation of theory tends still to be based on the fact that 'it works' and the consultant is hired again. The most important development in this field has been the recognition that innovation and change, initiated and brought about by management itself, is the central feature to be studied; authority, communications, payment, human relations and satisfactions gained from work—previously examined for their own sake or for the contribution they make to the maintenance of an equilibrium—are now being examined for the light they throw on this process.

The development of research in these fields demands a sophisticated appreciation of the concepts, methods and traditions of the various academic disciplines employed, and their social and moral implications. The logic of these enquiries calls for the attention of philosophers educated in handling

---

[1] Herbert A. Simon, *Administrative Behaviour*. (Second Edition.) New York, Macmillan, 1957, p. xii.

what are, in a broad sense, 'political' theories. This is not a job that can be done very effectively by outsiders; students of the processes we have discussed must do most of their own philosophizing. But philosophers who have given serious attention to the analysis of human institutions—not only to the analysis of ideas about these institutions—have contributed fruitfully to the conceptual framework within which such research proceeds.

Below is a selection of some of the best examples we are aware of in the fields we have outlined. It has deliberately been kept as short as possible. Included in it is a selection of the collected 'readings' available: these are unlikely to be of great help to those who confine their attention to them, but they offer a quick and useful introduction to a variety of approaches, and hence a guide to further exploration. Books in the list which contain useful surveys of the literature and extensive bibliographies have been marked with an asterisk.

Collected 'readings' and symposia

*Merton (Robert King) and others (eds.), *Reader in Bureaucracy*. Glencoe, Free Press. 1952.

Etzioni (Amitai), *Complex Organizations: a Sociological Reader*. New York, Holt, Rinehart & Winston. 1961.

Haire (Mason) (ed.), *Modern Organization Theory: a Symposium of the Foundation for Research on Human Behaviour*. New York, Wiley. 1959.

Dubin (Robert), *Human Relations in Administration*. Englewood Cliffs, Prentice-Hall. 1961.

Case studies and reports on particular developments

*Stein (Harold) (ed.), *Public Administration and Policy Development: a Case Book*. New York, Harcourt. 1952.

Willson (Francis Michael Glenn), *Administrators in Action: British Case Studies, Vol. 1*. London, Allen & Unwin. 1961.

Kaplan (Harold), *Urban Renewal Politics: Slum Clearance in Newark*. New York, Columbia University Press. 1963.

Grieve (Hilda), *The Great Tide: the Story of the 1953 Flood Disaster in Essex*. Chelmsford, County Council of Essex. 1959.

Caine (Sir Sydney), *The History of the Foundation of the London School of Economics and Political Science*. London, London School of Economics and Political Science. 1963.

The sociology of complex organizations

*Merton (Robert King), *Social Theory and Social Structure*. Glencoe, Free Press. 1961.

*Etzioni (Amitai), *A Comparative Analysis of Complex Organizations: on Power, Involvement and their Correlates*. Glencoe, Free Press. 1961.

*Blau (Peter Michael), *Bureaucracy in Modern Society.* New York, Random House. 1961.
*Blau (Peter Michael) and Scott (William Richard), *Formal Organizations: A Comparative Approach.* San Francisco, Chandler. 1962.

The development of economic organizations

Barna (Tibor), *Investment and Growth Policies in British Industrial Firms.* Cambridge, University Press. 1962.
*Penrose (Edith Tilton), *The Theory of the Growth of the Firm.* Oxford, Blackwell. 1959.

Various aspects of administrative organization

Wheare (Kenneth Clinton), *Government by Committee: an Essay on the British Constitution.* Oxford, Clarendon Press. 1955.
Chapman (Brian), *The Profession of Government: the Public Service in Europe.* London, Allen & Unwin. 1959.
*Simon (Herbert Alexander) and others, *Public Administration.* New York, Knopf. 1950.
Simon (Herbert Alexander), *Administrative Behaviour: a Study of Decision-Making Processes in Administrative Organization.* New York, Macmillan. 1961.
*March (James Gardner) and Simon (Herbert Alexander), *Organizations.* New York, Wiley. 1959.

Industrial organization

Jaques (Elliott), *The Changing Culture of a Factory.* London, Tavistock Publications. 1961.
Argyris (Chris), *Understanding Organizational Behaviour.* London, Tavistock Publications. 1960.
Jaques (Elliott), *Equitable Payment: a General Theory of Work, Differential Payment and Individual Progress.* London, Heinemann. 1961.
Brown (Wilfred Banks Duncan), *Exploration in Management.* London, Heinemann. 1962.

Political philosophy

Oakeshott (Michael Joseph), *Rationalism in Politics and Other Essays.* London, Methuen. 1962.
Benn (Stanley I.) and Peters (Richard Stanley), *Social Principles and the Democratic State.* London, Allen & Unwin. 1959.

APPENDIX 2

A NOTE FOR TEACHERS AND STUDENTS

The authors of a book can never foresee the uses to which others may put their work—uses that may well be more revealing and constructive than any they had envisaged. But those embarking on this kind of study for the first time may find it helpful to consider some of the questions which the cases presented in this book appear to us to pose. Most of the questions discussed at the London School of Economics and Political Science and elsewhere, when these cases have been used for teaching purposes, have already been dealt with in the concluding chapter of this book and in the notes attached to each case. We are indebted to many for extending and sharpening our appreciation of these issues, and we would be glad to hear from others who learn or teach anything with the aid of this material. Their experience will help to shape further studies of this kind that may be made in the future. Many of the assertions we make about these cases deserve to be critically questioned, and we have no doubt that the conclusions of other students will frequently diverge from our own. We give below a list of questions which may help to provoke further thought. They are by no means the only ones worth considering, nor do we suggest that clear or conclusive answers can be found for all of them.

1. Select any of the case studies presented in this book and prepare (a) a list of the principal events, arranged in chronological order, (b) an 'organization chart' showing the administrative relationships between the people playing a part in these events. Explain which you regard as the crucial events in this list, and who appear to have taken the crucial roles in the story.

2. Had you been one of the 'new young men' who joined the Children's Aid Society (Chapter 10), how would you have attempted to handle the situation confronting them?

3. Give an outline of the report you would have written, and any further information not provided in the study which you would have asked for, had you been called upon to act as a consultant advising the Education Committee of the new Borough of Croydon in 1965. (See Chapter 12.)

4. Explain the factors which determined the volume and distribution of the Home Help Services discussed in Chapter 6. How and why did these differ from the factors which operated in any of the other services dealt with in this series of cases?

5. What appear to be the principal strengths and weaknesses of the administrative structure described in the study of the National Assistance Board (Chapter 6)?

6. Compare the systems employed for financing the Children's Aid Society and the Family Welfare Association, so far as these are revealed by Chapters 10 and 11. Does this comparison suggest any general principles that may be helpful to those administering voluntary social work agencies?

7. Compare the parts played by the Ontario Director of Child Welfare in Chapter 10, and Croydon's Chief Education Officer in Chapter 12. What light do these comparisons throw on the timing of discussions and major decisions about the development of a service?

8. Compare the means employed for ensuring that the developments studied met the needs of clients of the Finsbury Housing Department (Chapter 9), the Children's Department (Chapter 8) and the Home Help Service (Chapter 7). Do you consider that any further procedures were required for this purpose in any of these services?

9. Compare the parts played by the Housing Committee in Bethnal Green (Chapter 5) and the Education Committee in Croydon (Chapter 12), and explain the differences you discern.

10. Select any case study and list the organizations *outside* the principal agency or authority involved which exerted an influence on the outcome of the development studied. Explain and contrast the character of these influences, and discuss the manner in which the principal agency handled its relationships with these external bodies.

11. Contrast the powers exercised and the part played by central government departments in the developments studied in the Children's Department (Chapter 8), Finsbury (Chapter 9) and Croydon (Chapter 12), explaining any differences that may appear.

12. Outline the different means that may be available to senior officials for controlling the actions of their subordinates. Contrast those that appear to have been available to the Regional Controller of the National Assistance Board (Chapter 6) and the General Secretary of the Family Welfare Association (Chapter 11).

13. What appear to you to be the principal skills and characteristics required for successful performance of the roles of the Deputy Town Clerk in the Bethnal Green case (Chapter 5), the head of the Policy and Casework Division in the Children's Department case (Chapter 8), and the architect in the Finsbury case (Chapter 9)?

14. Explain and contrast the principal factors playing a part in the initiation of the changes described in Bethnal Green (Chapter 5) and the Home Help Service (Chapter 7).

15. The solution of one problem often determines the character of subsequent problems. What new problems would you expect to emerge after the completion of the developments described in Bethnal Green (Chapter 5), and the Children's Department (Chapter 8)?

16. Explain the principal factors which determine the maximum rate at which an organization can bring about changes in the services it provides. Which of these appear to have operated in the cases of the Children's Aid Society (Chapter 10) and the Home Help Service (Chapter 7)?

INDEX

Part I of this Index lists administrative concepts and processes, and offers a guide to points in the book at which these are discussed, however briefly. Thus the pages listed under the heading of 'Conflict', for example, neither include all those on which the word is used, nor all those on which a conflict of some kind is described, but indicate points at which some generalization, conclusion or discussion dealing with this subject can be found. Part II of the Index lists references to organizations, services and professions. Part III lists the names of people.

PART I: ADMINISTRATIVE CONCEPTS AND PROCESSES

PART III: NAMES OF PEOPLE

GEORGE ALLEN & UNWIN LTD
Head Office
40 Museum Street, London W.C.1
Telephone: 01–405 8577

Sales, Distribution and Accounts Departments
Park Lane, Hemel Hempstead, Herts.
Telephone: 0442 3244

Athens: 7 Stadiou Street
Auckland: P.O. Box 36013, Northcote Central N.4
Barbados: P.O. Box 222, Bridgetown
Beirut: Deeb Building, Jeanne d'Arc Street
Bombay: 103/5 Fort Street, Bombay 1
Calcutta: 285J Bepin Behari Ganguli Street, Calcutta 12
Cape Town: 68 Shortmarket Street
Delhi: 1/18B Asaf-Ali, New Delhi 1
Hong Kong: 105 Wing On Mansion, 26 Hancow Road, Kowloon
Ibadan: P.O. Box 62
Karachi: Karachi Chambers, McLeod Road
Madras: 2/18 Mount Road, Madras
Mexico: Villalongin 32, Mexico 5, D.F.
Nairobi: P.O. Box 30583
Philippines: P.O. Box 157, Quezon City D-502
Rio de Janeiro: Caixa Postal 2537-Zc-00
Singapore: 36c Prinsep Street, Singapore 7
Sydney N.S.W.: Bradbury House, 55 York Street
Tokyo: C.P.O. Box 1728, Tokyo 100-91
Toronto: 81 Curlew Drive, Don Mills

1. SOCIAL WORK AND SOCIAL CHANGE
EILEEN YOUNGHUSBAND

'. . . should be compulsory reading for students of social work and social administration of any age.'   *Case Conference*
'. . . covers the subject in a most instructive and useful manner and should be studied by all interested in the subject.'   *Quarterly Review*
Demy 8vo.

2. INTRODUCTION TO A SOCIAL WORKER
NATIONAL INSTITUTE FOR SOCIAL WORK TRAINING

. . . an admirable pioneer of casework which packs a great deal into small compass. It is readable and commendably free of jargon, so, in addition to the student readers for whom it was written, it could serve a useful purpose by giving to committee members and administrators a clear and concise idea of the nature of the casework services for which they are responsible . . . should find a place in every library of schools of social work. It is a valuable addition to literature suitable for the beginning stage of social work training.'
Crown 8vo.

4. SOCIAL WORK WITH FAMILIES
EILEEN YOUNGHUSBAND

This book gathers together some outstanding contributions to various aspects of social work with families. This subject is now more than ever of concern to social workers as fresh knowledge adds to their understanding of the dynamics of family life and interaction. The papers which compose this book are by well-known authors on both sides of the Atlantic. They are arranged in three sections, dealing with normal and less normal families as a group, with particular crisis situations for children, and with some more theoretical concepts contributing to an understanding of family types.

This volume is the first in a series of READINGS IN SOCIAL WORK designed to collect together significant articles on different aspects of social work. This series will be of value not only to social workers but to others working in the field of human relations. A great deal of care and knowledge has gone into selecting from the substantial literature those papers which are of lasting value and which will be most helpful to social workers.
Demy 8vo.

GEORGE ALLEN AND UNWIN LTD